EVIDENCE CASES
AND PROBLEMS

**CONTEMPORARY
LEGAL EDUCATION SERIES**

LAW SCHOOL ADVISORY BOARD

CO-CHAIRS

Howard P. Fink
*Isadore and Ida Topper Professor
 of Law
Ohio State University
College of Law*

Stephen A. Saltzburg
*Howrey Professor of Trial Advocacy,
 Litigation and Professional
 Responsibility
George Washington University
National Law Center*

MEMBERS

Charles B. Craver
*Leroy S. Merrifield Research Professor
 of Law
George Washington University
National Law Center*

Jane C. Ginsburg
*Morton L. Janklow Professor of
 Literary and Artistic
 Property Law
Columbia University School of Law*

Edward J. Imwinkelried
*Professor of Law
University of California at Davis
School of Law*

Daniel R. Mandelker
*Howard A. Stamper Professor of Law
Washington University
School of Law*

Mark V. Tushnet
*Professor of Law
Georgetown University
National Law Center*

Evidence Cases and Problems

STEVEN I. FRIEDLAND
Professor of Law
Nova Southeastern University

MICHIE BUTTERWORTH
Law Publishers
CHARLOTTESVILLE, VIRGINIA

COPYRIGHT © 1995
BY
MICHIE BUTTERWORTH
A Division of Reed Elsevier Inc.

Library of Congress Catalog Card No. 95-75336
ISBN 1-55834-218-4

Printed in the United States of America
All rights reserved.

Preface

This book is intended to provide a somewhat unconventional addition to the body of existing materials on the law of evidence. While evidence text books usually contain a polyglot of cases, questions, problems, law review articles and other materials, this book focuses almost entirely on cases and problems.

The cases were selected for several reasons. First, some of the cases are "classics" and of great significance to the law of evidence — *Mutual Life Insurance Co. v. Hillmon*, for example, is probably found in just about every evidence case book. Other cases are particularly illustrative of specific areas of evidence. *People v. Zackowitz*, for instance, nicely shows the power and perils of character evidence. Second, in several cases, the court's opinion offers an especially instructive explanation of a concept or rule. One example of this is *Ault v. International Harvester*, a California case which describes why the rule prohibiting the introduction of subsequent remedial measures to show culpability or negligence does not apply in strict liability actions. (Of course, *Ault* also doubles as a classic, since it has been used endlessly to illustrate this point.) Finally, some of the cases, such as *Seiler v. Lucasfilm*, were included simply because of their general interest quotient — a case involving the film "The Empire Strikes Back" makes for interesting reading and, hopefully, will generate a more lively evidentiary discussion.

The problems also were designed with several different purposes in mind. Some of the problems parallel the cases and should be used in answering them. This was done to ensure and reinforce an adequate understanding of the principles illustrated or discussed in the cases. Other problems go beyond the cases and require a basic knowledge of the Federal Rules of Evidence. These problems will assist the professor in explaining basic evidentiary concepts, such as the distinctions between direct and cross examination, even though no case directly covers the specific subject matter.

Many of the problems are introductory, intended simply to welcome the novice problem-solver to a particular area of evidence; no prior knowledge is presumed or required. Several of the problems, however, are designed to be more challenging and to focus on some of the more subtle and advanced evidence issues. These problems take the reader on an excursion into either public policy or precedent analysis. For example, one of the problems seeks to discern a governing principle for novel expert testimony following the decision in *Daubert v. Merrell Dow Pharmaceuticals, Inc.*

Given its rather modest length, the book does not cover every evidentiary rule or principle. However, each of the major evidentiary areas, from relevance to witnesses, hearsay, privilege, and writings, is represented by at least one case and several problems. The book also omits questions directly about the cases and their meaning. This reflects an intent to have the teacher treat the cases as he or she desires. It is certainly expected that additional materials — such as the Federal Rules of Evidence and their associated legislative history — will also be utilized in a basic course on evidence law.

This book, like most, was the product of the hard work of many people. I would particularly like to thank my research assistant, Cathy Williams, for her efforts in seeing this project through to fruition.

Steven I. Friedland
Atlanta, Georgia
July, 1995

Summary Table of Contents

	Page
Preface	v
Table of Contents	ix

I. INTRODUCTION TO EVIDENCE 1
   A. The Purposes of Evidence 1
   B. The Rules of Evidence 1

II. RELEVANCE 7
   A. Relevance Cases 7
   B. Relevance Problems 13

III. RELEVANT BUT INADMISSIBLE EVIDENCE BECAUSE OF UNFAIR PREJUDICE, ETC. 17
   A. Unfair Prejudice Cases 17
   B. Unfair Prejudice Problems 26

IV. CHARACTER AND HABIT EVIDENCE 29
   A. Character and Habit Cases 29
   B. Character and Habit Evidence Problems 48

V. OTHER EXCLUSIONS OF RELEVANT EVIDENCE 53
   A. Other Exclusions of Relevant Evidence Cases 54
   B. Other Exclusions of Relevant Evidence Problems 63

VI. WITNESSES 67
   A. Examining Witnesses on Direct and Cross 67
   B. The Competency of Witnesses 69
   C. Opinions and Expert Testimony 74
   D. The Impeachment of Witnesses 103

VII. HEARSAY 111
   A. Non-Hearsay 111
   B. Statutory "Not-Hearsay" Cases (Special Prior Statements of Witnesses and Admissions of a Party-Opponent) 118
   C. Hearsay Exceptions 131

VIII. THE CONFRONTATION CLAUSE 153
   A. Confrontation Clause Cases 153
   B. Confrontation Clause Problems 172

	Page
IX. PRIVILEGES	173
A. Privilege Cases	173
B. Privilege Problems	183
X. AUTHENTICATION	185
A. Authentication Cases	185
B. Authentication Problems	188
XI. THE BEST EVIDENCE RULE	189
A. Best Evidence Rule Cases	189
B. Best Evidence Rule Problems	192
XII. PROOF ISSUES — PRESUMPTIONS AND JUDICIAL NOTICE	193
A. Issues of Proof Cases	193
B. Issues of Proof Problems	202
XIII. MISCELLANEOUS PROBLEMS	205
A. *The Answering Machine*	205
B. *"Not Again!"*	205
C. *A Marital Partnership*	205
D. *Tenth Avenue Punch-Out*	205
E. *Von Goodenough*	205

Table of Contents

	Page
Preface	v
Summary Table of Contents	vii

I. INTRODUCTION TO EVIDENCE 1
   A. The Purposes of Evidence 1
   B. The Rules of Evidence 1
      1. History 1
      2. Purposes of the Rules 2
      3. The Roles of Judge, Counsel and Trier of Fact 3
      4. Some Basic Principles Underlying the Rules 3

II. RELEVANCE 7
   A. Relevance Cases 7
      Knapp v. State 7
      United States v. Onumonu 8
      United States v. Hays 11
   B. Relevance Problems 13
      1. *"I Told You So"* 13
      2. *Greed* 13
      3. *"Friends Don't Let Friends ... "* 13
      4. *"The Smoking Gun"* 14
      5. *Rodney Runner* 14
      6. *"Conditionally Yours ... "* 15

III. RELEVANT BUT INADMISSIBLE EVIDENCE BECAUSE OF UNFAIR PREJUDICE, ETC. 17
   A. Unfair Prejudice Cases 17
      Fusco v. General Motors Corp. 17
      People v. Collins 19
      Schultz v. Butcher 25
   B. Unfair Prejudice Problems 26
      1. *Pre-Owned Clothes* 26
      2. *Heads Up* 27
      3. *"Wax On, Wax Off"* 27
      4. *Little Red Corvette* 28
      5. *"A Lot Is Riding on Your Tires ... "* 28
      6. *Lobster Bill of Lading* 28
      7. *Murder He Wrote* 28

IV. CHARACTER AND HABIT EVIDENCE 29
   A. Character and Habit Cases 29
      People v. Zackowitz 29
      Michelson v. United States 33

	Page
United States v. Beechum	35
Rex v. Smith	42
Dowling v. United States	43
Huddleston v. United States	45

    B. Character and Habit Evidence Problems 48
        1. *Rambo III* 48
        2. *The Wanderlust of Cows, and Other True Stories* 49
        3. *Crash Johnson* 49
        4. *"No Coke, Pepsi"* 49
        5. *"A Streetcar Named Desire"* 50
        6. *Defamaaaaaaaaation!* 50
        7. *"But Mom!"* 50
        8. *Muddy for the Defense* 51
        9. *I.M. Rich* 51

V. OTHER EXCLUSIONS OF RELEVANT EVIDENCE 53
    A. Other Exclusions of Relevant Evidence Cases 54
        Ault v. International Harvester Co. 54
        Moe v. Avions Marcel Dassault-Breguet Aviation 56
        Winchester Packaging, Inc. v. Mobil Chemical Co. 59
        United States v. Acosta-Ballardo 61
    B. Other Exclusions of Relevant Evidence Problems 63
        1. *No Breaks* 63
        2. *The Slippery Snake* 63
        3. *Stingray City* 63
        4. *"Two Utes"* 64
        5. *House Calls* 64
        6. *NYPD Red* 65

VI. WITNESSES 67
    A. Examining Witnesses on Direct and Cross 67
        1. Cases 67
            Suarez Matos v. Ashford Presbyterian Community Hospital 67
        2. Examination of Witness Problems 68
            1. *"A Witness Named Wanda"* 68
            2. *A Truly Cross Examination* 68
            3. *The Forgetful Witness* 69
    B. The Competency of Witnesses 69
        1. Competency Cases 69
            United States v. Phibbs 69
            Rock v. Arkansas 71
        2. Competency Problems 73
            1. *"What Shirley Saw"* 73
            2. *The Mugging* 73
            3. *The Dead Man* 74
    C. Opinions and Expert Testimony 74
        1. Opinions and Expert Testimony Cases 74

TABLE OF CONTENTS

Page

      United States v. Markum 74
      In re Air Disaster at Lockerbie Scotland on December 21, 1988 ... 77
      Frye v. United States 79
      United States v. Downing 80
      Daubert v. Merrell Dow Pharmaceuticals, Inc. 85
      United States v. Rincon 90
      Carroll v. Morgan 93
      Engebretsen v. Fairchild Aircraft Corp. 95
      United States v. Piccinonna 97
   2. Opinions and Expert Testimony Problems 101
      1. *"In My Opinion"* 101
      2. *Daughter of Ms. Jean Dixon* 102
      3. *Sister-in-Law* 102
      4. *Cops* 102
      5. *The Legacy of* Daubert 102
 D. The Impeachment of Witnesses 103
   1. Impeachment Cases 103
      United States v. Swanson 103
      United States v. Brackeen 105
   2. Impeachment Problems 107
      1. *"Betty Sue"* 107
      2. *Cliff and Norm* 108
      3. *Dr. Doctor* 108
      4. *Perjury* 109

VII. HEARSAY 111
 A. Non-Hearsay 111
   1. Non-Hearsay Cases 111
      United States v. Emmons 111
      Wright v. Doe Dem. Tatham 113
      United States v. Alosa 114
   2. Non-Hearsay Problems 116
      1. *Is It Hearsay?* 116
 B. Statutory "Not-Hearsay" Cases (Special Prior Statements of Witnesses and Admissions of a Party-Opponent) 118
   1. Statutory "Not-Hearsay" Cases 118
      United States v. Odom 118
      Lippay v. Christos 120
      Bourjaily v. United States 125
   2. Statutory "Not-Hearsay" Problems 129
      1. *Bribery* 129
      2. *Dognappers* 130
      3. *Translator* 130
      4. *Free Agent* 130
      5. *Just a Guess* 130
      6. *Confession* 131

	Page
C. Hearsay Exceptions	131
1. Hearsay Exception Cases	131
Mutual Life Insurance Co. v. Hillmon	131
Shepard v. United States	133
Palmer v. Hoffman	135
Beech Aircraft Corp. v. Rainey	136
Dallas County v. Commercial Union Assurance Co.	138
United States v. Salerno	140
Horne v. Owens-Corning Fiberglas Corp.	142
Williamson v. United States	144
2. Hearsay Exceptions Problems	150
1. "Missing ... "	150
2. Shepard's Pie	150
3. Records	150
4. "I Swear to Tell ... "	151
5. The Fugitive	151
6. Dead Overdrive	151
7. Grand Jury	151
VIII. THE CONFRONTATION CLAUSE	153
A. Confrontation Clause Cases	153
Bruton v. United States	153
Ohio v. Roberts	157
United States v. Inadi	159
Maryland v. Craig	163
Idaho v. Wright	166
White v. Illinois	170
B. Confrontation Clause Problems	172
1. Ready and Available	172
2. "I Confess"	172
3. Jogger	172
4. Baby Jessica	172
IX. PRIVILEGES	173
A. Privilege Cases	173
Upjohn Co. v. United States	173
Nix v. Whiteside	176
Trammel v. United States	179
B. Privilege Problems	183
1. CEO	183
2. The Client	184
3. "Till Death Do Us Part ... "	184
X. AUTHENTICATION	185
A. Authentication Cases	185
United States v. Paulino	185
B. Authentication Problems	188

TABLE OF CONTENTS

Page

    1. *A Piece of Paper* 188
    2. *"My Baby Just Wrote Me A ... "* 188
    3. *The Mall* 188

XI. THE BEST EVIDENCE RULE 189
  A. Best Evidence Rule Cases 189
    Seiler v. Lucasfilm, Ltd. 189
    United States v. Duffy 191
  B. Best Evidence Rule Problems 192
    1. *Blow-Up* 192
    2. *Through Rain, Sleet or Hail ...* 192

XII. PROOF ISSUES — PRESUMPTIONS AND JUDICIAL NOTICE 193
  A. Issues of Proof Cases 193
    Sandstrom v. Montana 193
    County Court of Ulster County, N.Y. v. Allen 195
    Meredith v. Beech Aircraft Corp. 201
  B. Issues of Proof Problems 202
    1. *Credit Card Balance* 202
    2. *A Question of Criminal Law* 203
    3. *On a Roll* 203
    4. *Judicially Noticed* 203

XIII. MISCELLANEOUS PROBLEMS 205
  A. *The Answering Machine* 205
  B. *"Not Again!"* 205
  C. *A Marital Partnership* 205
  D. *Tenth Avenue Punch-Out* 205
  E. *Von Goodenough* 205

I. INTRODUCTION TO EVIDENCE

A. THE PURPOSES OF EVIDENCE

Why offer evidence at a trial or hearing? Evidence is generally offered to prove the case, the meaning of one the elements of the claim, cause of action, or defense. Thus, in an armed robbery case, the prosecution must offer evidence that a robbery took place in that particular jurisdiction, that the perpetrator was armed, and that the defendant was the perpetrator.

Simply because a party offers evidence on an element does not mean that party will prevail. The trier of fact — often a jury — must have confidence in the reliability and accuracy of the evidence. In this broader sense, the evidence is used to paint a picture of a prior event, person or thing and to persuade the trier that that version of the event, person or thing is accurate. Evidence offered to impeach a witness is an apt example of evidence used to help colorize the way the trier of fact views and weighs that witness' testimony.

Not all evidence is admitted for the trier of fact's consideration. Some evidence, deemed irrelevant, is not useful to the jury's determination of the issues in the case. Other evidence may be useful but has countervailing considerations, such as unfair prejudice, that warrants its exclusion. Still other evidence may be useful and not harmful but may, nevertheless, be excluded for independent policy reasons. This category of evidence includes privileges for confidential communications between attorney and client and between priest and penitent.

B. THE RULES OF EVIDENCE

1. HISTORY

The Federal Rules of Evidence did not take effect until 1975, after President Gerald Ford signed them into law. Prior to that time in federal courts, the common law supplied the rules governing the admissibility of evidence. While efforts prior to that time were made to codify the law of evidence, the impetus necessary to adopt such significant legislation was lacking.

States have adopted their own codes of evidence, some in special free-standing codes and others with parts integrated into areas of substantive law. In fact, many of the state codes were patterned after the Federal Rules of Evidence. However, the rules have not remained static since their adoption. In the 1990s, changes have added a notice requirement to Rule 404(b) (the provision permitting evidence of other crimes, wrongs or acts), clarifying the uses of convictions to impeach in Rule 609(a), and extending Rule 412 (dealing with the sexual history of a sex crime victim) to civil cases. It also appears that several new rules, Rules

413-415, concerning the use of other offenses in sexual molestation cases, will, barring Congressional modification, soon take effect.

The adoption of the original Federal Rules was neither sudden nor simple. In 1965, Chief Justice Earl Warren appointed an Advisory Committee to draw up an evidence code for federal courts. The Committee's proposal was considered by the Supreme Court and in 1972 sent to Congress for its approval. It was intended to go into effect in July of 1973. Instead, the rules were further shaped, refined and appended by Congress. The code was adopted in its modified form and became effective July 1, 1975.

Various sources of legislative history exist which aid the understanding of the Federal Rules of Evidence. The Advisory Committee, for example, created Notes to each provision to explain and support the rule. When changes were made by the House Committee on the Judiciary or the Senate Committee on the Judiciary, explanatory notes were created by the respective legislative committee. Further, when the modifications of the House and Senate committees conflicted, a Conference Report reflected the Conference Committee's resolution. The legislative history of a given rule is instructive both for the novice reader and courts assigned the difficult job of interpreting a subtlety in the law.

2. PURPOSES OF THE RULES

Not all evidence is admissible. The Federal Rules limit both what may be admitted and what the jury may take back with them for their deliberations. These limitations are based on various policies, including fairness, efficiency, predictability and consistency. For example, the rules ensure an equal playing field for the parties in the combat of the courtroom. If an accused introduces character evidence under Rule 404(a), the prosecution is allowed to rebut it; if a party introduces part of a writing, the opponent is permitted to introduce its remainder (see Rule 106). The exclusions of some otherwise relevant evidence in the 400 series of the rules (irrelevant evidence, unfair prejudice, subsequent remedial measures, offers to compromise or pay medical expenses, plea bargaining, liability insurance, or — "in any civil or criminal proceeding involving alleged sexual misconduct" — the victim's past sexual behavior or sexual predisposition), occur not only to ensure fairness in results but to promote efficiency in the trial process.

With the various policies that inform the rules, it is easy to explore the underlying tensions that exist. Should privilege exclude otherwise important relevant evidence? Does other-acts evidence prejudice the jury? Do limiting instructions really limit prejudice? These questions can only be answered based on logic and experience. Ironically, they reveal what experienced observers of the judicial system have known for a long time — there are often no absolutely correct answers as to whether evidence is admissible; it depends on the context of the offer. Important factors may include other evidence in the case, the nature of the case, and the people involved in the offer and decision. That is why

B. THE RULES OF EVIDENCE 3

viewing evidence law as an exact science, with "rights and wrongs," often fundamentally misconceives the subject matter and why the rules give the judge considerable discretion in many admissibility decisions.

3. THE ROLES OF JUDGE, COUNSEL AND TRIER OF FACT

The Federal Rules create fairly well-defined roles for the participants in a trial. The judge rules on the admissibility of evidence, instructs the jury on the relevant law, and is generally responsible for overseeing the smooth operation of the trial or hearing (much like a police officer directing traffic). The trier of fact is responsible for deciding the facts of the case and applying the pertinent substantive law to those facts to determine liability, guilt, or some other legal conclusion.

The attorneys have a dual role. On the one hand, the attorneys must zealously advocate their client's position in an effort to persuade the jury to decide the case in their favor (or even argue that the court should dismiss the case prior to sending it to the hearing of a jury). On the other hand, it is the attorney's responsibility to create a record for a potential appeal. To preserve an appeal, counsel must generally object when impermissible evidence is offered (unless the error is considered "plain error") or proffer what excluded evidence would have shown had it been allowed. Thus, during a trial counsel must keep one eye on the proceedings and one eye on the record that is being made.

4. SOME BASIC PRINCIPLES UNDERLYING THE RULES

Several basic principles or building blocks of evidence exist. All evidence must at a minimum be relevant. While the relevance threshold is a low one and does not ensure admissibility, irrelevant evidence is unequivocally excluded from trial. (Rule 402)

Relevant evidence is defined by the Federal Rules as evidence that has any tendency to make a fact of consequence to the action more or less probable. (Rule 401) This definition is given a broad construction. There is no limit to the number of inferences that can be used to connect evidence to the case. Nor does the evidence have to make the fact of consequence more or less likely — any little bit will suffice. This notion of logical relevance stands, therefore, as a shallow moat, not a crocodile-infested river, around admissibility.

All evidence must be authenticated. In this sense, authenticity merely means that there is some reason to believe the thing is what it purports to be. If not, the evidence may very well be irrelevant. For example, a witness must have some evidence to contribute about the facts in issue through her perception, memory or narration. Real evidence must also be shown to somehow relate to the case. A knife found near the scene of a robbery, for instance, must be shown to have some relationship to the robbery.

The authenticity requirement is founded on a broader principle of reliability. If evidence cannot be fairly or accurately evaluated by the trier of fact, then it may be excluded. Thus, evidence of excessive violence, various forms of other allegedly similar occurrences, happenings or events, some statistical probability evidence, and novel scientific evidence all may mislead the jury and be subject to exclusion.

Perhaps the best known evidence fraught with dangers of unreliability is hearsay. As the definition states, hearsay is the out-of-court statement of a declarant offered for the truth of the matter asserted. (Rule 801) This rule excludes out-of-court declarations dependent upon the credibility of the speaker unless there are independent reasons indicating that the statement is reliable. The numerous exceptions delineated in Federal Rules 803 and 804 are believed by the drafters to possess the requisite reliability.

An important component of evidence law involves the testimony of witnesses. An entire series of the rules (the 600s) is devoted to witnesses. (Another series of the rules, the 700s, deals with a special type of witness testimony, opinions, and an important type of witness, the expert witness.) Many formalities exist in the way witnesses can be questioned. On direct examination of a witness, leading questions (those that suggest an answer) are generally disallowed. On cross examination by the opponent of the witness, however, leading questions are not only permitted, but preferred.

The purpose of direct examination is to elicit the witness' capacity — what he or she perceived, remembers, and now communicates to the jury. The purposes of cross examination are somewhat different. Cross examination is not intended generally to beat the witness into submission. Instead, it serves to fill in gaps on direct, corroborate the cross examiner's case, and impeach the witness' credibility.

However, not all testimony is received with the same enthusiasm. The particular weight of testimony often depend on whether and how the witness is impeached. To this end, the credibility of witnesses is often attacked through various methods of impeachment. A witness may be impeached by contradicting her about the facts of her testimony, by showing her bias, by introducing certain types of her prior criminal convictions (such as felonies and crimes of dishonesty or false statement), by certain prior acts bearing on the witness' truthfulness or veracity, by attacking defects in her testimonial capacities such as poor perception or memory, and by her prior inconsistent statements. If a direct attack on the witness' credibility has occurred, she may be rehabilitated either through a second direct examination called "redirect" or by calling another witness.

While the rules on witnesses coalesce in the 600 series, the rules concerning another important area, writings, are disbursed in various parts of the code. Writings sometimes may only be read to the jury (see Rule 803(5)), or used to refresh the witness' memory and simply not seen or heard by the jury at all (see Rule 612). Generally, however, when a writing is introduced, it may be taken back to the jury room for the jury's deliberations (see Rule 803(6) or Rule 803(8)). Other than to refresh a witness' memory, writings generally are not permitted to be used by witnesses while testifying (see generally Rule 612). If

B. THE RULES OF EVIDENCE

offered in evidence, writings often are challenged on grounds of authentication, best evidence, and hearsay.

A major focus of the Federal Rules of Evidence is the exclusion of otherwise relevant evidence. Unfair prejudice, improper character evidence, privilege, hearsay, and the "best evidence" rule are but some examples of how the rules bar pertinent evidence. These exclusions are based on various grounds, from the effect the evidence would have on the jury (e.g., unfair prejudice), to extrinsic policies deemed more important than the particular case (e.g., privilege). Evidence is admitted for the jury's consideration only if it survives all of the possible exclusions placed in its way by the rules.

II. RELEVANCE

> Problems of relevancy call for an answer to the question whether an item of evidence, when tested by the processes of legal reasoning, possesses sufficient probative value to justify receiving it in evidence.... The standard of probability ... is "more ... probable than it would be without the evidence." Any more stringent requirement is unworkable and unrealistic.

Fed. R. Evid. 401 Advisory Committee's Note

A. RELEVANCE CASES

KNAPP v. STATE
79 N.E. 1076 (Ind. 1907)

GILLETT, J.:

Appellant appeals from a judgment in the above-entitled cause, under which he stands convicted of murder in the first degree. Error is assigned on the overruling of a motion for a new trial.

Appellant, as a witness in his own behalf, offered testimony tending to show a killing in self-defense. He afterwards testified, presumably for the purpose of showing that he had reason to fear the deceased, that before the killing he had heard that the deceased, who was the marshall of Hagerstown, had clubbed and seriously injured an old man in arresting him, and that he died a short time afterwards. On appellant being asked, answered: "Some people around Hagerstown there. I can't say as to who it was now." The state was permitted, on rebuttal, to prove by a physician, over the objection and exception of the defense, that the old man died of senility and alcoholism, and that there were no bruises or marks on his person. Counsel for appellant contend that it was error to admit this testimony; that the question was as to whether he had, in fact, heard the story, and not as to its truth or falsity. While it is laid down in the books that there must be an open and visible connection between the fact under inquiry and the evidence by which it is sought to be established, yet the connection this required is in the logical processes only, for to require an actual connection between two facts would be to exclude all presumptive evidence.... Within settled rules, the competency of testimony depends largely upon its tendency to persuade the judgment....

We are of the opinion that the testimony referred to was competent. While appellant's counsel are correct in their assertion that the question was whether appellant had heard a story to the effect that the deceased had offered serious violence to the old man, yet it does not follow that the testimony complained of did not tend to negative the claim of appellant as to what he had heard. One of the first principles of human nature is the impulse to speak the truth. "This principle ... has a powerful operation, even in the greatest liars; for where they lie once they speak the truth 100 times." Truth-speaking preponderating, it follows that to show that there was no basis in fact for the statement appellant claims to have heard had a tendency to make it less probable that his testimony on this point was true. Indeed, since this court has not, in cases where self-defense is asserted as a justification for homicide, confined the evidence concerning the deceased to character evidence, we do not perceive how, without the possibility of a gross perversion of right, the state could be denied the opportunity to meet in the manner indicated the evidence of the defendant as to what he had heard, where he, cunningly perhaps, denies that he can remember who gave him the information. The fact proved by the state tended to discredit appellant, since it showed that somewhere between the fact and the testimony there was a person who was not a truth speaker, and, appellant being unable to point to his informant, it must at least be said that the testimony complained of had a tendency to render his claim as to what he had heard less probable....

Judgment affirmed.

UNITED STATES v. ONUMONU

967 F.2d 782 (2d Cir. 1992)

GEORGE C. PRATT, CIRCUIT JUDGE:

We have recently seen a significant increase in alimentary-canal drug smugglers who, by swallowing drug-filled condoms, use their bodies to shield illegal drugs from the eyes of customs inspectors. Because of this unusual practice, our courts have been faced with novel legal issues in guiding law enforcement officials who seek to discover and apprehend the smugglers....

Ojiabo Onumonu, another accused "balloon swallower," was convicted by a jury in the United States District Court for the Eastern District of New York, Raymond J. Dearie, Judge, of knowingly importing heroin into the United States in violation of 21 U.S.C. § 952(a), and of knowingly possessing heroin with an intent to distribute in violation of 21 U.S.C. § 841(a). Judge Dearie sentenced him to concurrent terms of 66 months' imprisonment, plus the mandatory special assessment.

At trial, Onumonu did not deny bringing contraband into the United States. His only defense was that he believed that the condoms he had swallowed had contained packets of diamonds, not heroin. In short, he claimed he did not have the requisite intent to be convicted of the knowing importation and possession of heroin.

On appeal Onumonu argues that the district court erred when it excluded the testimony of his expert regarding the prevalence and feasibility of internally smuggling diamonds into this country....

While we hold that the district court correctly denied Onumonu's motion to suppress the contraband, we conclude that it erred in excluding the expert

A. RELEVANCE CASES 9

testimony proffered by Onumonu on the subject of diamond smuggling from Nigeria to this country. Because we are reversing Onumonu's conviction for this evidentiary ruling, which we conclude was an abuse of discretion, and because we are remanding for a new trial, we do not reach the sentencing issue.

Background

... After a trip to Nigeria, Onumonu returned on Nigeria Airway Flight 850 to John F. Kennedy International Airport in the early morning hours of August 8, 1990. As he walked through the airport's International Arrivals Building, Onumonu approached a plainclothes customs inspector, Glenn Washington, who is a member of the Customs Service's Contraband Enforcement Team which, as Washington testified at trial, "target[s] individuals who may be trying to smuggle narcotics into the United States." When Onumonu asked Washington for help in locating the areas where he could be cleared through customs, Washington identified himself as a customs official and told Onumonu that he would assist him.

As he observed Onumonu, however, Washington grew suspicious. Onumonu sweated profusely, even though "it wasn't particularly warm" in the air-conditioned International Arrivals Building, and his hands were shaking when he presented his passport and customs declaration. Washington noted that Onumonu had paid cash for his one-way ticket from Nigeria to New York. Asked about his travel plans, Onumonu said he had traveled to Nigeria for his stepfather's funeral and that he planned to return to Detroit after he cleared customs, yet he had no airplane ticket to Detroit, nor hotel reservations in New York. Washington found Onumonu's answers to questions to be vague and evasive, and noted that during their conversation, Onumonu failed to make eye contact.

Washington escorted Onumonu into a search room and conducted a pat-down search. When this failed to reveal any contraband, Washington told Onumonu that he believed him to be an internal drug carrier who was bringing narcotics into the United States. Onumonu declined the opportunity to undergo an x-ray.

At this point Washington administered Miranda warnings to Onumonu and escorted him to a mobile van located at the airport so that customs agents could monitor Onumonu's bowel movements....

After four days in the medical van, Onumonu had a bowel movement and passed a few condoms that, according to inspector Melvin Pincus, contained hard, opaque, hollow containers which held a substance that field-tested as heroin. Pincus then administered Miranda warnings and placed Onumonu under arrest. After two more days, Onumonu had passed a total of 83 condoms containing similarly-packaged heroin. The total amount of heroin was 576 grams, which had a wholesale value of $100,000....

Before trial, Judge Dearie authorized Onumonu to retain, at government expense, an expert witness, a gemologist by the name of Samuel Beizer, who was chairman of the Jewelry Design Institute at New York City's Fashion Institute of Technology. Onumonu's attorney informed the court that Beizer would testify about: 1) the feasibility of smuggling diamonds by ingesting them in the same manner that drug smugglers swallow their contraband; 2) the value of the amount of diamonds that could have been concealed in the 83 condoms Onumonu had swallowed; 3) the amount of duty that someone would have to pay to legally import those diamonds from Nigeria; and 4) the substantial profit to be derived from smuggling diamonds from Nigeria....

After the government concluded the direct examination of its first witness, however, Judge Dearie announced that he was granting the government's motion to exclude the testimony of Onumonu's gemologist....

Expert testimony must be relevant, *see* Fed.R.Evid. 401, 402, but even relevant expert testimony, like all relevant evidence, may be excluded under Fed. R. Evid. 403, if its probative value is outweighed by the danger that it would confuse the jury, be unfairly prejudicial, cause undue delay, waste judicial resources, or be cumulative. *See* Fed R. Evid. 403. Thus, where relevant testimony from a qualified expert would help a jury determine a fact in issue, and where the testimony does not fall under one of the rule 403 exceptions, such testimony should normally be admitted where the district court fails to provide, "a legitimate basis for excluding the proffered evidence." *McBride*, 786 F.2d at 51.

1. *Rule 401 — Relevance*

We first assess the relevance of the proffered testimony. All relevant evidence is admissible unless excluded because of the constitution, a statute, or a rule.... As the government accurately notes, Onumonu's subjective belief was the critical issue in this case where Onumonu had conceded the objective, physical facts, and the prosecution had the burden of proving only that Onumonu "knowingly or intentionally import[ed]" the heroin. *See* 21 U.S.C. §§ 952(a)(1), 960(a)(1).

Onumonu testified that his friend and fellow tribesman, Michael Amparo, had asked him to swallow diamonds and carry them on his flight from Nigeria into the United States for $5,000. When Onumonu agreed, his friend presented him with a thick soup made of okra, which was slippery and resembled a native dish, "foo-foo". Lubricated by the "foo-foo", the small, hard opaque package inside the condoms were easily swallowed. Onumonu testified that he believed that the packets in the condoms contained diamonds. In order to corroborate this testimony and to relate it to both the physical and economic realities of doing what Onumonu testified he believed he was doing, Onumonu proffered the expert testimony of gemologist Beizer. In the context of this case, that testimony certainly met the relevancy standard of rule 401 because it made the existence of Onumonu's belief about diamonds more probable than it would have been without the evidence....

....

Judge Dearie made no reference to rule 403, and our review of the record leads us to conclude that the evidence could not be excluded under that rule.

A. RELEVANCE CASES

First, the proposed testimony of the expert Beizer could not be termed unfairly prejudicial, as Judge Dearie permitted Onumonu himself to testify as to diamond smuggling....

....

... [T]he district court abused its discretion when it excluded Onumonu's proffered expert testimony about the prevalence of diamond smuggling out of Nigeria, and about the physical and economic feasibility of smuggling diamonds in swallowed condoms.

We reverse the judgment of conviction and remand for a new trial.

UNITED STATES v. HAYS
872 F.2d 582 (5th Cir. 1989)

JOHNSON, CIRCUIT JUDGE:

Defendants-appellants James L. Hays and Weldon J. Hays appeal their convictions for conspiracy, misapplication of funds and making false entries in the records of a federally insured savings and loan association. Concluding that the district courts' admission of unnecessarily cumulative, prejudicial and irrelevant evidence impermissibly affected substantial rights of the defendants, we are constrained to reverse.

I. *Facts and Procedural History*

In 1982, an appellant-defendant in this case, James Hays, became the president of Lancaster First Federal Savings and Loan Association (hereinafter Lancaster) in Lancaster, Texas. Prior to assuming that position, James Hays, a former Texas Savings and Loan bank examiner, had been Lancaster's vice-president and a member of its board. James Hays' son, Weldon Hays, also a former Texas Savings and Loan bank examiner and the other appellant-defendant in this case, likewise was involved in the savings and loan business as an employee at Lancaster and also as president of the Colony Savings and Loan (hereinafter Colony). This appeal arises from the criminal convictions of James and Weldon Hays for improper activities regarding certain loans and deposits involving the Lancaster's funds....

II. *Discussion*

On appeal the appellants contend that the district court made a substantial number of evidentiary rulings that were in error. Specifically, appellants contend that the trial court improperly allowed the Government to introduce an overwhelming amount of irrelevant evidence. They also argue that even if some of the challenged evidence was relevant, that it was highly prejudicial, and as such was improperly admitted under Fed.R.Evid. 403....

....

As defined by the Federal Rules of Evidence, relevant evidence is that evidence which has "any tendency to make the existence of any fact that is of consequence to the determination of the action more probable or less probable than it would be without the evidence." Fed.R.Evid. 401. Evidence which meets this broad standard is known as "logically relevant" evidence. The Federal Rules of Evidence further provide that "[a]ll relevant evidence is admissible," and that "[e]vidence which is not relevant is not admissible." Fed.R.Evid. 402.

In determining whether evidence should be admitted or excluded on the basis of relevancy, however, the trial court's decision does not always turn upon a simple determination that the standard enunciated in Rule 401 is satisfied. Instead, the focus may turn to a determination of whether the proffered evidence is "legally relevant." Fed.R.Evid. 403 provides that "[relevant] evidence may be excluded if its probative value is substantially outweighed by the danger of unfair prejudice, confusion of the issues, or misleading the jury, or by considerations of undue delay, waste of time, or needless presentation of cumulative evidence." Thus, while the trial court's discretion in admitting evidence under Rule 401 is necessarily quite broad, Rule 403 requires a balancing of interests to determine whether *logically relevant* evidence is also *legally relevant* evidence. [Emphasis added.]

In reviewing the district court's rulings on matters of relevancy, this Court is guided by the principle that district courts have wide discretion in determining relevancy under Rule 401. The district court's decision will not be disturbed absent a substantial abuse of discretion. *United States v. Brown*, 692 F.2d 345, 349 (5th Cir.1982). Similarly, the decision of the district court with regard to the admissibility of evidence under the standards set forth in Rule 403 is subject to considerable deference. In the absence of an abuse of discretion, the district court's ruling on matters involving Rule 403 will not be overruled....

Nevertheless, our review of erroneous evidentiary rulings in criminal trials is necessarily heightened. As the Supreme Court has instructed, evidence in criminal trials must be "strictly relevant to the particular offense charged." *Williams v. New York*, 337 U.S. 241, 247 (1949). "The admission of irrelevant facts that have a prejudicial tendency is fatal to a conviction, even through there was sufficient relevant evidence to sustain the verdict." ...
....

At trial, the Government presented eleven witnesses who testified at length regarding Weldon Hays' allegedly improper activities during the time he was attempting to secure sufficient deposits to ensure the continued operation of Colony. The testimony of those eleven witnesses required almost 200 pages of the record on appeal. Little, if any, of that testimony is relevant to the offenses with either Weldon Hays or his father were charged. Instead, the evidence consists primarily of testimony regarding the unscrupulous conduct of Weldon Hays at or about the time he was attempting to get Colony chartered....
....

Accordingly, the only glimmer of possible relevance of this testimony to the offenses charged is fleeting at best. Thus, we must conclude that its admission was error....

B. RELEVANCE PROBLEMS

... [A] review of the record leaves us with the impression that the evidence was cumulative, unduly prejudicial and inflammatory. Had the evidence been restricted to a limited number of witnesses, or had the testimony taken a more modest number of pages of the record, the result might have been different.... Having so concluded, we must view the error as having impermissibly affected substantial rights of the defendants....

B. RELEVANCE PROBLEMS

1. "I Told You So"

Diego, while leaving his evening Biology class at Calistoga College, was told "the guy in the Crips gang who sits several rows away from you in Near Ancient Civilizations 101, Jean Claude Von Swarzenger, said he's going to tear you apart." Diego ran into Jean Claude later that day and a fight ensued. Diego is charged with assault, but claims self defense.

   a. Is what Diego was told after Biology class relevant? To what? What does the warning make more likely?
   b. Does it matter whether Diego knew the person who told Diego that Jean Claude was out to get him? Why?
   c. Is it relevant if the person who informed Diego that Jean Claude was "going to tear you apart" is known around school as a liar?

2. Greed

Xenobia Evanston, the Chief Executive Officer of Eastern Southwest Central Savings and Loan, is sued by the investors of the bank for embezzling millions of dollars of the bank's money, causing it to fail. At trial, the plaintiffs attempt to introduce various items of evidence. Which of the items, if any, are admissible?

   a. Xenobia routinely borrowed money from wealthy friends and would never pay them back.
   b. Xenobia gambled illegally in Las Vegas several times a year.
   c. Xenobia flirted with a loan officer under false pretenses to secure a loan for the bank.

3. "Friends Don't Let Friends ..."

After working all day at the airport as a mechanic, Ulysses spent from 6:30 to 9:30 p.m. at a local bar, Aundra's Place. While driving home, Ulysses was stopped by a police officer for speeding and charged with driving under the influence of alcohol. Which of the following evidence is relevant to the case?

   a. Ulysses was seen in a different bar, Tony's Place, earlier on the same day of the incident.
   b. Ulysses collects beer cans.

c. Ulysses is married with two young children, Monique and Les.
d. Ulysses was convicted of driving under the influence of alcohol in 1993.
e. Ulysses also was convicted of reckless driving in 1992.
f. Ulysses was a high level executive of a Fortune 500 company at the time of the arrest.
g. Ulysses keeps a six-pack of beer in his refrigerator.
h. Ulysses likes psychedelic rock music such as the songs of Jimi Hendrix.
i. Ulysses runs an extremely important meeting every Friday morning at 7:30 a.m.
j. Ulysses is out of shape and has a protruding stomach, also sometimes called a "beer belly."

4. "The Smoking Gun"

Ivy is charged with the unregistered possession of a firearm. The firearm, a pistol, was found in the unlocked closet of a motel room. Which of the following evidence is relevant to the case? Explain.

a. Ivy was found with a key to the motel room, a "Motel 7", in her purse.
b. Three other people, Sam, Woody and Rebecca, were found with keys to the motel room on their persons.
c. Ivy was observed in the motel lobby earlier on the day the gun was found.
d. Ivy's birth certificate was found in the same closet as the gun.
e. Ivy has been convicted of disorderly conduct and battery.
f. Ivy is a recovering alcoholic.
g. A housekeeping employee at the motel, Carla, entered the room to clean it on the day the gun was discovered.
h. The pistol apparently had been purchased in Kansas (the identity of the purchaser was unknown); the motel room and Ivy's residence are in New York.

5. *Rodney Runner*

Rodney Runner brought suit against the Wily Coyote Corporation for disabling injuries. The only issue in this worker's compensation action was whether Runner was injured on the job. Which of the following evidence is relevant? Explain.

a. The Wily Coyote Corp. shows that Rodney was a poor worker.
b. The Wily Coyote Corp. offers evidence that Rodney was reprimanded on three occasions for drinking alcoholic beverages during company time.
c. The Wily Coyote Corp. offers evidence that Rodney often ran to work over uneven terrain.
d. The defendant company offers evidence that Rodney attempted to bribe the central defense witness not to testify.

B. RELEVANCE PROBLEMS

6. "Conditionally Yours ..."

Leandra was brutally knifed and killed at approximately 11 p.m. as she was opening the door to her apartment. At the crime scene, police found the following evidence. What fact must exist for each piece of evidence to be relevant? Explain.

   a. A serrated knife purchased at the local Sweig & Halmut knife store was found in the bushes near the front door to the condominium.
   b. Tire prints were discovered on the gravel approximately 15 feet away from the front door.
   c. A love letter by a spurned suitor signed "conditionally yours, Ray," was found in Leandra's purse.
   d. A single latex rubber glove was discovered in the alley near several broken bottles on the side of the apartment.
   e. An answering machine on Leandra's kitchen counter had three messages on it, one at the alleged time of the killing.

III. RELEVANT BUT INADMISSIBLE EVIDENCE BECAUSE OF UNFAIR PREJUDICE, ETC.

[C]ertain circumstances call for the exclusion of evidence which is of unquestioned relevance. These circumstances entail risks which range all the way from inducing decision on a purely emotional basis, at one extreme, to nothing more harmful than merely wasting time, at the other extreme. Situations in this area call for balancing the probative value of and need for the evidence against the harm likely to result from its admission....

Fed. R. Evid. 403 Advisory Committee's Note

A. UNFAIR PREJUDICE CASES

FUSCO v. GENERAL MOTORS CORP.

11 F.3d 259 (1st Cir. 1993)

BOUDIN, CIRCUIT JUDGE:

Carol Fusco was injured in a car accident and brought suit against General Motors, the car's manufacturer. A jury awarded Fusco $1 million in damages and General Motors has appealed, challenging rulings on evidence and discovery made by the district judge. We affirm.

I.

On December 15, 1986, Fusco was driving her car, a Chevrolet Chevette, near Pelham, New Hampshire. Her car suddenly left the roadway, slid across an ice-covered embankment, and hit a telephone pole somewhere along the front left side of the car. Fusco was injured.

Fusco brought suit against General Motors in state court in New Hampshire, claiming that a key component in the steering system — the front left "ball stud" — had broken from metal fatigue and caused the disaster.[1] General Motors removed the case to federal district court and took the position that the ball stud had not been the cause of the accident but rather had fractured when the car hit the telephone pole. A jury trial, begun on July 7, 1992, resulted in an evenly divided hung jury, and the district court promptly ordered a second trial for November 6, 1992.

---

[1] It appears that the ball is a spherical object with a protruding stud; that the ball and stud together form part of the elaborate connection (via the tie rod and steering gear) between the tire wheel or axle and the steering wheel. If the stud breaks entirely, the tire wheel is no longer controlled by the steering wheel.

III. RELEVANT BUT INADMISSIBLE EVIDENCE: UNFAIR PREJUDICE, ETC.

At the second trial Fusco offered eyewitness testimony that the car had abruptly veered off the highway and collided with a telephone pole. A state trooper who arrived first at the accident testified that the car was resting against the pole near the hinge pillar on the driver's side, a location between the door and the left front fender. Fusco offered two experts (Robert Walson and Carl Thelin) who, based in part on this testimony and their examination of the broken ball stud, concluded that metal fatigue had caused the stud to break, causing the steering apparatus to fail and the car to veer into the pole....

....

II.

General Motors' first claim on appeal is that the district court erred in ruling, prior to the first trial, that two videotapes — the "driving tapes" — were inadmissible. The main tape made in 1992 has two parts. In the indoor part, Ulman used a car mounted on a lift to display the function of the ball stud and tie rod and showed how in this demonstration the connection between the stud and the tire wheel or axle had been altered in the test vehicle so that the stud could be released deliberately from inside the car.

In the outdoor part, filmed at a General Motors test track, Ulman drove the Chevette while Willis, sitting in the passenger seat, intentionally disconnected the tie rod from the tire wheel. The film showed that, when the left wheel finally separated from the rod, the wheel flopped out of alignment with the right wheel and dragged on the highway apparently creating a long black skid mark. The car did not veer out of control or hit the track barrier. The other tape, made in 1986, simply showed a similar test track demonstration with a different driver and passenger. Thus, there is no need for an independent discussion of this tape....

....

... [W]e turn to the merits of the ruling excluding the driving tapes. The oral ruling was terse ("You don't have to argue it. I'm not going to let it in.") but the district judge had a written motion from Fusco, and a written response from General Motors, and made the ruling only after allowing both sides to argue their points orally. Fusco's main objection was that the taped scene on the test track did not adequately replicate the conditions of the accident. Merely to state the obvious, no one claimed that the accident had occurred when a jury-rigged cotter pin was pulled from the ball stud by a wire leading into the passenger seat. Another facially obvious difference is that the test car was driven by an experienced driver who expected the break to occur.

General Motors readily admitted that the conditions were not the same but argued that the tape was admissible to show general scientific principles and that the dissimilarities went to weight and not admissibility.[4] It repeats this

---

[4] General Motors does not claim that the indoor portion of the tape was admissible independently; and indeed most of the indoor portion was merely to lay the groundwork for the test. The

argument on appeal, adding that under Fed. R. Evid. 403 the burden was upon Fusco (as the opponent of the evidence) to show that prejudice substantially outweighed probative value. General Motors says that not only did Fusco fail to show that the dissimilarities were important but, in addition, General Motors' own experts would have said that the dissimilarities were not significant.

The problems raised by demonstrations of this kind are interesting and important....

The case law in this area is muddled, as one might expect, but the tendency of the court is to treat this class of demonstrative evidence more skeptically than would the lay juror. The concern lies not with use of tape or film (the issue would be largely the same if the jurors were taken to the test track for a live demonstration) but with the deliberate re-creation of an event under staged conditions. Where that re-creation could easily seem to resemble the actual occurrence, courts have feared that the jurors may be misled because they do not fully appreciate how variations in the surrounding conditions, as between the original occurrence and the staged event, can alter the outcome.

In such cases the solution of many courts, including this one, has been to call for substantial similarity in conditions, or to stress the great discretion of the trial judge to exclude the evidence where similarity is not shown or both.... This case law largely undercuts General Motors' claim that the burden lay with Fusco to show undue prejudice; instead, courts have created a doctrine, predating and now loosely appended to Rule 403, that requires a foundational showing of substantial similarity in circumstances....

Here the test track demonstration was rife with the risk of misunderstanding. Whatever Fusco's counsel or experts said to the jury about differing circumstances, the drama of the filmed re-creation could easily overcome the logic of the distinctions. Our case is scarcely different than the re-creating in *Swajian* involving a broken rear axle in a similarly staged demonstration by General Motors. We there affirmed the trial judge's exclusion of such evidence, pointing to "the sound and broad discretion of the trial judge" in policing such videotaped evidence. *Id.* at 36. We reaffirm here the principle and the result....

PEOPLE v. COLLINS

438 P.2d 33 (Cal. 1968)

SULLIVAN, JUSTICE:

We deal here with the novel question whether evidence of mathematical probability has been properly introduced and used by the prosecution in a criminal case. While we discern no inherent incompatibility between the disciplines of law and mathematics and intend no general disapproval or

---

indoor portion did show Ulman using a straw, in place of the stud, to show how the stud could be bent by an impact on the rear portion of the wheel, but General Motors does not claim that this brief sequence justified the tape, and it could easily have been replicated in court with a mock-up.

III. RELEVANT BUT INADMISSIBLE EVIDENCE: UNFAIR PREJUDICE, ETC.

disparagement of the latter as an auxiliary of the fact-finding processes of the former, we cannot uphold the technique employed in the instant case. As we explain in detail ... the testimony as to mathematical probability infected the case with fatal error and distorted the jury's traditional role of determining guilt or innocence according to long-settled rules. Mathematics, a veritable sorcerer in our computerized society, while assisting the trier of fact in the search for truth, must not cast a spell over him. We conclude that on the record before us defendant should not have had his guilt determined by the odds and that he is entitled to a new trial. We reverse the judgment....

On June 18th, 1964, at about 11:30 a.m., Mrs. Juanita Brooks, who had been shopping, was walking home along an alley in the San Pedro area of the City of Los Angeles.... As she stooped down to pick up an empty carton, she was suddenly pushed to the ground by a person whom she neither saw nor heard approach.... She managed to look up and saw a young woman running from the scene. According to Mrs. Brooks the latter appeared to weigh about 145 pounds, was wearing "something dark," and had hair "between a dark blond and a light blond," but lighter than the color of the defendant Janet Collins' hair as it appeared at trial. Immediately after the incident, Mrs. Brooks discovered that her purse, containing between $35 and $40, was missing.

About the same time as the robbery, John Bass, who lived on the street at the end of the alley, was in front of his house watering his lawn.... [H]e saw a woman run out of the alley and enter a yellow automobile parked across the street from him.... The latter then saw that it was being driven by a male Negro, wearing a mustache and beard. At the trial Bass identified defendant as the driver of the yellow automobile....

....

At the seven-day trial the prosecution experienced difficulty in establishing the identities of the perpetrator of the crime. The victim could not identify Janet and had never seen the defendant. The identification by the witness Bass, who observed the girl run out of the alley and get into the automobile, was incomplete as to Janet and may have been weakened as to the defendant....

In an apparent attempt to bolster the identifications, the prosecutor called an instructor of mathematics at a state college. Through this witness he sought to establish that assuming the robbery was committed by a Caucasian woman with a blond ponytail who left the scene accompanied by a Negro with a beard and mustache, there was an overwhelming probability that the crime was committed by any couple answering such distinctive characteristics. The witness testified, in substance, to the "product rule," which states that the probability of the joint occurrence of a number of mutually independent events is equal to the product of the individual probabilities that each of the events will occur.... Without presenting any statistical evidence whatsoever in support of the probabilities for the factors selected, the prosecutor then proceeded to have the witness assume probability factors for the various characteristics which he deemed to be shared

A. UNFAIR PREJUDICE CASES

by the guilty couple and all other couples answering to such distinctive characteristics.[10]

Applying the product rule to his own factors the prosecutor arrived at a probability that there was but one chance in 12 million that any couple possessed the distinctive characteristics of the defendants. Accordingly, under this theory, it was to be inferred that there could be but one chance in 12 million that defendants were innocent and that another equally distinctive couple actually committed the robbery. Expanding on what he had thus purported to suggest as a hypothesis, the prosecutor offered the completely unfounded and improper testimonial assertion that, in his opinion, the factors he had assigned were "conservative estimates" and that, in reality "the chances of anyone else besides these defendants being there, ... having every similarity, ... is somewhat like one in a billion."

Objections were timely made to the mathematician's testimony on the grounds that it was immaterial, that it invaded the province of the jury, and that it was based on unfounded assumptions. The objections were "temporarily overruled" and the evidence admitted subject to a motion to strike. When that motion was made at the conclusion of the direct examination, the court denied it, stating that the testimony had been received only for the "purpose of illustrating the mathematical probabilities of various matters, the possibilities for them occurring or re-occurring."

....

As we shall explain, the prosecution's introduction and use of mathematical probability statistics injected two fundamental prejudicial errors into the case: (1) The testimony itself lacked an adequate foundation both in evidence and in

---

[10] Although the prosecutor insisted that the factors he used were only for illustrative purposes — to demonstrate how the probability of the occurrence of mutually independent factors affected the probability that they would occur together — he nevertheless attempted to use factors which he personally related to the distinctive characteristics of the defendants. In his argument to the jury he invited the jurors to apply their own factors, and asked defense counsel to suggest what the latter would deem reasonable. The prosecutor himself proposed the individual probabilities set out in the table below. Although the transcript of the examination of the mathematics instructor and the information volunteered by the prosecutor at that time create some uncertainty as to precisely which of the characteristics the prosecutor assigned to the individual probabilities, he restated in his argument to the jury that they should be as follows:

	Characteristic	Individual Probability
A.	Partly yellow automobile	1/10
B.	Man with mustache	1/4
C.	Girl with ponytail	1/10
D.	Girl with blond hair	1/3
E.	Negro man with beard	1/10
F.	Interracial couple in car	1/1000

In his brief on appeal the defendant agrees that the foregoing appeared on a table presented in the trial court.

statistical theory; and (2) the testimony and the manner in which the prosecution used it distracted the jury from its proper and requisite function of weighing the evidence on the issue of guilt, encouraged the jurors to rely upon an engaging but logically irrelevant expert demonstration, foreclosed the possibility of an effective defense by an attorney apparently unschooled in mathematical refinements, and placed the jurors and defense counsel at a disadvantage in sifting relevant fact from inapplicable theory.

We initially consider the defects in the testimony itself. As we have indicated, the specific technique presented through the mathematician's testimony and advanced by the prosecutor to measure the probabilities in question suffered from two basic and pervasive defects — an inadequate evidentiary foundation and an inadequate proof of statistical independence. First, as to the foundation requirement, we find the record devoid of any evidence relating to any of the six individual probability factors used by the prosecutor and ascribed by him to the six characteristics as we have set them out in footnote 10, *ante*. To put it another way, the prosecution produced no evidence whatsoever showing, or from which it could be in any way inferred, that only one out of every ten cars which might have been at the scene of the robbery was partly yellow, that only one out of every four men who might have been there wore a mustache, that only one out of every ten girls who might have been there wore a ponytail, or that any of the other individual probability factors listed were even roughly accurate....

. . . .

We can hardly conceive of a more fatal gap in the prosecution's scheme of proof. A foundation for the admissibility of the witness' testimony was never even attempted to be laid, let alone established. His testimony was neither made to rest on his own testimonial knowledge nor presented by proper hypothetical questions based upon valid data in the record....

But, as we have indicated, there was another glaring defect in the prosecution's technique, namely an inadequate proof of the statistical independence of the six factors. No proof was presented that the characteristics selected were mutually independent, even though the witness himself acknowledged that such condition was essential to the proper application of the "product rule" or "multiplication rule." ... To the extent that the traits or characteristics were not mutually independent (e.g., Negroes with beards and men with mustaches obviously represent overlapping categories ...), the "product rule" would inevitably yield a wholly erroneous and exaggerated result even if all of the individual components had been determined with precision....

. . . .

In the instant case, therefore, because of the aforementioned two defects — the inadequate evidentiary foundations and the inadequate proof of statistical independence — the technique employed by the prosecutor could only lead to wild conjecture without demonstrated relevancy to the issues presented. It acquired no redeeming quality from the prosecutor's statement that it was being used only "for illustrative purposes" since, as we shall point out, the prose-

A. UNFAIR PREJUDICE CASES

cutor's subsequent utilization of the mathematical testimony was not confined within such limits.

We know turn to the second fundamental error caused by the probability testimony. Quite apart from our foregoing objections to the specific technique employed by the prosecution to estimate the probability in question, we think that the entire enterprise upon which the prosecution embarked, and which was directed to the objective of measuring the likelihood of a random couple possessing the characteristics allegedly distinguishing the robbers, was gravely misguided. At best, it might yield an estimate as to how infrequently bearded Negroes drive yellow cars in the company of blonde females with ponytails.

The prosecution's approach, however, could furnish the jury with absolutely no guidance on the crucial issue: *Of the admittedly few such couples, which one, if any, was guilty of committing this robbery?* Probability theory necessarily remains silent on that question, since no mathematical equation can prove beyond a reasonable doubt (1) that the guilty couple *in fact* possessed the characteristics described by the People's witnesses, or even (2) that only *one* couple possessing those distinctive characteristics could be found in the entire Los Angeles area.

As to the first inherent failing we observe that the prosecution's theory of probability rested on the assumption that the witnesses called by the People had conclusively established that the guilty couple possessed the precise characteristics relied upon by the prosecution. But no mathematical formula could ever establish beyond a reasonable doubt that the prosecution's witnesses correctly observed and accurately described the distinctive features which were employed to link defendants to the crime.... Conceivably, for example, the guilty couple might have included a light-skinned Negress with bleached hair rather than a Caucasian blonde; or the driver of the car might have been wearing a false beard as a disguise; or the prosecution's witnesses might simply have been unreliable. (Footnote omitted.)

The foregoing risks of error permeate the prosecution's circumstantial case. Traditionally, the jury weighs such risks in evaluating the credibility and probative value of trial testimony, but the likelihood of human error or of falsification obviously cannot be quantified; that likelihood must therefore be excluded from any effort to assign a *number* to the probability of guilt or innocence. Confronted with an equation which purports to yield a numerical index of probable guilt, few juries could resist the temptation to accord disproportionate weight to that index; only an exceptional juror, and indeed only a defense attorney schooled in mathematics, could successfully keep in mind the fact that the probability computed by the prosecution can represent, *at best*, the likelihood that a random couple would share the characteristics testified to by the People's witnesses — *not necessarily the characteristics of the actually guilty couple*.

As to the second inherent failing in the prosecution's approach, even assuming that the first failing could be discounted, the most a mathematical computation could *ever* yield would be a measure of the probability that a random couple

III. RELEVANT BUT INADMISSIBLE EVIDENCE: UNFAIR PREJUDICE, ETC.

would possess the distinctive features in question. In the present case, for example, the prosecution attempted to compute the probability that a random couple would include a bearded Negro, a blonde girl with a ponytail, and a partly yellow car; the prosecution urged that this probability was no more than one in 12 million. Even accepting this conclusion as arithmetically accurate, however, one still could not conclude that the Collinses were probably *the* guilty couple. On the contrary, as we explain in the Appendix, the prosecution's figures actually imply a likelihood of over 40 percent that the Collinses could be "duplicated" by at least *one other couple who might equally have committed the San Pedro robbery*. Urging that the Collinses be convicted on the basis of evidence which logically establishes no more than this seems as indefensible as arguing for the conviction of X on the ground that a witness saw either X or X's twin commit the crime.

Again, few defense attorneys, and certainly few jurors, could be expected to comprehend this basic flaw in the prosecution's analysis. Conceivably even the prosecutor erroneously believed that his equation established a high probability that *no* other bearded Negro in the Los Angeles area drove a yellow car accompanied by a ponytailed blonde. In any event, although his technique could demonstrate no such thing, he solemnly told the jury that he had supplied mathematical proof of guilt.

Sensing the novelty of that notion, the prosecutor told the jurors that the traditional idea of proof beyond a reasonable doubt represented "the most hackneyed, stereotyped, trite, misunderstood concept in criminal law." He sought to reconcile the jury to the risk that, under his "new math" approach to criminal jurisprudence, "on some rare occasion ... an innocent person may be convicted." "Without taking that risk," the prosecution continued, "life would be intolerable ... because ... there would be immunity for the Collinses, for people who chose not to be employed to go down and push old ladies down and take their money and be immune because how could we ever be sure they are the ones who did it?"

In essence this argument of the prosecutor was calculated to persuade the jury to convict defendants whether or not they were convinced of their guilt to a moral certainty and beyond a reasonable doubt.... Undoubtedly the jurors were unduly impressed by the mystique of the mathematical demonstration but were unable to assess its relevancy or value. Although we make no appraisal of the proper applications of mathematical techniques in the proof of facts, ... we have strong feelings that such applications, particularly in a criminal case, must be critically examined in view of the substantial unfairness to a defendant which may result from ill conceived techniques with which the trier of fact is not technically equipped to cope.... We feel that the technique employed in the case before us falls into the latter category.

We conclude that the court erred in admitting over defendant's objection the evidence pertaining to the mathematical theory of probability and in denying

A. UNFAIR PREJUDICE CASES

defendant's motion to strike such evidence.... The judgment against defendant must therefore be reversed ....

....

Appendix

....

Hence, even if we should accept the prosecution's figures without question, we would derive a probability of over 40 percent that the couple observed by the witnesses could be "duplicated" by at least one other equally distinctive interracial couple in the area, including a Negro with a beard and mustache, driving a partly yellow car in the company of a blonde with a ponytail. Thus the prosecution's computations, far from establishing beyond a reasonable doubt that the Collinses were the couple described by the prosecution's witnesses, imply a very substantial likelihood that the area contained *more than one* such couple, and that a couple *other* than the Collinses was the one observed at the scene of the robbery....

SCHULTZ v. BUTCHER

24 F.3d 626 (4th Cir. 1994)

CHAPMAN, SENIOR CIRCUIT JUDGE:

Karen Schultz was injured when the small boat in which she was riding crossed the wake created by The Spirit of Mount Vernon, a large passenger vessel, which caused the smaller boat to impact sharply upon the water. Schultz brought this action against the owner and the operator of the smaller boat, and against The Spirit Cruises, Inc. ("Spirit Cruises")....

On July 4, 1991, Karen Schultz was a passenger in a 16 foot pleasure boat, Gypsy, with a 65 horsepower outboard engine. She was injured when this craft crossed the wake of The Spirit of Mount Vernon and came down with great force, causing her to fall on the boat's hard inner surface. She suffered a fracture of her L-1 vertebra. This injury required extensive surgery, and her medical bills totaled $39,833.56.

Gypsy was owned by G. William Butcher, III and being operated by Edward H. Maass, neither of whom had any prior experience in the operation of small boats, particularly on the holiday crowded Potomac River. As Gypsy approached the three foot wake of The Spirit of Mount Vernon, Maass spotted the wake and reduced speed. After some discussion among Maass, Butcher and the passengers about the size of the wake and how to cross it, Maass increased the boat's speed to roughly ten knots and crossed the wake at a 45 degree angle. Prior to the accident, the five individuals who were on Gypsy, including Maass, consumed some alcoholic beverages....

Spirit Cruises claims the district court improperly excluded evidence of Maass's alcohol consumption the day of the accident. The court excluded the evidence and found that under Federal Rule of Evidence 403 it was more prejudicial than probative when Spirit Cruises could not make a proffer that the alcohol impaired Maass's operation of the boat or his memory. We review the district court's exclusion of the evidence for an abuse of discretion....

Schultz brought this action under admiralty jurisdiction, thus the Federal Rules of Evidence apply. Rule 403 provides that relevant evidence "may be excluded if its probative value is substantially outweighed by the danger of unfair prejudice, [or] confusion of the issues...." A district court has broad discretion under Rule 403 to exclude prejudicial evidence, but a court typically exercises this authority during jury trials.... Prejudicial evidence is excluded to protect the jury from drawing improper inferences. *Mullen v. Princess Anne Volunteer Fire Co.*, 853 F.2d 1130, 1134 (4th Cir. 1988) ("All relevant evidence is 'prejudicial' in the sense that it may prejudice the party against whom it is admitted. Rule 403, however, is concerned only with 'unfair' prejudice. That is, the possibility that the evidence will excite the jury to make a decision on the basis of a factor unrelated to the issues properly before it.")

In this case, we are faced with the exclusion of prejudicial evidence in a trial to the bench. In *Gulf States Utils. Co. v. Ecodyne Corp.*, 635 F.2d 517 (5th Cir. Unit A Jan. 1981), the Fifth Circuit found the district court's exclusion of prejudicial evidence to be in error since the matter was tried before the bench. In so doing, the Fifth Circuit stated,

> [e]xcluding relevant evidence in a bench trial because it is cumulative or a waste of time is clearly a proper exercise of the judge's power, but excluding relevant evidence on the basis of "unfair" prejudice is a useless procedure. Rule 403 assumes a trial judge is able to discern and weigh the improper inferences, and then balance those improprieties against probative value and necessity. Certainly, in a bench trial, the same judge can also exclude those improper inferences from his mind in reaching a decision.

Id. at 519.

Adopting the position taken in *Gulf States*, we hold that in the context of a bench trial, evidence should not be excluded under 403 on the ground that it is unfairly prejudicial.... Rule 403 was designed to keep evidence not germane to any issue outside the purview of the jury's consideration. For a bench trial, we are confident that the district court can hear relevant evidence, weigh its probative value and reject any improper inferences....

Reversed, Vacated and Remanded with Instructions.

B. UNFAIR PREJUDICE PROBLEMS

1. Pre-Owned Clothes

Jack is arrested and charged with burglary ("the breaking and entering of the dwelling house of another at night with the intent to commit a felony therein").

B. UNFAIR PREJUDICE PROBLEMS 27

He is accused of stealing five expensive men's suits. At trial the prosecution offers the following evidence:

   a. The closets and dresser drawers in Jack's apartment contained two hundred pairs of men's socks and three hundred towels (many of which had hotel monograms on them). Admissible? Why?
   b. Jack had 40 suits in his apartment closet. Admissible? Why?
   c. Jack had stolen twenty pairs of underwear the year before. Why would such evidence be offered? Admissible?

Note: this problem is based on an actual case.

2. Heads Up

Cars driven by Stanley Rodriguez and Frances DeLarue collide on Peachtree Street. Frances, who is injured, sues Stanley for negligence. At trial, she offers a video of Dr. Gupta suturing her scalp wound. The video highlights the bloody area of the wound.

   a. What is the basis for an objection to this evidence?
   b. What is the proponent of the evidence's best response to the objection?
   c. What ruling and why?

3. "Wax On, Wax Off"

Amy slips and falls in the lobby of the Armitron Corp. She sues the company for damages resulting from the negligent maintenance and repair of the floor.

   a. At trial, Amy offers evidence that in the past two weeks, at least nine other people slipped and fell in the same general area of the lobby. (Three of the people slipped and fell subsequent to Amy's fall.) Is this evidence admissible to show negligence or culpability? For a different purpose? Why?
   b. Amy offers the testimony of a professional floor cleaner, Carl, as an expert on "waxology and the general slipperiness of floors." The expert will testify that he performed an experiment in the lobby of another building on a similar floor that was two years older than the one in question — the original floor on which Amy fell had been destroyed and then remodeled in good faith. The expert found the floor to be highly slippery, much more so than the average floor. Admissible? Why?
   c. Amy also offers the maintenance and repair records of the Armitron Corp. on the lobby floors of other buildings it owns. Admissible? Why?
   d. The defendant corporation offers evidence that Amy slipped and fell twice before that same week, once in the supermarket and once while getting into her car. Admissible? Why?
   e. The defendant also offered evidence that its records reflected that no one had fallen on the floor in the three months preceding Amy's fall. Admissible? Why?

III. RELEVANT BUT INADMISSIBLE EVIDENCE: UNFAIR PREJUDICE, ETC.

4. Little Red Corvette

a. On a dark and remote foggy stretch of two-lane highway, Carlos' Astro Van collided with LeShawn's Corvette. There were no eyewitnesses to the crash and neither Carlos nor LeShawn remembered how the crash had occurred. Carlos later sued LeShawn for damages. At trial, Carlos called a statistics expert, Dr. Lenny Leonardo, to testify that "Corvette drivers are nine times more likely to cause an accident than other drivers, and are fourteen times more likely to cause an accident than Astro Van drivers." Admissible? Why?

b. Carlos is also prosecuted for holding up a Bloomingdale's Department Store earlier that same day. Several eyewitnesses swear they saw a person looking exactly like Carlos, dressed in the same polar-arctic sweater and with a beard and mustache, escape in an Astro Van after robbing the store. Carlos denies the charge. Dr. Leonardo is called to testify by the prosecution. Leonardo states that "the odds of another person fitting Carlos' description, wearing a similar sweater and driving an Astro Van in the same county is one in six million." Admissible? Why?

5. "A Lot Is Riding on Your Tires..."

Kate is charged with cocaine conspiracy. At trial, she testifies and mentions she has a daughter, age 5, named Becca. In rebuttal, the prosecution offers a photograph of Becca playing with large sums of money while sitting inside an empty tire in what looks like Becca's room. Admissible? Why?

6. Lobster Bill of Lading

In a breach of contract action between Noah's Lobsters Inc. and The Olde Edward Inn restaurant, the only issue at trial was the meaning of a term in the bill of lading guaranteeing "Maine lobsters for delivery." Noah's insisted that the term permitted the substitution of South African lobsters on a necessity basis. Noah's offered prior bills of lading for the sale of Maine lobsters with The Olde Edward Inn, and bills of lading for lobster sales involving Noah's and other restaurants. Admissible? Why?

7. Murder He Wrote

Jorge is charged with murder. At trial, the prosecution calls an expert to the witness stand, Dr. Denise Dart, who will testify that bite marks found on the victim were made by Jorge. Admissible? Why?

IV. CHARACTER AND HABIT EVIDENCE

> Character and habit are close akin. Character is a generalized description of one's disposition, or of one's disposition in respect to a general trait, such as honesty, temperance, or peacefulness. "Habit," in modern usage, both lay and psychological, is more specific. It describes one's regular response to a repeated specific situation.

Fed. R. Evid. 406 Advisory Committee's Note (quoting McCormick, § 162 at 340 (1st ed.))

> Character questions arise in two fundamentally different ways. (1) Character may itself be an element of a crime, claim, or defense. A situation of this kind is commonly referred to as "character in issue."... (2) Character evidence is susceptible of being used for the purpose of suggesting an inference that the person acted on the occasion in question consistently with his character. This use of character is often described as "circumstantial."...
>
> In most jurisdictions today, the circumstantial use of character is rejected but with important exceptions: (1) an accused may introduce pertinent evidence of good character ... in which event the prosecution may rebut with evidence of bad character; (2) an accused may introduce pertinent evidence of the character of the victim ... and the prosecution may introduce similar evidence in rebuttal of the character evidence, or, in a homicide case, to rebut a claim that deceased was the first aggressor; and (3) the character of a witness may be gone into as bearing on his credibility....

Fed. R. Evid. 404(a) Advisory Committee's Note (citing McCormick, §§ 155-61)

> Under Rule 404(b), "other crimes" evidence may be offered by any party for a purpose other than proving criminal propensity or conforming conduct. None of these rules permits evidence of prior bad acts when the sole purpose is to show propensity toward criminal conduct.

United States v. McCourt, 925 F.2d 1229 (9th Cir. 1990)

A. CHARACTER AND HABIT CASES

PEOPLE v. ZACKOWITZ
172 N.E. 466 (N.Y. 1930)

CARDOZO, C.J.:

On November 10, 1929, shortly after midnight, the defendant in Kings county shot Frank Coppola and killed him without justification or excuse. A crime is admitted. What is doubtful is the degree only.

Four young men, of whom Coppola was one, were at work repairing an automobile in a Brooklyn street. A woman, the defendant's wife, walked by on the opposite side. One of the men spoke to her insultingly, or so at least she understood him. The defendant, who had dropped behind to buy a newspaper, came up to find his wife in tears. He was told she had been insulted, though she did not then repeat the words. Enraged, he stepped across the street and upbraided the offenders with words of coarse profanity. He informed them, so the survivors testify, that "if they did not get out of there in five minutes, he would come back and bump them all off." Rejoining his wife, he walked with her to their apartment house located close at hand.... With rage aroused again, the defendant went back to the scene of the insult and found the four young men still working at the car. In a statement to the police, he said that he had armed himself at the apartment with a .25-caliber automatic pistol. In his testimony at the trial he said that this pistol had been in his pocket all the evening. Words and blows followed, and then a shot.... The pistol came from the pocket, and from the pistol a single shot, which did its deadly work. The defendant walked away and at the corner met his wife who had followed him from the home. The two took a taxicab to Manhattan, where they spent the rest of the night at the dwelling of a friend. On the way the defendant threw his pistol into the river. He was arrested on January 7, 1930, about two months following the crime.

At the trial the vital question was the defendant's state of mind at the moment of the homicide. Did he shoot with a deliberate and premeditated design to kill? Was he so inflamed by drink or by anger or by both combined that, though he knew the nature of his act, he was the prey to sudden impulse, the fury of the fleeting moment? *People v. Caruso*, 246 N.Y. 437, 446, 159 N.E. 390. If he went forth from his apartment with a preconceived design to kill, how is it that he failed to shoot at once? How reconcile such a design with the drawing of the pistol later in the heat and rage of an affray? These and like questions the jurors were to ask themselves and answer before measuring the defendant's guilt.... There must be no blurring of the issues by evidence illegally admitted and carrying with it in its admission an appeal to prejudice and passion.

Evidence charged with that appeal was, we think, admitted here. Not only was it admitted, and this under objection and exception, but the changes were rung upon it by prosecutor and judge. Almost at the opening of the trial the people began the endeavor to load the defendant down with the burden of an evil character. He was to be put before the jury as a man of murderous disposition. To that end they were allowed to prove that at the time of the encounter and at that of his arrest he had in his apartment, kept there in a radio box, three pistols and a tear-gas gun. There was no claim that he had brought these weapons out at the time of the affray, no claim that with any of them he had discharged the fatal shot. He could not have done so, for they were all of different caliber. The

A. CHARACTER AND HABIT CASES 31

end to be served by laying the weapons before the jury was something very different. The end was to bring persuasion that here was a man of vicious and dangerous propensities, who because of those propensities was more likely to kill with deliberate and premeditated design than a man of irreproachable life and amiable manners. Indeed, this is the very ground on which the introduction of the evidence is now explained and defended. The district attorney tells us in his brief that the possession of the weapons characterized the defendant as "a desperate type of criminal," a "person criminally inclined." The dissenting opinion, if it puts the argument less bluntly, leaves the substance of the thought unchanged. "Defendant was presented to the jury as a man having dangerous weapons in his possession, making a selection therefrom and going forth to put into execution his threats to kill." The weapons were not brought by the defendant to the scene of the encounter. They were left in his apartment where they were incapable of harm. In such circumstances, ownership of the weapons, if it has any relevance at all, has relevance only as indicating a general disposition to make use of them thereafter, and a general disposition to make use of them thereafter is without relevance except as indicating a "desperate type of criminal," a criminal affected with a murderous propensity.

We are asked to extenuate the error by calling it an incident; what was proved may have an air of innocence if it is styled the history of the crime. The virus of the ruling is not so easily extracted. There was no passing reference to something casually brought out in the narrative of the killing, as if an admission had been proved against the defendant that he had picked one weapon out of several. Here in the forefront of the trial, immediately following the statement of the medical examiner, testimony was admitted that weapons, not the instruments of the killing, had been discovered by the police in the apartment of the killer; and the weapons with great display were laid before the jury, marked as exhibits, and thereafter made the subject of animated argument. Room for doubt there is none that in the thought of the jury, as in that of the district attorney, the tendency of the whole performance was to characterize the defendant as a man murderously inclined. The purpose was not disguised. From the opening to the verdict, it was flaunted and avowed.

If a murderous propensity may be proved against a defendant as one of the tokens of his guilt, a rule of criminal evidence, long believed to be of fundamental importance for the protection of the innocent, must be first declared away. Fundamental hitherto has been the rule that character is never an issue in a criminal prosecution unless the defendant chooses to make it one.... In a very real sense a defendant starts his life afresh when he stands before a jury, a prisoner at the bar. There has been a homicide in a public place. The killer admits the killing, but urges self-defense and sudden impulse. Inflexibly the law has set its face against the endeavor to fasten guilt upon him by proof of character or experience predisposing to an act of crime.... The endeavor has been often made, but always it has failed. At times, when the issue has been self-defense, testimony has been admitted as to the murderous propensity of the deceased, the victim of the homicide, ... but never of such a propensity on the part of the killer. The principle back of the exclusion is one, not of logic, but of policy.... There may be cogency in the argument that a quarrelsome defendant is more likely to start a quarrel than one of milder type, a man of dangerous mode of life more likely than a shy recluse. The law is not blind to this, but equally it is not blind to the peril to the innocent if character is accepted as probative of crime. "The natural and inevitable tendency of the tribunal — whether judge or jury — is to give excessive weight to the vicious record of crime thus exhibited, and either to allow it to bear too strongly on the present charge, or to take the proof of it as justifying a condemnation irrespective of guilt of the present charge." (Citations omitted.)

A different question would be here if the pistols had been bought in expectation of this particular encounter. They would then have been admissible as evidence of preparation and design.... A different question would be here if they were so connected with the crime as to identify the perpetrator, if he had dropped them, for example, at the scene of the affray. *People v. Hill*, 198 N.Y. 64, 91 N.E. 272. They would then have been admissible as tending to implicate the possessor (if identity was disputed), no matter what the opprobrium attached to his possession. Different, also, would be the question if the defendant had been shown to have gone forth from the apartment with all the weapons on his person. To be armed from head to foot at the very moment of an encounter may be a circumstance worthy to be considered, like acts of preparation generally, as a proof of preconceived design. There can be no such implication from the ownership of weapons which one leaves behind at home.

The endeavor was to generate an atmosphere of professional criminality. It was an endeavor the more unfair in that, apart from the suspicion attaching to the possession of these weapons, there is nothing to mark the defendant as a man of evil life. He was not in crime as a business. He did not shoot as a bandit shoots in the hope of wrongful gain. He was engaged in a decent calling, an optician regularly employed, without criminal record, or criminal associates. If his own testimony be true, he had gathered these weapons together as curios, a collection that interested and amused him. Perhaps his explanation of their ownership is false. There is nothing stronger than mere suspicion to guide us to an answer. Whether the explanation be false or true, he should not have been driven by the people to the necessity of offering it. Brought to answer a specific charge, and to defend himself against it, he was placed in a position where he had to defend himself against another, more general and sweeping. He was made to answer to the charge, pervasive and poisonous even if insidious and covert, that he was a man of murderous heart, of criminal disposition....

The judgment of conviction should be reversed, and a new trial ordered....

A. CHARACTER AND HABIT CASES

MICHELSON v. UNITED STATES

335 U.S. 469 (1948)

MR. JUSTICE JACKSON delivered the opinion of the Court:

In 1947 petitioner Michelson was convicted of bribing a federal revenue agent. The Government proved a large payment by the accused to the agent for the purpose of influencing his official action. The defendant, as a witness on his own behalf, admitted passing the money but claimed it was done in response to the agent's demands, threats, solicitations, and inducements that amounted to entrapment. It is enough for our purposes to say that determination of the issue turned on whether the jury should believe the agent or the accused....

. . . .

Defendant called five witnesses to prove that he enjoyed a good reputation. Two of them testified that their acquaintance with him extended over a period of about thirty years and the others said they had known him at least half that long. A typical examination in chief was as follows:

"Q. Do you know the defendant Michelson?
"A. Yes
"Q. How long did you know Mr. Michelson?
"A. About 30 years.
"Q. Do you know other people who know him?
"A. Yes.
"Q. Have you had occasion to discuss his reputation for honesty and truthfulness and for being a law-abiding citizen?
"A. It is very good.
"Q. You have talked to others?
"A. Yes.
"Q. And what is his reputation.
"A. Very good."

These are representative of answers by three witnesses; two others replied, in substance, that they never had heard anything against Michelson.

On cross-examination, four of the witnesses were asked in substance, this question: "Did you ever hear that Mr. Michelson on March 4, 1927, was convicted of a violation of the trademark law in New York City in regard to watches?" This referred to the twenty-year-old conviction about which defendant himself had testified on direct examination. Two of them had heard of it and two had not.

To four of these witnesses the prosecution also addressed the question the allowance of which, over defendant's objection, is claimed to be reversible error.

"Did you every hear that on October 11th, 1920, the defendant, Solomon Michelson, was arrested for receiving stolen goods?"

None of the witnesses appears to have heard of this.

The trial court asked counsel for the prosecution, out of presence of the jury, "Is it a fact according to the best information in your possession that Michelson was arrested for receiving stolen goods?" Counsel replied that it was, and to support his good faith exhibited a paper record which defendant's counsel did not challenge.

The judge also on three occasions warned the jury, in terms that are not criticized, of the limited purpose for which this evidence was received....
....

Courts that follow the common-law tradition almost unanimously have come to disallow resort by the prosecution to any kind of evidence or a defendant's evil character to establish a probability of his guilt....
....

When the defendant elects to initiate a character inquiry, another anomalous rule comes into play. Not only is he permitted to call witnesses to testify from hearsay, but indeed such a witness is not allowed to base his testimony on anything but hearsay. What commonly is called "character evidence" is only such when "character" is employed as a synonym for "reputation." The witness may not testify about defendant's specific acts or courses of conduct or his possession of a particular disposition, or of benign mental and moral traits; nor can he testify that his own acquaintance, observation, and knowledge of defendant leads to his own independent opinion that defendant possesses a good general or specific character inconsistent with commission of acts charged. The witness is, however, allowed to summarize what he has heard in the community, although much of it may have been said by persons less qualified to judge than himself....
....

... The price a defendant must pay for attempting to prove his good name is to throw open the entire subject which the law has kept closed for his benefit and to make himself vulnerable where the law otherwise shields him. The prosecution may pursue the inquiry with contradictory witnesses to show that damaging rumors, whether or not well-grounded, were afloat — for it is not the man that he is, but the name that he has which is put in issue. Another hazard is that his own witness is subject to cross-examination as to the contents and extent of the hearsay on which he bases his conclusions, and he may be required to disclose rumors and reports that are current even if they do not affect his own conclusion. It may test the sufficiency of his knowledge by asking what stories were circulating concerning events, such as one's arrest, about which people normally comment and speculate. Thus, while the law gives defendant the option to show as a fact that his reputation reflects a life and habit incompatible with commission of the offense charged, it subjects his proof to tests of credibility designed to prevent him from profiting by a mere parade of partisans....

Arrest without more does not, in law any more than in reason, impeach the integrity or impair the credibility of a witness. It happens to the innocent as well as the guilty. Only a conviction, therefore, may be inquired about to undermine the trustworthiness of a witness.

Arrest without more may nevertheless impair or cloud one's reputation. False arrest may do that. Even to be acquitted may damage one's good name if the community receives the verdict with a wink and chooses to remember defendant as one who ought to have been convicted. A conviction, on the other hand, may be accepted as a misfortune or an injustice, and even enhance the standing of one who mends his ways and lives it down. Reputation is the net balance of so many debits and credits that the law does not attack the finality to a conviction, when the issue is reputation, that is given to it when the issue is credibility.

The inquiry as to an arrest is permissible also because the prosecution has a right to test the qualifications of the witness to bespeak the community opinion. If one never heard the speculations and rumors in which even one's friends indulge upon his arrest, the jury may doubt whether he is capable of giving any very reliable conclusions as to his reputation....

....

... However, limiting instructions on this subject are no more difficult to comprehend or apply than those upon various other subjects; for example, instructions that admissions of a co-defendant are to be limited to the question of his guilt and are not to be considered as evidence against other defendants, and instructions as to other problems in the trial of conspiracy charges. A defendant in such a case is powerless to prevent his cause from being irretrievably obscured and confused; but, in cases such as the one before us, the law foreclosed this whole confounding line of inquiry, unless defendant thought the net advantage from opening it up would be with him. Given this option we think defendants in general and this defendant in particular have no valid complaint at the latitude which existing law allows to the prosecution to meet by cross examination an issue voluntarily tendered by the defense.

We end as we began, with the observation that the law regulating the offering and testing of character testimony may merit many criticisms ....

The judgement is

Affirmed.

UNITED STATES v. BEECHUM

582 F.2d 898 (5th Cir. 1978),
cert. denied, 440 U.S. 920 (1979)

TJOFLAT, CIRCUIT JUDGE:

....

I. *Facts*

Orange Jell Beechum had been a substitute letter carrier in South Dallas, Texas for approximately two and one-half years prior to his arrest on September 16, 1975. Because Beechum had been suspected of rifling the mail on several occasions, postal inspectors planted in a mailbox on Beechum's route a letter containing the silver dollar, a greeting card, and sixteen dollars in currency. According to the testimony of one of the inspectors, the currency had been dusted with a powder visible only under ultraviolet light. A postal inspector observed Beechum retrieving the mail from the mailbox in which the letter had been planted and noted that Beechum stopped at a record shop for approximately one hour before returning to the South Dallas Postal Station. At the station, Beechum turned in the raw mail containing the test letter, and it was discovered that the letter had been opened and resealed. The silver dollar and the currency were missing.

....

... The inspector then asked Beechum to empty his pockets. Standing with his front pockets everted, Beechum professed to have relinquished all, but a frisk revealed the silver dollar in his hip pocket. At this time, the inspector discovered in Beechum's wallet the two Sears credit cards, which, as we have noted, were not issued to Beechum and had not been signed.

The arresting inspector questioned Beechum about the credit cards, and Beechum responded first that the only credit cards he possessed were his own. Later, when confronted with the Sears cards, he stated that he had never used them. The inspector testified that in response to further questioning concerning the cards, Beechum said, "Since you have all the answers, you tell me." The inspector inquired no further....

....

On direct examination Beechum testified that the silver dollar fell out of the mailbox as he was raking out the mail and that he picked it up and placed it first in his shirt pocket, and later (after it had fallen out) in his hip pocket, where he claimed to keep his change. Beechum also testified that, upon return to the postal station, he intended to turn in the silver dollar to Cox [Beechum's supervisor] but that he could not find Cox. Beechum also stated that he was not leaving the station when he was arrested. No mention was made of the credit cards.

On cross-examination the Government asked Beechum if the credit cards were in his wallet when he was arrested. Defense counsel objected on the basis that inquiry about the cards was outside the scope of cross-examination, and the court overruled the objection. On reassertion of the question, Beechum invoked his fifth amendment rights, but the prosecutor continued questioning on the subject of the cards. This occasioned repeated invocation of the fifth amendment by Beechum and vehement objection by defense counsel. Eventually, Beechum did admit to stating shortly after his arrest that the inspector could "answer his own questions" when the inspector quizzed him about the cards and that the only credit cards he had were his own....

A. CHARACTER AND HABIT CASES

II. *Issues*

As we have noted, the central issue in this case is whether the district court properly allowed the credit cards to be admitted as extrinsic offense evidence going to the issue of Beechum's intent to possess the silver dollar unlawfully....

....

... We conclude that the credit cards were highly probative of Beechum's intent and therefore properly admissible to attack the plausibility of his exculpatory testimony....

....

C. *The Extrinsic Offense*

At the time of his arrest, Beechum possessed a silver dollar and two credit cards, none of which belonged to him. The only contested issue concerning the silver dollar was whether Beechum intended to turn it in, as he claimed, or to keep it for himself. Apparently, he had possessed the credit cards for some time, perhaps ten months, prior to his arrest. The obvious question is why would Beechum give up the silver dollar if he kept the credit cards. In this case, the Government was entitled to an answer....

....

In this case, the jury was entitled to assess the credibility of Beechum's explanation but was deprived of the most effective vehicle for determining the veracity of Beechum's story when the judge erroneously allowed Beechum to invoke the fifth amendment and avoid the critical question on cross-examination. The Government was relegated to the inferences the jury might draw from the credit cards themselves and the additional evidence relating to them. The panel held that the cards and this evidence were insufficient to satisfy the strict standards for admissibility of extrinsic offense evidence established by *United States v. Broadway*, 477 F.2d 991 (5th Cir. 1973). We agree that *Broadway* dictates that the credit cards should not have been admitted; because this is so, we must reject the *Broadway* standards.

Broadway established two prerequisites to the admissibility of extrinsic offense evidence. First, it required that the physical elements of the extrinsic offense include the essential physical elements of the offense for which the defendant was indicted. Second, the case mandated that each of the physical elements of the extrinsic offense be established by plain, clear, and convincing evidence (footnote omitted)....

....

We must overrule *Broadway* because a straightforward application of the Federal Rules of Evidence calls for admission of the cards. The directly applicable rule is Fed.R.Evid. 404(b), which provides as follows:

> *Other crimes, wrongs, or acts.* Evidence of other crimes, wrongs, or acts is not admissible to prove the character of a person in order to show that he acted in conformity therewith. It may, however, be admissible for other

purposes, such as proof of motive, opportunity, intent, preparation, plan, knowledge, identity, or absence of mistake or accident.

The rule follows the venerable principle that evidence of extrinsic offenses should not be admitted solely to demonstrate the defendant's bad character.... Where, however, the extrinsic offense evidence is relevant to an issue such as intent, it may well be that the evidence has probative force that is not substantially outweighed by its inherent prejudice. If this is so, the evidence may be admissible (footnote omitted)....

What the rule calls for is essentially a two-step test. First, it must be determined that the extrinsic offense evidence is relevant to an issue other than the defendant's character. Second, the evidence must possess probative value that is not substantially outweighed by its undue prejudice and must meet the other requirements of rule 403.... The test for relevancy under the first step is identical to the one we have already encountered. The standards are established by rule 401, which deems evidence relevant when it has "any tendency to make the existence of any fact that is of consequence to the determination of the action more probable or less probable than it would be without the evidence." Where the evidence sought to be introduced is an extrinsic offense, its relevance is a function of its similarity to the offense charged. In this regard, however, similarity means more than that the extrinsic and charged offense have a common characteristic. For the purposes of determining relevancy, "a fact is similar to another only when the common characteristic is the significant one for the purpose of the inquiry at hand." Stone, The Rule of Exclusion of Similar Fact Evidence: England, 46 Harv. L. Rev. 954, 955 (1933). Therefore, similarity, and hence relevancy, is determined by the inquiry or issue to which the extrinsic offense is addressed.

Where the issue addressed is the defendant's intent to commit the offense charged, the relevancy of the extrinsic offense derives from the defendant's indulging himself in the same state of mind in the perpetration of both the extrinsic and charged offenses. The reasoning is that because the defendant had unlawful intent in the extrinsic offense, it is less likely that he had lawful intent in the present offense ....

Obviously, the line of reasoning that deems an extrinsic offense relevant to the issue of intent is valid only if an offense was in fact committed and the defendant in fact committed it. Therefore, as a predicate to a determination that the extrinsic offense is relevant, the Government must offer proof demonstrating that the defendant committed the offense. If the proof is insufficient, the judge must exclude the evidence because it is irrelevant. The issue we must decide is by what standard the trial court is to determine whether the Government has come forward with sufficient proof....

....

... The standard for the admissibility of extrinsic offense evidence is that of rule 104(b): "the preliminary fact can be decided by the judge against the

A. CHARACTER AND HABIT CASES

proponent only where the jury could not reasonably find the preliminary fact to exist.'' 21 Wright & Graham, Federal Practice and Procedure: Evidence § 5054, at 269 (1977).

Once it is determined that the extrinsic offense requires the same intent as the charged offense and that the jury could find that the defendant committed the extrinsic offense, the evidence satisfies the first step under rule 404(b). The extrinsic offense is relevant (assuming the jury finds the defendant to have committed it) to an issue other than propensity because it lessens the likelihood that the defendant committed the charged offense with innocent intent .... Therefore, we turn to the second step of the analysis required by rule 404(b), whether the evidence satisfies rule 403.

As we have stated, the central concern of rule 403 is whether the probative value of the evidence sought to be introduced is "substantially outweighed by the danger of unfair prejudice." *Broadway* would reverse this standard by requiring a high degree of similarity between the extrinsic and charged offenses and a stringent standard of proof.... Demanding that the Government prove by excessive evidence each physical element of the extrinsic offense does not necessarily enhance its probative value and may in fact increase its unfair prejudice....

....

The task for the court in its ascertainment of probative value and unfair prejudice under rule 403 calls for a common sense assessment of all the circumstances surrounding the extrinsic offense. As the Advisory Committee Notes to rule 404(b) state: "No mechanical solution is offered. The determination must be made whether the danger of undue prejudice outweighs the probative value of the evidence in view of the availability of other means of proof and other facts appropriate for making decision of this kind under Rule 403." 28 U.S.C.A. Rules of Evidence at 109 (1975).

Probity in this context is not an absolute; its value must be determined with regard to the extent to which the defendant's unlawful intent is established by other evidence, stipulation, or inference. It is the incremental probity of the evidence that is to be balanced against its potential for undue prejudice.... Thus, if the Government has a strong case on the intent issue, the extrinsic offense may add little and consequently will be excluded more readily.... If the defendant's intent is not contested, then the incremental probative value of the extrinsic offense is inconsequential when compared to its prejudice; therefore, in this circumstance the evidence is uniformly excluded. In measuring the probative value of the evidence, the judge should consider the overall similarity of the extrinsic and charged offenses. If they are dissimilar except for the common element of intent, the extrinsic offense may have little probative value to counterbalance the inherent prejudice of this type of evidence. Of course, equivalence of the elements of the charged and extrinsic offenses is not required. But the probative value of the extrinsic offense correlates positively with its likeness to the offense charged. Whether the extrinsic offense is sufficiently similar in its physical elements so that its probative value is not substantially outweighed by its undue prejudice is a matter within the sound discretion of the trial judge. The judge should also consider how much time separates the extrinsic and charged offenses: temporal remoteness depreciates the probity of the extrinsic offense....

....

We shall now apply the precepts we have set forth to the facts of this case. As we have demonstrated above, the credit card evidence is relevant to Beechum's intent with respect to the silver dollar. That Beechum possessed the credit cards with illicit intent diminishes the likelihood that at the same moment he intended to turn in the silver dollar. If there is sufficient evidence to establish that Beechum wrongfully possessed the credit cards, the requirement of the first step under rule 404(b), that the evidence be relevant to an issue other than propensity, is met. This is so even if the evidence were insufficient for a finding that the cards were stolen from the mail. As we have said, relevancy is established once the identity of the significant state of mind is established. The similarity of the physical elements of the extrinsic and charged offenses is a measure of probity....

....

... We think the evidence in the record clearly supports a finding that Beechum possessed the credit cards with the intent not to relinquish them to their rightful owners. Beechum possessed the credit cards of two different individuals. Neither card had been signed by the person to whom it was issued. When asked about the cards, Beechum answered first that the only cards he had were his own. When confronted with the credit cards, which were obviously not his own, Beechum responded that they had never been used. He refused to respond further because the inspector "had all the answers." The logical inference from this statement is that Beechum was attempting to mitigate his culpability, having been caught red-handed. The undisputed evidence indicated that he could have possessed the cards for some ten months. The jury would have been wholly justified in finding that Beechum possessed these cards with the intent permanently to deprive the owners of them. This is all the rules require the court to determine to establish the relevancy of the extrinsic offense evidence.

We move now to the second step of the rule 404(b) analysis, the application of rule 403. The incremental probity of the extrinsic offense evidence in this case approaches its intrinsic value. Indeed, the posture of this case and the nature of the Government's proof with respect to the intent issue present perhaps the most compelling circumstance for the admission of extrinsic offense evidence. From the very inception of trial, it was clear that the crucial issue in the case would be Beechum's intent in possessing the silver dollar. He took the stand to proclaim that he intended to surrender the coin to his supervisor. The issue of intent was therefore clearly drawn, and the policies of justice that require a defendant to explain evidence that impugns his exculpatory testimony were in full force. As we have seen, these policies dictate that a defendant waive his fifth amendment privilege against self-incrimination as to cross-examination relevant to his

A. CHARACTER AND HABIT CASES

testimony. Where a privilege so central to our notions of fairness and justice yields to the search for truth, we should not lightly obstruct that quest. The credit card evidence bore directly on the plausibility of Beechum's story; justice called for its admission....

That the posture of this case demanded the admission of the credit card evidence is reinforced by the nature of the Government's proof on the issue of intent apart from that evidence. This proof consisted of the following. The Government called Cox, Beechum's supervisor, who testified that Beechum had had several opportunities to surrender the coin to him. Beechum denied this, and called two fellow employees who testified that Beechum had asked them if they had seen Cox. Absent the credit card evidence, the issue would have been decided wholly by the jury's assessment of the credibility of these witnesses. The Government, therefore, did not make out such a strong case of criminal intent that the credit card evidence would have been of little incremental probity. In fact, the credit card evidence may have been determinative.

The overall similarity of the extrinsic and charged offenses in this case generates sufficient probity to meet the rule 403 test that the probative value of the evidence not be substantially outweighed by its unfair prejudice. We think this to be true even if it could not be established that the credit cards were stolen from the mail. At the least, there was sufficient evidence for the jury to find that Beechum possessed property belonging to others, with the specific intent to deprive the owners of their rightful possession permanently. That Beechum entertained such intent with respect to the credit cards renders less believable the story that he intended to turn in the coin in this instance. The force of this inference is not appreciably diminished by the failure of the Government to prove that the cards actually were stolen from the mail.

The probity of the credit card evidence in this case is augmented by the lack of temporal remoteness. Although Beechum may have obtained the cards as much as ten months prior to his arrest for the possession of the silver dollar, he kept the cards in his wallet where they would constantly remind him of the wrongfulness of their possession. In effect, Beechum's state of mind with respect to the credit cards continued through his arrest. He maintained contemporaneously the wrongful intent with respect to the cards and the intent as regards the coin. The force of the probity of this circumstance is illustrated by what Beechum would have had to convince the jury in order to avoid it. He would have been forced to argue that his state of mind was schizoid — that he intended at the same time to relinquish the coin but to keep the cards. This situation does not differ significantly from one in which a thief is caught with a bag of loot, is charged with the larceny as to one of the items, but claims that he intended to return that item. Would any reasonable jury believe this story when it is established that he had stolen the rest of the loot?

....

Having examined at length the circumstances of this case, we conclude that the credit card evidence meets the requirements of rule 403. Therefore, the conditions imposed by the second step of the analysis under rule 404(b) have been met, and the extrinsic offense evidence in this case was properly admitted at trial.

IV. *Conclusion*

For the reasons stated above, we *Affirm* Beechum's conviction....

REX v. SMITH
11 Cr. App. R. 229, 84 LJKB 2153 (1915)

LORD READING, C.J.:

The appellant was convicted of the murder of Bessie Munday. His appeal to this court is based on point of law relating to the admission of evidence and to the summing-up of the judge at the trial. On the charge of murder preferred against the appellant evidence was admitted showing that he murdered two other women at a later date. The first question raised by appeal is whether the judge acted rightly on admitting evidence of the deaths of two other women ....

The principles of law governing the admission of evidence of this nature have been often under the consideration of this court and depend chiefly on the statement of law in the case of *Makin v. Attorney-General for the New South Wales*, where Lord Herschell says: "It is undoubtedly not competent for the prosecution to adduce evidence tending to show that the accused has been guilty of criminal acts other than those covered by the indictment for the purpose of leading to the conclusion that the accused is a person likely from his criminal conduct or character to have committed the offence for which he is being tried. On the other hand, the mere fact that the evidence adduced tends to show that the commission of other crimes does not render it inadmissible if it be relevant to an issue before the jury, and it may be so relevant if it bears upon the question whether the acts alleged to constitute the crime charged in his indictment were designed or accidental, or to rebut a defence which would otherwise be open to the accused." In the present case the prosecution tendered evidence relating to the other two women, and it was admitted by the judge as tending to show that the act charged was committed with design. It is sufficient to say that it is not disputed and cannot be disputed, that if as a matter of law there was *prima facie* evidence that the appellant committed the acts charged evidence of similar acts become admissible. We have come to conclusion that undoubtedly there was as a matter of law *prima facie* evidence that the appellant committed the act charged. The point, therefore, taken by the defence under this head fails.

The second point taken is that, even assuming that evidence of the other two women was admissible, the prosecution should not have been allowed to give evidence beyond the fact that the two women were found dead in their baths. Obviously, for the reasons given in dealing with the first point, it would not have been of any assistance to cut short the evidence in this way. We think that the

A. CHARACTER AND HABIT CASES

prosecution were entitled to give, and the judge rightly admitted, evidence of the circumstances relating to the deaths of the two women ....

DOWLING v. UNITED STATES

493 U.S. 342 (1990)

JUSTICE WHITE delivered the opinion of the Court:

At petitioner's trial for various offenses arising out of a bank robbery, testimony was admitted under Rule 404(b) of the Federal Rules of Evidence, relating to an alleged crime that the defendant had previously been acquitted of committing. We conclude that neither the Double Jeopardy nor the Due Process Clause barred the use of this testimony.

I

On the afternoon of July 8, 1985, a man wearing a ski mask and armed with a small pistol robbed the First Pennsylvania Bank in Frederiksted, St. Croix, Virgin Islands, taking over $7,000 in cash from a bank teller, approximately $5,000 in cash from a customer, and various personal and travelers' checks. The culprit ran from the bank, scurried around in the street momentarily, and then commandeered a passing taxi van. While driving away from the scene, the robber pulled off his ski mask. An eyewitness, who had slipped out of the bank while the robbery was taking place, saw the maskless man and at trial identified him as petitioner, Rueben Dowling. Other witnesses testified that they had seen Dowling driving the hijacked taxi van outside of Frederiksted shortly after the bank robbery....

....

... After a third trial, Dowling was convicted on most of the counts; the trial judge sentenced him to 70 years' imprisonment.

During petitioner's third trial, the Government, over petitioner's objection, called a woman named Vena Henry to the stand. Ms. Henry testified that a man wearing a knitted mask with cutout eyes and carrying a small handgun had, together with a man named Delroy Christian, entered her home in Frederiksted approximately two weeks after the First Pennsylvania Bank robbery. Ms. Henry testified that a struggle ensued and that she unmasked the intruder, whom she identified as Dowling. Based on this incident, Dowling had been charged, under Virgin Islands law with burglary, attempted robbery, assault, and weapons offenses, but had been acquitted after a trial held before his third trial in the bank robbery case.

....

... We granted certiorari to consider Dowling's contention that Henry's testimony was inadmissible under both the Double Jeopardy and the Due Process Clause of the Fifth Amendment....

There is no claim here that the acquittal in the case involving Ms. Henry barred further prosecution in the present case. The issue is the inadmissibility of Henry's testimony....

....

For present purposes, we assume for the sake of argument that Dowling's acquittal established that there was a reasonable doubt as to whether Dowling was the masked man who entered Vena Henry's home with Delroy Christian two weeks after the First Pennsylvania Bank robbery trial. But to introduce evidence on this point at the bank robbery trial, the Government did not have to demonstrate that Dowling was the man who entered the home beyond a reasonable doubt; the Government sought to introduce Henry's testimony under Rule 404(b), and, as mentioned earlier, in *Huddleston v. United States*, 485 U.S., at 681, we held that "[i]n the Rule 404(b) context, similar act evidence is relevant only if the jury can reasonably conclude that the act occurred and that the defendant was the actor."...

Even if we agreed with petitioner that the lower burden of proof at the second proceeding does not serve to avoid the collateral-estoppel component of the Double Jeopardy Clause, we agree with the Government that the challenged evidence was nevertheless admissible because Dowling did not demonstrate that his acquittal in his first trial represented a jury determination that he was not one of the men who entered Ms. Henry's home....

....

There are any number of possible explanations for the jury's acquittal verdict at Dowling's first trial. As the record stands, there is nothing at all that persuasively indicates that the question of identity was at issue and was determined in Dowling's favor at the prior trial; at oral argument, Dowling conceded as much.... As a result, even if we were to apply the Double Jeopardy Clause to this case, we would conclude that petitioner has failed to satisfy his burden of demonstrating that the first jury concluded that he was not one of the intruders in Ms. Henry's home.

Besides arguing that the introduction of Henry's testimony violated the Double Jeopardy Clause, petitioner also contends that the introduction of this evidence was unconstitutional because it failed the due process test of "fundamental fairness." ... The question ... is whether it is acceptable to deal with the potential for abuse through nonconstitutional sources like the Federal Rules of Evidence (footnote omitted), or whether the introduction of this type of evidence is so extremely unfair that its admission violates "fundamental conceptions of justice." ...

....

... Especially in the light of limiting instructions provided by the trial judge, we cannot hold that the introduction of Henry's testimony merits this kind of condemnation. Plainly Henry's testimony was at least circumstantially valuable in providing petitioner's guilt.

....

A. CHARACTER AND HABIT CASES

Because we conclude that the admission of Ms. Henry's testimony was constitutional and the Court of Appeals therefore applied that correct harmless-error standard, we affirm the judgment of the Court of Appeals.

HUDDLESTON v. UNITED STATES

485 U.S. 681 (1988)

CHIEF JUSTICE REHNQUIST delivered the opinion of the Court:
Federal Rule of Evidence 404(b) provides:

> "Other crimes, wrongs, or acts. — Evidence of other crimes, wrongs, or acts is not admissible to prove the character of a person in order to show action in conformity therewith. It may, however, be admissible for other purposes, such as proof of motive, opportunity, intent, preparation, plan, knowledge, identity, or absence, of mistake or accident."

This case presents the question whether the district court must itself make a preliminary finding that the Government has proved the "other act" by a preponderance of the evidence before it submits the evidence to the jury. We hold that it need not do so.

Petitioner, Guy Rufus Huddleston, was charged with one count of selling stolen goods in interstate commerce, 18 U.S.C. § 2315, and one count of possessing stolen property in interstate commerce, 18 U.S.C. § 659. The two counts related to two portions of a shipment of stolen Memorex videocassette tapes that petitioner was alleged to have possessed and sold, knowing that they were stolen.

The evidence at trial showed that a trailer containing over 32,000 blank Memorex videocassette tapes with a manufacturing cost of $4.53 per tape was stolen from the Overnight Express yard in South Holland, Illinois, sometime between April 11 and 15, 1985. On April 17, 1985, petitioner contacted Karen Curry, the manager of the Magic Rent-to-Own in Ypsilanti, Michigan, seeking her assistance in selling a large number of blank Memorex videocassette tapes. After assuring Curry that the tapes were not stolen, he told her he wished to sell them in lots of at least 500 at $2.75 to $3 per tape. Curry subsequently arranged for the sale of a total of 5,000 tapes, which petitioner delivered to the various purchasers — who apparently believed the sales were legitimate....

....

... The first piece of similar act evidence offered by the Government was the testimony of Paul Toney, a record store owner. He testified that ... petitioner offered to sell new 12" black and white televisions for $28 apiece....

The second piece of similar act evidence was the testimony of Robert Nelson, an undercover FBI agent posing as a buyer for an appliance store. Nelson testified that in May 1985, petitioner offered to sell him a large quantity of Amana appliances ....

Petitioner testified that the Memorex tapes, the televisions, and the appliances had all been provided by Leroy Wesby, who had represented that all of the merchandise was obtained legitimately.... Petitioner maintained that ... he had no knowledge that any of the goods were stolen....

....

... A divided panel of the United States Court of Appeals for the Sixth Circuit initially reversed the conviction, concluding that because the Government had failed to prove by clear and convincing evidence that the televisions were stolen, the District Court erred in admitting the testimony concerning the televisions. The panel subsequently granted rehearing to address the decision in *United States v. Ebens*, 800 F.2d 1422 (6th Cir. 1986), which held: "Courts may admit evidence of prior bad acts if the proof shows by a preponderance of the evidence that the defendant did in fact commit the act." ... On rehearing the court affirmed the conviction....

We granted certiorari, 484 U.S. 894 (1987), to resolve a conflict among the Courts of Appeals as to whether the trial court must make a preliminary finding before "similar act" and other Rule 404(b) evidence is submitted to the jury. We conclude that such evidence should be admitted if there is sufficient evidence to support a finding by the jury that the defendant committed the similar act.

Federal Rule of Evidence 404(b) — which applies in both civil and criminal cases — generally prohibits the introduction of evidence of extrinsic acts that might adversely reflect on the actor's character, unless that evidence bears upon a relevant issue in the case such as motive, opportunity, or knowledge. Extrinsic acts evidence may be critical to the establishment of the truth as to a disputed issue, especially when that issue involves the actor's state of mind and the only means of ascertaining that mental state is by drawing inferences from conduct. The actor in the instant case was a criminal defendant, and the act in question was "similar" to the one with which he was charged. Our use of these terms is not meant to suggest that our analysis is limited to such circumstances.

....

Petitioner argues from the premise that evidence of similar acts has a grave potential for causing improper prejudice. For instance, the jury may choose to punish the defendant for the similar rather than the charged act, or the jury may infer that the defendant is an evil person inclined to violate the law. Because of this danger, petitioner maintains, the jury ought not to be exposed to similar act evidence until the trial court has heard the evidence and made a determination under Federal Rules of Evidence 104(a) that the defendant committed the similar act.

....

We reject petitioner's position, for it is inconsistent with the structure of the Rules of Evidence and with the plain language of Rule 404(b). Article IV of the Rules of Evidence deals with the relevancy of evidence. Rules 401 and 402 establish the broad principle that relevant evidence — evidence that makes the existence of any fact at issue more or less probable — is admissible unless the

A. CHARACTER AND HABIT CASES 47

Rules provide otherwise. Rule 403 allows the trial judge to exclude relevant evidence if, among other things, "its probative value is substantially outweighed by the danger of unfair prejudice." Rules 404 through 412 address specific types of evidence that have generated problems. Generally, these latter Rules do not flatly prohibit the introduction of such evidence but instead limit the purpose for which it may be introduced. Rule 404(b), for example, protects against the introduction of extrinsic act evidence when that evidence is offered solely to prove character. The text contains no intimation, however, that any preliminary showing is necessary before such evidence may be introduced for a proper purpose. If offered for such a proper purpose, the evidence is subject only to general strictures limiting admissibility such as Rules 402 and 403.

Petitioner's reading of Rule 404(b) as mandating a preliminary finding by the trial court that the act in question occurred not only superimposes a level of judicial oversight that is nowhere apparent from the language of that provision, but it is simply inconsistent with the legislative history behind Rule 404(b). The Advisory Committee specifically declined to offer any "mechanical solution" to the admission of evidence under 404(b). Advisory Committee's Notes on Fed.Rule Evid. 404(b), 28 U.S.C. App., p. 691. Rather, the Committee indicated that the trial court should assess such evidence under the usual rules for admissibility: "The determination must be made whether the danger of undue prejudice outweighs the probative value of the evidence in view of the availability of other means of proof and other facts appropriate for making decisions of this kind under Rule 403." (Citation omitted.)

. . . .

Such questions of relevance conditioned on a fact are dealt with under Federal Rule of Evidence 104(b).... Rule 104(b) provides:

> "When the relevance of evidence depends upon the fulfillment of a condition of fact, the court shall admit it upon, or subject to, the introduction of evidence sufficient to support a find of the fulfillment of the condition."

In determining whether the Government has introduced sufficient evidence to meet Rule 104(b), the trial court neither weighs credibility nor makes a finding that the government has proved the conditional fact by a preponderance of the evidence. The court simply examines all the evidence in the case and decides whether the jury could reasonably find the conditional fact — here, that the televisions were stolen — by a preponderance of the evidence.... The trial court has traditionally exercised the broadest sort of discretion in controlling the order of proof at trial, and we see nothing in the Rules of Evidence that would change this practice. Often the trial court may decide to allow the proponent to introduce evidence concerning a similar act, and at a later point in the trial assess whether sufficient evidence has been offered to permit the jury to make the requisite finding.[7] If the proponent has failed to meet this minimal standard of proof, the trial court must instruct the jury to disregard the evidence.

We emphasize that in assessing the sufficiency of the evidence under Rule 104(b), the trial court must consider all evidence presented to the jury. "[I]ndividual pieces of evidence, insufficient in themselves to prove a point, may in cumulation prove it. The sum of an evidentiary presentation may well be greater than its constituent parts." *Bourjaily v. United States*, 483 U.S. 171, 179-180 (1987). In assessing whether the evidence was sufficient to support a finding that the televisions were stolen, the court here was required to consider not only the direct evidence on that point — the low price of the televisions, the large quantity offered for sale, and petitioners inability to produce a bill of sale — but also the evidence concerning petitioner's involvement in the sales of other stolen merchandise obtained from Wesby, such as the Memorex tapes and the Amana appliances. Given this evidence, the jury reasonably could have concluded that the televisions were stolen, and the trial court therefore properly allowed the evidence to go to the jury.

. . . .

Affirmed.

B. CHARACTER AND HABIT EVIDENCE PROBLEMS

1. Rambo III

Houston Rambo III collects exotic weapons as a hobby, participates in bodybuilding competitions, loves the film *Natural Born Killers* (which is about several serial killers), and was a professional wrestler for several years. At approximately 3 a.m. on Saturday, July 14th, Rambo was involved in a brawl outside of a local bar named The Varsity.

a. If Rambo is sued for assault and battery by Betty, a person injured in the fight, can Betty introduce evidence of Rambo's hobby, bodybuilding activities or prior employment? Why?

b. If Rambo is prosecuted for assault as a result of the same brawl, can the prosecution introduce evidence of Rambo's hobby, bodybuilding or prior employment? Explain.

---

[7] "When an item of evidence is conditionally relevant, it is often not possible for the offeror to prove the fact upon which relevance is conditioned at the time the evidence is offered. In such cases it is customary to permit him to introduce the evidence and 'connect it up' later. Rule 104(b) continues this practice, specifically authorizing the judge to admit the evidence 'subject to' proof of the preliminary fact. It is, of course, not the responsibility of the judge sua sponte to insure that the foundation evidence is offered; the objector must move to strike the evidence if at the close of the trial the offeror has failed to satisfy the condition." 21 C. Wright & K. Graham, Federal Practice and Procedure § 5054, pp. 269-270 (1977) (footnotes omitted).

B. CHARACTER AND HABIT EVIDENCE PROBLEMS

    c.   Can Rambo's business partner, Manny, testify for the defense if he states that for the past five years Rambo has been a responsible accountant/attorney and that Rambo has a very meek personality?

    d.   Can Rambo's mother testify that Rambo has a reputation in the community for being a very peaceful person, so peaceful that he refused to fight others on at least eight separate occasions when challenged?

    e.   If Rambo's mother testifies, can the prosecution ask her on cross examination whether she has heard that Rambo was arrested for attempted murder six years ago? Can she still be questioned if the attempted murder charges were eventually dropped?

    f.   If Rambo's mother testifies, can the prosecution call Rambo's former music teacher, Martha, in rebuttal to testify that Rambo has a reputation in the community as a very violent individual?

2. The Wanderlust of Cows, and Other True Stories

Farmer Stephanie brought suit against Jesse for running over and killing one of her cows. Jesse counterclaimed. Jessie alleged that Stephanie inadequately supervised her cows, and negligently allowed them to escape. At trial, Stephanie called another farmer, John, to testify. John stated that in his expert opinion, based on 30 years of experience in raising and herding cows, cows have a propensity to wander. Is farmer John's opinion on this inadmissible character evidence? Why?

3. Crash Johnson

Cars driven by Johnny "Crash" Johnson and Buford Gump collided at the intersection of Haight and Ashbury. Crash was charged with reckless driving.

    a.   Can the prosecution offer evidence that Crash had been in an alcohol treatment program the previous year?

    b.   Can Crash testify that "I am a terrific driver, better than Petty, Ernhardt, Elliot or the rest"?

    c.   Can Crash say, "Just look at my driving record; no blemishes whatsoever!"?

4. "No Coke, Pepsi"

Sherri is prosecuted for the distribution of cocaine after she allegedly sold one gram of the substance to an undercover police officer.

    a.   The prosecution offers evidence in its case in chief that Sherri had sold cocaine on four prior occasions. Sherri objects. What is the basis for her objection? What ruling and why?

    b.   What if Sherri had been acquitted after a jury trial about two of the alleged sales? Admissible? Explain.

    c.   If the prior sales are otherwise admissible, what is the quantum of proof required before a court appropriately admits the evidence?

5. "A Streetcar Named Desire"

Debbie, a cabbie, gave Eldridge a ride across town, from 7th Street to Piedmont. While Debbie was telling Eldridge that she would one day be famous because of her great desire to succeed, she forgot to pay attention to the road and crashed. In the ensuing law suit brought by Eldridge, Eldridge offers evidence that Debbie had received twelve citations for reckless driving in the past two years.

   a. If all of the citations were issued on Mondays, would this evidence be admissible to show habit? Why?
   b. Is this evidence admissible to show Debbie's propensity to drive carelessly? Why?

6. Defamaaaaaaaaation!

Television news reporter Alain Prather is sued for defamation by the State Water Commissioner, Carol Young, after Prather called her "an incompetent thief." At trial, the plaintiff offers the following evidence. Which evidence, if any, is admissible?

   a. Plaintiff was given an award for excellence in her position as Water Commissioner by the Boy Scouts of America six years ago.
   b. The plaintiff is known in the community for her honesty.
   c. In 1992, the plaintiff voluntarily returned an erroneous bank draft that gave her a windfall of thirty thousand dollars.

The defendant then offers evidence in its case-in-chief. Which evidence, if any, is admissible?

   d. The plaintiff was charged with disorderly conduct after attending an R.E.M. concert two years ago.
   e. The plaintiff shoplifted a dress from a Bloomingdale's five years earlier.
   f. The water supply decreased by 35 percent during the plaintiff's tenure as commissioner.

7. "But Mom!"

Wayne is charged with assaulting his estranged brother Michael. At trial, Wayne testifies in his own behalf. He concedes punching Michael and breaking his nose, but claims "I only did so after he swung a chain saw at me!"

   a. If Michael swung the chain saw almost simultaneously with Wayne's punch, would the evidence about the chain saw be admissible? Why?
   b. If Michael swung the chain saw at Wayne several hours earlier that same day, would the evidence about the chain saw be admissible? Why?

B. CHARACTER AND HABIT EVIDENCE PROBLEMS

8. *Muddy for the Defense*

Mark Muddy, attorney at law, was prosecuted for filing a false statement with the Securities and Exchange Commission on behalf of a local bank. He defends the suit by claiming that he mistakenly filed the erroneous statements.

a. In rebuttal, can the prosecutor introduce other false statements filed by Muddy?

b. Can the prosecutor, to show that Muddy is a greedy person, offer evidence of shady transactions in which Muddy took financial advantage of his siblings?

c. Can the prosecutor offer Muddy's sudden preference for untraceable financial transactions to show Muddy's intent regarding the statements he filed with the Securities and Exchange Commission?

9. *I.M. Rich*

Cindy Ford was charged with passing bad checks, which she signed "I. M. Rich." Can the prosecution introduce the fact that on three prior occasions, Cindy wrote checks signed "I. M. Rich"? Explain.

V. OTHER EXCLUSIONS OF RELEVANT EVIDENCE

[E]vidence of subsequent remedial measures [are excluded] as proof of an admission of fault. The rule rests on two grounds. (1) The conduct is not in fact an admission.... (2) The other, and more impressive, ground for exclusion rests on a social policy of encouraging people to take, or at least not discouraging them from taking, steps in furtherance of added safety.

Fed. R. Evid. 407 Advisory Committee's Note

As a matter of general agreement, evidence of an offer to compromise a claim is not receivable in evidence as an admission of, as the case may be, the validity or invalidity of the claim.... The evidence is irrelevant, since the offer may be motivated by a desire for peace rather than from any concession of weakness of position.... A more consistently impressive ground is promotion of the public policy favoring the compromise and settlement of disputes.

Fed. R. Evid. 408 Advisory Committee's Note

[G]enerally, evidence of payment of medical, hospital, or similar expenses of an injured party by the opposing party, is not admissible, the reason often given being that such payment or offer is usually made from humane impulses and not from an admission of liability, and that to hold otherwise would tend to discourage assistance to the injured person.

Fed. R. Evid. 409 Advisory Committee's Note (citing 20 A.L.R. 2d 291, 293 (1951))

... [T]he purpose of Fed. R. Evid. 410 and Fed. R. Crim. P. 11(e)(6) is to permit the unrestrained candor which produces effective plea discussions between the "attorney for the government and the attorney for the defendant or the defendant when acting pro se...." Withdrawn pleas of guilty were held inadmissible in federal prosecutions in *Kercheval v. United States,* 274 U.S. 220, 47 S.Ct. 582, 71 L.Ed. 1009 (1927).

Fed. R. Evid. 410 Advisory Committee's Note

The effect of this legislation [Rule 412], therefore, is to preclude the routine use of evidence of specific instances [or reputation or opinion evidence] of a rape victim's prior sexual behavior. Such evidence will be admitted only in clearly and narrowly defined circumstances and only after an in camera hearing.

Statement by Representative Mann before the House of Representatives, concerning Fed. R. Evid. 412

A. OTHER EXCLUSIONS OF RELEVANT EVIDENCE CASES

AULT v. INTERNATIONAL HARVESTER CO.

528 P.2d 1148 (Cal. 1974)

MOSK, JUSTICE:

Plaintiff was injured in an accident involving a motor vehicle known as a "Scout," manufactured by defendant. He brought an action alleging that the accident was caused by a defect in the design of the vehicle, asserting that he was entitled to recovery under theories of strict liability, breach of warranty, and negligence.

The gear box of the Scout involved in the accident was manufactured of aluminum 380, a material which plaintiff asserts was defective for that purpose....

....

It was plaintiff's contention that the gear box broke because the aluminum 380 out of which it was made suffered from metal fatigue, and he produced a number of expert witnesses in support of this theory. Plaintiff's witnesses also testified that aluminum 380 was an unsuitable material out of which to build the gear box, that malleable iron was stronger than aluminum 380, that a gear box made of malleable iron would have been less likely to fail, and that in 1967, three years after the accident, defendant substituted malleable iron for aluminum 380 in the manufacture of Scout's gear box.

Defendant asserts that the admission of the evidence it changed from aluminum 380 to malleable iron after the accident violated the proscription of section 1151. In our view, however, the language and the legislative history of section 1151 demonstrate that the section is designed for cases involving negligence or culpable conduct on the part of the defendant, rather than to those circumstances in which a manufacturer is alleged to be strictly liable for placing a defective product on the market. Furthermore, we are not persuaded that the rationale which impelled the Legislature to adopt the rule set forth in the section for cases involving negligence is applicable to suits founded upon strict liability, and we therefore decline to judicially extend the application of the section to litigation founded upon that theory.

Section 1151 by its own terms excludes evidence of subsequent remedial or precautionary measures only when such evidence is offered to prove negligence or culpable conduct. In an action based upon strict liability against a manufacturer, negligence or culpability is not a necessary ingredient. The plaintiff may recover if he establishes that the produce was defective, and he need not show that the defendants breached a duty of due care....

A. OTHER EXCLUSIONS OF RELEVANT EVIDENCE CASES 55

Defendant maintains that the phrase "culpable conduct" in section 1151 is sufficiently broad to encompass strict liability. It concedes that the term "culpable" implies blameworthiness, and that a manufacturer in a strict liability action may not be blameworthy in a legal sense. However, asserts defendant, a manufacturer who has placed a defective product on the market is blameworthy in a moral sense, and is therefore guilty of "culpable conduct" within the meaning of section 1151. We are unpersuaded by this tenuous construction. It is difficult to escape a contrary conclusion: if the Legislature had intended to encompass cases involving strict liability within the ambit of section 1511, it would have used an expression less related to and consistent with affirmative fault than "culpable conduct" — a term which, under defendant's theory, would embrace a moral rather than a legal duty.

. . . .

Nevertheless, courts and legislatures have frequently retained the exclusionary rule in negligence cases as a matter of "public policy," reasoning that the exclusion of such evidence may be necessary to avoid deterring individuals from making improvements or repairs after an accident has occurred. Section 1151 rests explicitly on this "public policy" rationale. In explaining the purpose of the section, the draftsmen's comment states: "The admission of evidence of subsequent repairs to *prove negligence* would substantially discourage persons from making repairs after the occurrence of an accident." (Emphasis added.) (Citation omitted.)

While the provisions of section 1151 may fulfill this anti-deterrent function in the typical negligence action, the provisions plays no comparable role in the products liability field. Historically, the common law rule codified in section 1151 was developed with reference to the usual negligence action, in which a pedestrian fell into a hole in a sidewalk ... or a plaintiff was injured on unstable stairs ...; in such circumstances, it may be realistic to assume that a landowner or potential defendant might be deterred from making repairs if such repairs could be used against him in determining liability for the initial accident.

When the context is transformed from a typical negligence setting to the modern products liability field, however, the "public policy" assumptions justifying this evidentiary rule are no longer valid. The contemporary corporate mass producer of goods, the normal products liability defendant, manufactures tens of thousands of units of goods; it is manifestly unrealistic to suggest that such a producer will forego making improvements in its product, and risk innumerable additional lawsuits and the attendant adverse effect upon its public image, simply because evidence of adoption of such improvement may be admitted in an action founded on strict liability for recovery on an injury that preceded the improvement. In the products liability area, the exclusionary rule of section 1151 does not affect the primary conduct of the mass producer of goods, but serves merely as a shield against potential liability. In short, the purpose of section 1151 is not applicable to a strict liability case and hence its exclusionary rule should not be gratuitously extended to that field.

This view has been advanced by others. It has been pointed out that not only is the policy of encouraging repairs and improvements of doubtful validity in an action for strict liability since it is in the economic self interest of a manufacturer to improve and repair defective products, but that the application of the rule would be contrary to the public policy of encouraging the distributor of mass-produced goods to market safer products....

Given the purpose of section 1151, and the difference between negligence and products liability actions noted above, it is not surprising that in drafting the provision the Legislature confined the section to actions in which the defendant's "negligence" or "culpable conduct" is at issue. Neither the Legislature nor the Law Revision Commission which drafted the section could have been oblivious to the likely evidentiary use of subsequent design changes in strict liability cases. Thus, the limitation of the section to essentially negligence causes of action must be deemed deliberate and significant....

....

Under these circumstances, the trial court correctly refused to admit examination of plaintiff on the basis of the prior pleading ....

....

The judgment is affirmed....

MOE v. AVIONS MARCEL DASSAULT-BREGUET AVIATION

727 F.2d 917 (10th Cir.),
cert. denied, 469 U.S. 853 (1984)

BARRETT, CIRCUIT JUDGE:

The plaintiffs-appellants appeal from a judgment entered on jury verdicts for the defendants-appellees in an action for damages for wrongful deaths, personal injuries and property damages on theories of negligence and strict product liability arising from an airplane crash near Denver, Colorado at 4:52 a.m. on April 3, 1977. Jurisdiction vests by virtue of diversity of citizenship under 28 U.S.C. § 1332. Plaintiffs claimed multiple theories of negligence and defect as the cause of the crash, including defective design of the autopilot system, runaway to the high position of the artificial feel system (Arthur Q), clogging of the suction filters for both of the two independent hydraulic systems, or a combination of the above, together with defect of the powerplant system and a failure to warn.

....

... At the outset, we observe some basic rules governing our appellate review.... In *Miller v. City of Broken Arrow, Okl.*, (citations omitted), we said, *inter alia*:

... In a diversity of citizenship case the federal district court sits as a state trial court and applies the law of the forum state.... The federal district court [or jury if tried to jury], as trier of fact, has the responsibility of weighing the credibility of the witnesses.... On appeal, the reviewing court

A. OTHER EXCLUSIONS OF RELEVANT EVIDENCE CASES 57

must view the evidence in the light most favorable to the prevailing party.... A judgment may be affirmed on any ground arising from the record.... Findings of a trial court will not be disturbed on appeal unless they are clearly erroneous....

Appellants argue that the trial court erred in applying Rule 407, *supra*, in light of the law of Colorado then controlling as set forth in *Good v. A.B. Chance Co.*, *supra*, which followed the reasoning of *Ault v. International Harvester*, 13 Cal.3d 113, 117 Cal.Rptr. 812, 528 P.2d 1148 (1974). *Ault* held, in a products liability action, that evidence of a manufacturer's post-accident warning had a direct bearing on liability as tending to establish knowledge of the defect, feasibility of giving warnings, duty to warn, and breach of that duty. The *Good v. Chance* court referred to *Hiigel v. General Motors Corp.*, *supra*, for the rule that failure to warn may render a product defective when that failure is a proximate cause of the injury, but it also relied on *Hiigel* for the rule that, "[a] [sic] affirmative defense in a products liability case exists when it can be shown that the injured party knew of the dangerous defect in the product and voluntarily and unreasonably encountered the known danger it presented." (Citation omitted.)

The trial court ruled that Rule 407, *supra*, is not governed by or made applicable by state law. On this predicate, the court did not view the *Good* decision as binding. The trial court stated that Rule 407 should not discourage defendants to take remedial measures following an accident. We respectfully disagree with the trial court's conclusion that the admissibility of evidence in diversity actions is governed exclusively by federal law — that is, the Federal Rules of Evidence....

. . . .

It is our view that when state courts have interpreted Rule 407 or its equivalent state counterpart, the question whether subsequent remedial measures are excluded from evidence is a matter of state policy.... The purpose of Rule 407 is not to seek the truth or to expedite trial proceedings; rather, in our view, it is one designed to promote state policy in a substantive law area.... For example, the State of Maine has adopted a rule of evidence which repudiates the rule of exclusion with regard to subsequent remedial repairs. This creates a conflict between Rule 407 and the Maine rule. We hold that when such conflicts arise, because Rule 407 is based primarily on policy considerations rather than relevancy or truth seeking, the state rule controls because (a) there is no federal products liability law, (b) the elements and proof of a products liability action are governed by the law of the state where the injury occurred and these may, and do, for policy reasons, vary from state to state, and (c) an announced state rule in variance with Rule 407 is so closely tied to the substantive law to which it relates (product liability) that it must be applied in a diversity action in order to effect uniformity and to prevent forum shopping.... We are not unmindful of the rule laid down in *Hanna v. Plummer*, 380 U.S. 460, 85 S.Ct. 1136, 14 L.Ed.2d

8 (1965), that where the federal and state rules both govern the issue in dispute and are in direct conflict, the federal rule applies in a diversity based case if the federal rule is arguably procedural in nature. However, we observe that while the sufficiency of the evidence is tested against the federal standard in a diversity case, *Hidalgo Properties, Inc. v. Wachovia Mortgage Co.*, 617 F.2d 196, 198 (10th Cir.1980), the underlying cause of action, with its attendant elements and requirement of proof in a diversity case, is governed by state law.... The ground for exclusion of remedial measures under Rule 407 rests on the social policy of encouraging people to take steps in furtherance of safety. The decision is necessarily a state policy matter. Product liability is not a federal cause of action but, rather, a state cause of action with varying degrees of proof and exclusion from state to state. If a state has not announced controlling rules, such as New Mexico (*Herndon, supra*) the federal district court, sitting as a state court in a product liability diversity case, must determine whether Rule 407 applies. Where the state law is expressed in product liability cases, these expressions control the application of Rule 407.... If the law of the state supplies the rule of decision, there is no justification for reliance on Rule 407. We recognize that, by its terms, Rule 407, when read in conjunction with Rules 401 and 402, does appear to apply in these cases. However, such a result is an unwarranted incursion into the *Erie* doctrine.... The crux of this conclusion is well stated, as follows:

> The constitutional meaning of the *Erie* doctrine seems to be this: The enumerated powers set forth for the Congress in Article II and for the Judiciary in Article III are by implication limited powers, and the notion of limited federal authority is reinforced by the Tenth Amendment. Therefore, the federal judiciary may not "find" or "create" general law to resolve controversies merely because they are litigated in federal court. One difficulty in advancing such an argument against the application of Rule 407 lies in the fact that the constitutional boundaries of congressional power, where there are competing state rules, have not been clearly defined .... Although *Erie* itself holds that there is no federal general common law of torts, nothing in the case suggests Congress could not pass a statute governing the rights of the parties on the very facts of *Erie* .... Despite the problems noted ... there may well be valid constitutional reasons why Rule 407 cannot be applied in cases where state law supplies the rule of decision. Even if Congress *could* constitutionally enact statutes to govern the rights of parties in a given instance, it does not necessarily follow that the Congress, in codifying the law of evidence, may constitutionally enact a narrow statute governing a single substantive issue in a lawsuit which is otherwise to be resolved by reference to state law .... It is unlikely that the Congress intended, in enacting Rule 407 along with the other rules, to make any incursion whatsoever in the *Erie* doctrine. [Footnotes omitted].

Louisell and Mueller, Federal Evidence, Vol. 2, § 166, pp. 261-264.

Notwithstanding our view that the trial court erred in ruling that Fed.Rule of Evid. Rule 407 applies in diversity actions without regard to state law, we hold that no harm resulted therefrom because the trial court's actions were proper and correct on other grounds....

....

WINCHESTER PACKAGING, INC. v. MOBIL CHEMICAL CO.

14 F.3d 316 (7th Cir. 1994)

POSNER, CHIEF JUDGE:

Mobil Chemical Company, the defendant in a diversity breach of contract suit brought by Winchester Packaging, Inc., appeals from a judgment for the plaintiff of more than half a million dollars, arguing that it was entitled to judgment notwithstanding the verdict, or alternatively to a new trial.

Mobil owned a business that manufactured a plastic wrapping "paper" for gifts. The last stage in producing "gift wrap" is called "rewinding," and consists of transferring the gift wrap from the very large rolls on which it is initially wound to the much smaller rolls on which it is sold to the consumer. Mobil contracted out the rewinding stage to Winchester, a small manufacturer of plastic bags. Winchester had done no rewinding previously but was experienced in working with plastic. In order to do the work called for by the contract, Winchester had to purchase a "winding line," which it did with the aid of a $300,000 loan from a local bank. According to testimony that the jury was entitled to believe, Mobil assured both Winchester and the bank that if Mobil got out of the wrap business it would buy back the equipment that Winchester had purchased with the loan. This was in 1987. By 1989, Winchester had borrowed a total of $8,000,000 with which to buy equipment for rewinding gift wrap for Mobil.

In March 1989 Mobil entered into a three-year contract with Winchester for the continued purchase of rewinding services....

Five months after signing this contract Mobil sold its gift-wrap business because of disappointing sales and terminated the contract. But it made no payments to Winchester, which in January 1990 wrote in some exasperation to Mobil that it had not been able to replace the lost Mobil business (later it did obtain some replacement business, but not enough to utilize all the winding lines that it had bought to service the contract with Mobil) and warning that "in view of our current position, and since there appears to be a reluctance on Mobil's part to get on with the settlement of the details of stopping production and the terms of the contract, I have engaged the services of John Hofeldt and Gomer Walters of Haight & Hofeldt, Attorneys at Law, in Chicago, Illinois. I would prefer to get this resolved, as I am sure you would, without getting the lawyers involved." Mobil replied that it had been waiting for Winchester to submit a settlement statement, that is, a bill. Winchester responded in a long letter that ended by saying: "our losses are great enough that I don't want to incur any additional legal costs. I hope that we will be able to come up with a settlement that the attorneys can put their stamp of approval [on]." This was followed up by a memo entitled "Contract Settlement" that listed "the points that need agreement in order to close out our contract." The sum total of the "points" came to only $302,000 even though one of the items was the $250,000 agreed termination fee, yet at trial the largest item of damages sought was for the unpaid balance (almost $800,000) of the bank loans that Winchester had taken out to buy winding lines....

....

... The judge excluded this correspondence under Fed. R. Evid. 408, which renders evidence regarding settlement offers and settlement negotiations inadmissible, save for special purposes not involved here.

....

... But we do not think the district judge exceeded permissible bounds in excluding the correspondence, although the question is so close that had the judge admitted it we would uphold that ruling as readily.

Two senses of "settlement" must be kept distinct. To settle a bill is to pay it. But a bill that itemizes what the sender thinks the recipient owes him and demands — even under threat of legal action — payment is not an offer in settlement or a document in settlement negotiations and hence is not excludable by force of Rule 408.... Dunning a deadbeat by threatening to sue is not the same thing as making an offer or demand in the context of a settlement negotiation. Likewise a statement of a condemnor as to what just compensation is due the condemnee is different from an offer for the purchase of the condemnee's property. *United States v. 320 Acres of Land,* 605 F.2d 762, 804-05 (5th Cir. 1979).... The settlement of legal disputes out of court would be discouraged if settlement offers and other documents in settlement negotiations were admissible in evidence.... For although parties typically are willing to settle for less than they would demand at trial, in order to avoid the expenses and uncertainty of a full-blown litigation, this strategy might be difficult to make credible to a jury, which might treat the settlement offer as the party's highest true estimate of its damage. That at least is the theory of the rule. It may well underestimate the intelligence of the average jury. On the other hand, if it is widely believed it could deter settlement negotiations even if the fear of what a jury would make of the demand and offers made in such negotiations is groundless. And there are below-average juries.

....

Although a reference to lawyers is not decisive on the issue of characterization, we know that in this case the reference was not merely a sign of impatience or the making explicit of what is after all implicit in every bill for a substantial amount of money. Winchester had already engaged lawyers, and from this plus Mobil's own evidence that there were telephone conversations following the initial, unanswered letters from Winchester to Mobil we can infer that Franseen envisaged a substantial likelihood of legal action when he sent the first letter from which we quoted. It is speculative but not implausible that in that and successive letters he was groping for a sum to charge Mobil that would be low enough to induce Mobil to pay rather than fight; so viewed, the letters were indeed settlement offers and not merely computations of the bill owed by Mobil. Mobil is not your average deadbeat. The contract fixed a termination fee but the fixed fee was only a part of the moneys to which the contract entitled Winchester upon termination in fewer than three years. The total amount to which Winchester was entitled was unspecified and highly contestable, and it would make sense for Winchester in submitting a bill to Mobil in an atmosphere in which the threat of a lawsuit was looming to offer an inducement that would avoid the necessity of "incurring any additional legal costs." If this is a correct interpretation of the correspondence, it would run contrary to the letter and spirit of Rule 408 to penalize Winchester for the inducement by allowing Mobil to treat it as an admission that Winchester was owed no more. It may not be a correct interpretation, but we cannot say that the judge abused his discretion in adopting it and excluding the correspondence.

....

UNITED STATES v. ACOSTA-BALLARDO

8 F.3d 1532 (10th Cir. 1993)

SEYMOUR, CIRCUIT JUDGE:
Defendant-appellant Armando Acosta-Ballardo (Acosta) appeals from convictions for conspiracy to possess cocaine with intent to distribute in violation of 21 U.S.C. 846 (1988), and possession of cocaine with intent to distribute in violation of 21 U.S.C. 841(a)(1) (1988). He was sentenced concurrently on the conspiracy and possession counts to sixty months. Mr. Acosta contends that his convictions must be reversed because the trial court erred in admitting statements made during plea discussions....

I.

Detective Oscar Medrano, posing as a cocaine dealer, was introduced to Sanio Silva-Manriquez (Silva). Mr. Silva stated that he represented a group individuals who had cocaine for sale. At a November 5th meeting in Mr. Silva's home, Detective Medrano was introduced to Mr. Acosta, Jose Manuel Carranza-Sanchez (Carranza), and Humberto Montes-Vallalba (Montes). Mr. Acosta set the price for a kilogram of cocaine and arranged to deliver it the next day. On November 6, Mr. Acosta, Mr. Silva, and Mr. Carranza again met at Mr. Silva's residence. Mr. Acosta removed a briefcase from his car and went inside. When Mr. Silva came inside, Mr. Acosta told him that the cocaine was in a stereo speaker inside the house. Mr. Acosta and Mr. Silva went back outside where Mr. Acosta gave Mr. Silva a pistol and instructions to sell the cocaine for $16,500 if he did not return. Mr. Acosta then left the house. Detective Medrano arrived and Mr. Silva gave him the cocaine after removing it from the stereo speaker. The men in the house were then arrested. Detective Medrano later arrested Mr. Acosta.

....

II.

We first address Mr. Acosta's argument concerning the admissibility of his statements made during the plea discussions. On direct examination, Mr. Acosta testified that he met Mr. Carranza on the night before the cocaine sale. During the plea discussions, however, Mr. Acosta stated that he knew Mr. Carranza from Arizona and that Mr. Carranza had brought the cocaine from Arizona. We are thus faced with a situation in which the defendant testified inconsistently with previous statements made in plea discussions.

We review the trial court's admission of evidence under the abuse of discretion standard. *Durtsche v. America Colloid Co.,* 958 F.2d 1007, 1011 (10th Cir. 1992). Under this standard, "a trial court's decision will not be disturbed unless the appellate court has a definite and firm conviction that the lower court made a clear error judgment or exceeded the bounds of permissible choice in the circumstances." *United states v. Ortiz,* 804 F.2d 1161, 1164 n.2 (10th Cir. 1986).

....

Commentators agree that Rule 410 and Rule 11 prohibit use of statements made in the course of plea discussions for impeachment purposes. "The legislative history makes it clear beyond any doubt that Congress, in deleting the impeachment provision from the original rule, intended that Rule 410 should bar the use of pleas and plea related statements for impeachment." 23 Charles A. Wright & Kenneth W. Graham, Jr., Federal Practice and Procedure: Evidence 5349 at 416 (1980) (footnotes omitted). "Statements made by a defendant in connection with a plea or an offer to plead may not be used substantively or for impeachment in any civil or criminal proceeding against the person who made the plea or offer." 2 Jack B. Weinstein and Margaret A. Berger, Weinstein's Evidence ¶ 410[02] at 410-30 (1992) (footnotes omitted).

....

We ... hold that statements made during plea negotiations are inadmissible for impeachment purposes under Rule 11(e)(6)(D). The district court therefore abused its discretion in allowing Detective Medrano to testify regarding the statements Mr. Acosta made in plea discussions....

....

Because the inadmissible impeachment evidence affected the credibility determinations made by the jury, we cannot say the error was harmless. We therefore *Reverse* Mr. Acosta's conviction for possession with intent to distribute and *Affirm* Mr. Acosta's conviction for conspiracy.

B. OTHER EXCLUSIONS OF RELEVANT EVIDENCE PROBLEMS

1. No Breaks ...

Deborah, Bonnie, and Sharlene take a ride in Deborah's new car, a General Chrysford Van. All three are injured when the brakes on the van mysteriously failed.

- a. In their subsequent product liability suit against the manufacturer, can the plaintiffs offer the fact that in the following year's model, General Chrysford, Inc., changed the design of the brakes? Why?
- b. Can the plaintiffs offer the fact that General Chrysford, Inc., subsequently fired their chief engineer, who had designed the brakes?
- c. Does it matter whether the plaintiffs' suit is based on negligence or strict liability? Why?
- d. In a diversity action, does Fed. R. Evid. 407 or state law apply?

2. The Slippery Snake

Janet visited the Snake Street Grille, a favorite Pittsburgh night spot, on a cold winter night when the temperature dropped to 21 degrees Fahrenheit. As she was leaving, she slipped and fell on the sidewalk immediately outside of the Grille and directly under the Grille's sidewalk awning. Janet brought a suit for damages against the Grille on a theory of negligence.

- a. Janet offers evidence that on each succeeding cold night below 32 degrees, the Grille placed a wooden sign on the sidewalk that stated "Watch your step — slippery as a Snake." Admissible? Why? (Is this habit evidence? Why?)
- b. If the Grille asserts in its defense that the City owns the sidewalk in question and the Grille has no control over it, could Janet show that an employee sprinkled salt on the sidewalk on succeeding cold days? Could Janet offer evidence of the sign stating "Watch your step — slippery as a Snake"? Explain.

3. Stingray City

Heather, driving a classic Corvette Stingray, crashes into City Hall one blustery, rainy night after sideswiping two parked cars and a pedestrian, Ethel. Heather is charged with driving under the influence of alcohol.

- a. Assume Heather had blurted out to the injured Ethel immediately after hitting her, "Oh, I am so terribly sorry, I don't know what I was thinking about, but it certainly was not about driving safely. Let me take you to the hospital and pay for everything there. Again, please forgive me." If Ethel later files suit for damages, can Ethel offer Heather's statements in evidence? Explain.

b. If Heather pleads guilty to the charges, is her plea of guilty admissible in a later civil action for damages brought by the owners of the parked cars?
   c. Assume Heather attempted to plea bargain with the assistant prosecutor. During the negotiations, she admitted she had consumed two bottles of Carlsberg beer right before driving. The plea bargaining process failed, however, and a trial ensued. Heather testified at trial stating "I only drank two Coca Colas that evening; nothing stronger I swear to you." What can the prosecutor do in response?
   d. Assume Heather had settled the civil suits with the owners of the damaged parked cars prior to her criminal trial for driving under the influence of alcohol. Could statements made by Heather in the settlement negotiations of the civil suits be used against her in the criminal case? Could the settlement agreements in the civil suits be used in the criminal case? Explain your reasoning.

4. "Two Utes"

A youth named Ernest borrowed $1,000 from a youth named Ira. Prior to the date Ernest was supposed to return the money, Ernest said to Ira, "you know, I won't have the dough for you at the agreed time, so don't count on it. How about letting me give you $500 and my baseball card collection right now, instead?"

   a. Are these statements admissible in a subsequent action brought by Ira for nonpayment?
   b. Assume Ernest had said on the day the money was due, "I know you think I owe you $1,000 and I heard you loud and clear when you said you would sue me if you did not get the full payment from me, but with the $400 I already gave you for the sneakers and clothes, I only really owe you $600." Are these statements admissible in the trial for nonpayment?

5. *House Calls*

In a medical malpractice action against Dr. Zhivago, Dr. Strangeglove testifies for the defense. She is an excellent witness with unimpeachable qualifications. After extremely articulate and believable testimony, she is cross-examined.

Plaintiff's counsel: "Doctor, you are employed?"
Doctor Strangeglove: "Yes."
Plaintiff's counsel: "By whom?"
Doctor Strangeglove: "An insurance company."
Plaintiff's counsel: "Which company employs you?"
Doctor Strangeglove: "Northeast Mutual Insurance."
Plaintiff's counsel: "Why, the very company representing the defendant?"

B. OTHER EXCLUSIONS OF RELEVANT EVIDENCE PROBLEMS

Defense counsel: "Your honor, I object to this entire line of questioning. It is improper under the Federal Rules of Evidence!"

What ruling and why?

6. NYPD RED

Louis is charged with raping an acquaintance, Sarah, after the two collegians had attended a party together.

a. If another woman had accused Louis of rape two years earlier, will that accusation be admissible in Louis' rape trial? Why?
b. If Sarah had dated two other men that same year, will that evidence be admissible if offered by Louis? Why?
c. Should Louis be permitted to offer evidence that Sarah used a condom to show consent? Why?
d. Will the rule adopted by Antioch College in Yellow Springs, Ohio, which essentially provides that a person must request permission to touch another, both for the initial touch and for each escalating touch, have an impact on social relationships? Explain.

VI. WITNESSES

A. EXAMINING WITNESSES ON DIRECT AND CROSS

... Spelling out detailed rules to govern the mode and order of interrogating witnesses and presenting evidence is neither desirable nor feasible. The ultimate responsibility for the effective working of the adversary system rests with the judge....

Fed. R. Evid. 611(a) Advisory Committee's Note

1. CASES

SUAREZ MATOS v. ASHFORD PRESBYTERIAN COMMUNITY HOSPITAL
4 F.3d 47 (1st Cir. 1993)

ALDRICH, SENIOR CIRCUIT JUDGE:

Plaintiff Karen Suarez Matos, a resident of New York vacationing in Puerto Rico, was taken to defendant Ashford Presbyterian Community Hospital in San Juan on October 30, 1989 on an emergency basis. A uterine tumor, or myoma, was removed the following day, and thereafter examined by defendant Doctor Jose Carrasco, a pathologist on the staff of the hospital. He, allegedly, reported it was benign. On discharge with that diagnosis plaintiff was advised to follow up with a New York doctor, two names being given. Beyond a clinic visit, this she failed to do, but after five months she again felt pain and was found, too late, cancerous beyond cure. It was concluded that her tumor had been an unusual type, and malignant or in danger of becoming so, calling for careful watching. Concededly she had not been so advised. A district court jury found Doctor Carrasco guilty of malpractice, and that the hospital was chargeable for his conduct. It awarded $1,325,000 against both, which included $650,000 for future medicals and care, with an additional $250,000 in favor of plaintiff Carmen Matos, Karen's mother....

....

In this contest of credibility defendants were hurt by two improprieties. The first was the court's allowing plaintiffs, after calling a Doctor Miranda, to cross-examine him as a hostile witness because defendants had named him, at pretrial, as their proposed expert. This was error.

....

This is an enlargement of a prior rule, and necessarily involves some factual interpretation, but we divide it into two categories; a witness who is an adverse party or identified with one, or is affirmatively viewable as hostile because of the situation, viz., classifiable in advance as hostile ... and witnesses who demonstrate hostility during trial. Doctor Miranda had no prior connection as part of the scene, or otherwise ... as, for example, an employee ... or a defendant's girlfriend. (Citation omitted.) We find no case involving the adversary's proposed expert, or suggesting that simply because a party expects favorable testimony from a witness, the opponent is entitled to call him, or her, as hostile. If a party proposes to call a happenstance witness to an accident, does that mean the other can call him and cross-examine? The obligation to name witnesses, about to be expanded, is intended to give opportunity to prepare, not to afford procedural advantages. We add that the court's rule would tend to make experts who are reluctant to appear in the first place even more reluctant if they are to start with rigorous cross-examination before they have even made their statement....

....

... The verdicts and judgments are vacated and the case remanded for further proceedings not inconsistent with this opinion....

2. EXAMINATION OF WITNESS PROBLEMS

1. "A Witness Named Wanda"

The Wankle Co. brought an action against Feckless Turbide, Inc. Wanda, a witness to the oral agreement, testified for the plaintiff.

    a.   On direct examination, Wanda is asked numerous questions. Which, if any, of these questions are permissible?
1. "What occurred at approximately 4 p.m. on January 29th?" [The parties agreed to a restructuring of the debt.]
2. "Did you observe the parties shake hands on the agreement?" [No.]
3. "Why were you there?" [To provide business advice.]
4. "What did Bernie Parmetton, the CEO of Wankle Co., say and do at that time?" [He stormed out of the room.]
5. "Could you repeat for me how the agreement occurred?" [Well, ...]

    b.   On cross examination, counsel asks Wanda numerous questions. Which, if any, of the questions that follow are permissible? Why?
1. "So you were present at the time of the so-called 'agreement'?"
2. "You were not in the room where the alleged handshake occurred during the entire meeting, were you?"
3. "You often dress in out-dated fashions, don't you?"
4. "Shantay also was at the meeting, wasn't she?"

2. A Truly Cross Examination

A gun fight occurred after a dispute at a card game. One of the players was killed. Two people were located as eyewitnesses, fellow card players Kramer and Jerry. Both admitted to the prosecutor that they disliked the police and did not want to testify against their fellow card player, Elaine, who was charged with the crime.

a. Can the prosecutor use leading questions on the direct examination of either Kramer or Jerry? Why?
b. If the prosecution asks Kramer about the evening in question, particularly the incident following the card game leading to the gun fight, can the defense counsel ask about the card game and events that occurred during the game on cross examination? Why?
c. Is it beyond the scope of the direct examination if, on cross examination, Kramer is asked whether he had recently been convicted of armed robbery? Why?
d. Is the cross examination of Kramer or Jerry important to the defense? Why? What might be the objectives of defense counsel in conducting such a cross examination?

3. *The Forgetful Witness*

Rohan testified in a land condemnation action for the defense. On direct examination, he is asked where he first heard discussions about the government initiating eminent domain proceedings on the property in question, located in a neighborhood of modest means. Rohan responded by saying "I forget."

a. Can counsel ask Rohan to read his notes on the question to the jury?
b. Can Rohan rely on his notes during the testimony? Why?
c. Can counsel suggest to Rohan that "it might have been the International House of Pancakes?"
d. Can counsel show Rohan a note that states "It was IHOP, Mr. Scatterbrained!"? If this method is permissible, why would it not be used?
e. What documents or items may be used to refresh Rohan's memory? Can inadmissible evidence be used to refresh memory? Why?

B. THE COMPETENCY OF WITNESSES

No mental or moral qualifications for testifying as a witness are specified.

Fed. R. Evid. 601 Advisory Committee's Note

1. COMPETENCY CASES

UNITED STATES v. PHIBBS

999 F.2d 1053 (6th Cir. 1993),
cert. denied, 114 S. Ct. 1070 (1994)

RALPH B. GUY, CIRCUIT JUDGE:

Defendants, Raymond Huckelby, Diane Whited, Robert Phibbs, Victor Rojas, and Robert Murr appeal their convictions arising from their participation in a cocaine distribution ring operating in Tennessee and Kentucky....

....

Whited raises the following allegations of error: ... (5) two key government witnesses should have been declared incompetent to testify....

....

Whited claims that witnesses Jerry Parks and Tommy McKeehan were incompetent to give testimony on grounds of mental incapacity. In the case of Parks, he had previously been found incompetent to stand trial, had a history of auditory delusions, and had spent time in mental health facilities. As for McKeehan, Whited cites an affidavit filed with the district court by his treating psychiatrist that he could not assist his counsel in an upcoming trial because he suffered from "confusion, agitation, paranoia and hallucinations." This affidavit was dated four days prior to McKeehan having entered into a plea agreement with the government. Because of such information, Whited contends that, at the very least, it was error for the court not to conduct a preliminary examination of Parks' and McKeehan's competency as witnesses.

Under Rule 601 of the Federal Rules of Evidence (General Rule of Competency), "[e]very person is competent to be a witness except as otherwise provided in these rules." The Advisory Committee Notes to Rule 601 explain that "[t]his general ground-clearing eliminates all grounds of incompetency not specifically recognized in the rules of this Article." Accordingly, "[n]o mental or moral qualifications for testifying as a witness" are specified. *Id.* This is because "[s]tandards of mental capacity have proved elusive in actual application." *Id.*

Thus, the Federal Rules of Evidence strongly disfavor barring witnesses on competency grounds due to mental incapacity. As we wrote in *United States v. Ramirez,* 871 F.2d 582, 584 (6th Cir.), *cert. denied,* 493 U.S. 841, 110 S.Ct. 127, 107 L.Ed.2d 88 (1989):

> What must be remembered, and is often confused, is that "competency" is a matter of status not ability. Thus, the only two groups of persons specifically rendered incompetent as witnesses by the Federal Rules of Evidence are judges (Rule 605) and jurors (Rule 606)....

Likewise, it addressed the question of McKeehan's mental capacity during a bench conference held after he had begun to testify. The court stated that it had "observed Mr. McKeehan, and he appears to the Court to be sober, cogent. He appears to the Court to know exactly where he is and what he is doing...."

....

Hence, the district court did not find that Parks and McKeehan were incapable of understanding their oath and obligation to testify truthfully. Nor did the court find, based on its observations, that their mental abilities were so limited that they did not have sufficient capacity to perceive events, to remember them, and to describe them for the benefit of the trier of fact. *See* Fed.R.Evid. 602. The court was not required, as Whited would have it, to conduct a special examination into their competency. If either Parks' or McKeehan's behavior raised concerns stemming from Rule 602 or 603, it could have excluded their testimony

B. THE COMPETENCY OF WITNESSES

(or portions thereof) without any examination whatsoever. Furthermore, the court had the additional authority, pursuant to Rule 403, to exclude their testimony in light of their past or present mental state....

After carefully reviewing the record, we conclude that the district court did not abuse its discretion .... As long as a witness appreciates his duty to tell the truth, and is minimally capable of observing, recalling, and communicating events, his testimony should come in for whatever it is worth. It is then up to the opposing party to dispute the witness' powers of apprehension, which well may be impaired by mental illness or other factors. As we are persuaded that Parks and McKeehan were at least minimally capable of offering reliable evidence, the possible weaknesses in their testimony went to its credibility, and so were to be assessed by the jury....

....

ROCK v. ARKANSAS

483 U.S. 44 (1987)

JUSTICE BLACKMUN delivered the opinion of the Court:

....

Petitioner Vickie Lorene Rock was charged with manslaughter in the death of her husband, Frank Rock, on July 2, 1983. A dispute had been simmering about Frank's wish to move from the couple's small apartment adjacent to Vickie's beauty parlor to a trailer she owned outside town. That night a fight erupted when Frank refused to let petitioner eat some pizza and prevented her from leaving the apartment to get something else to eat.... When police arrived on the scene they found Frank on the floor with a bullet wound in his chest. Petitioner urged the officers to help her husband, TR 230, and cried to a sergeant who took her in charge, "please save him" and "don't let him die."...

Because petitioner could not remember the precise details of the shooting, her attorney suggested that she submit to hypnosis in order to refresh her memory. Petitioner was hypnotized twice by Doctor Bettye Back, a licensed neuropsychologist with training in the field of hypnosis....

When the prosecutor learned of the hypnosis sessions, he filed a motion to exclude petitioner's testimony. The trial judge held a pretrial hearing on the motion and concluded that no hypnotically refreshed testimony would be admitted

....

On appeal, the Supreme Court of Arkansas rejected petitioner's claim that the limitations on her testimony violated her right to present her defense....

Petitioner's claim that her testimony was impermissibly excluded is bottomed on her constitutional right to testify in her own defense. At this point in the development of our adversary system, it cannot be doubted that a defendant in a criminal case has the right to take the witness stand and to testify in his or her own defense. This, of course, is a change from the historic common-law view, which was that all parties to litigation, including criminal defendants, were disqualified from testifying because of their interest in the outcome of the trial....

....

... The necessary ingredients of the Fourteenth Amendment's guarantee that no one shall be deprived of liberty without due process of law include a right to be heard and to offer testimony:

> "A person's right to reasonable notice of a charge against him, and *an opportunity to be heard in his defense* — a right to his day in court — are basic in our system of jurisprudence; and these rights include, as a minimum, a right to examine the witnesses against him, to offer testimony, and to be represented by counsel." (Emphasis added.)

In re Oliver, 333 U.S. 257, 273 (1948)....

The right to testify is also found in the Compulsory Process Clause of the Sixth Amendment, which grants a defendant the right to call "witness in his favor," a right that is guaranteed in the criminal courts of the States by the Fourteenth Amendment.... Logically included in the accused's right to call witnesses whose testimony is "material and favorable to his defense," ... is a right to testify himself, should he decide it is in his favor to do so. In fact, the most important witness for the defense in many criminal cases is the defendant himself....

....

The Arkansas rule enunciated by the state courts does not allow a trial court to consider whether posthypnosis testimony may be admissible in a particular case; it is a *per se* rule prohibiting the admission at trial of any defendant's hypnotically refreshed testimony on the ground that such testimony is always unreliable. Thus, in Arkansas, an accused's testimony is limited to matters that he or she can prove were remembered before hypnosis. This rule operates to the detriment of any defendant who undergoes hypnosis, without regard to the reasons for it, the circumstances under which it took place, or any independent verification of the information it produced....

Responses of individuals to hypnosis vary greatly. The popular belief that hypnosis guarantees the accuracy of recall is as yet without established foundation and, in fact, hypnosis often has no effect at all on memory. The most common response to hypnosis, however, appears to be an increase in both correct and incorrect recollections. Three general characteristics of hypnosis may lead to the introduction of inaccurate memories: the subject becomes "suggestible" and may try to please the hypnotist with answers the subject thinks will be met with approval; the subject is likely to "confabulate," that is, to fill in details from the imagination in order to make an answer more coherent and complete; and, the subject experiences "memory hardening," which gives him great confidence in both true and false memories, making effective cross-examination more difficult.... Despite the unreliability that hypnosis concededly may introduce,

however, the procedure has been credited as instrumental in obtaining investigative leads or identifications that were later confirmed by independent evidence....
....

We are not now prepared to endorse without qualifications the use of hypnosis as an investigative tool; scientific understanding of the phenomenon and of the means to control the effects of hypnosis is still in its infancy. Arkansas, however, has not justified the exclusion of *all* of a defendant's testimony that the defendant is unable to prove to be the product of prehypnosis memory. A State's legitimate interest in barring unreliable evidence does not extend to *per se* exclusions that may be reliable in an individual case. Wholesale inadmissibility of a defendant's testimony is an arbitrary restriction on the right to testify in the absence of clear evidence by the State repudiating the validity of all posthypnosis recollections....

In this case, ... [t]he tape recordings provided some means to evaluate the hypnosis and the trial judge concluded that Doctor Back did not suggest responses with leading questions .... Those circumstances present an argument for admissibility of petitioner's testimony in this particular case, an argument that must be considered by the trial court. Arkansas' *per se* rule excluding all posthypnosis testimony infringes impermissibly on the right of a defendant to testify on his own behalf.

The judgment ... is vacated, and the case is remanded ... for further proceedings not inconsistent with this opinion.

2. COMPETENCY PROBLEMS

1. "What Shirley Saw"

Shirley Brown, age 4, was the only eyewitness to a homicide that occurred one night at 10 p.m. in the parking lot of the local convenience store, "Burt's Take Out." Shirley's mom had entered the store to get some milk and pay for gas while Shirley sat in the car. Her mother said, "stay here in the car for a minute, Shirley; I'll be right back."

    a.   What must occur for Shirley to be competent to testify?
    b.   Can Shirley's mother, Annie, who admits to knowing and intensely disliking the defendant, testify?
    c.   If Shirley's mother also had been an eyewitness, but she admitted to being intoxicated at the time of the homicide, could she still testify?

2. The Mugging

Andrew was mugged early one evening after eating at Fat Matt's Ribs. He was too shaken up to identify the perpetrator and had a mental block about the assailant's description for months. The police, through certified hypnotist Dr. Roberto Crizuelo, hypnotized Andrew and obtained a fresh identification of a suspect. The identification resulted in an arrest and trial. Can Andrew testify at trial about the perpetrator's identity? If the defendant had been hypnotized, could the defendant still have testified? Explain.

3. The Dead Man

Jonah died after a protracted battle with cancer. While his will was being probated, a woman who identified herself as "Jonah's friend Mary" claimed that Jonah had promised her $1 million if she provided accounting services for one year. Mary claimed that she had performed her part of this oral bargain, but that Jonah had not performed his. Can Mary collect if she brings an action based on diversity of citizenship in federal court? Why?

C. OPINIONS AND EXPERT TESTIMONY

> [Lay witnesses must have] first-hand knowledge or observation.... [Furthermore, their testimony must be] helpful in resolving issues.... If ... attempts are made to introduce meaningless assertions which amount to little more than choosing up sides, exclusion for lack of helpfulness is called for by the rule.

Fed. R. Evid. 701 Advisory Committee's Note

> Expert evidence is admissible under Rule 702 if "scientific, technical, or other specialized knowledge will assist the trier of fact to understand the evidence or to determine a fact in issue." Fed. R. Evid. 702. The court must determine whether (1) the subject at issue is beyond the common knowledge of the average layman, (2) the witness has sufficient expertise, and (3) the state of the pertinent art or scientific knowledge permits the assertion of a reasonable opinion.... An expert may offer an opinion or inference as to the ultimate issue to be decided by the trier of fact....

Maffei v. Northern Ins. Co. of New York, 12 F.3d 892, 897 (9th Cir. 1993)

> "The Federal Rules of Evidence provide that expert witnesses may give opinion evidence even without hypothetical questions. [If a hypothetical question is used, however, it cannot omit a] 'material fact essential to the formation of a rational opinion....'"

Piotrowski v. Southworth Prods. Corp., 15 F.3d 748 (8th Cir. 1994) (quoting in part *Iconco v. Hensen Constr. Co.*, 622 F.2d 1291, 1301 (8th Cir. 1980))

1. OPINIONS AND EXPERT TESTIMONY CASES

UNITED STATES v. MARKUM

4 F.3d 891 (10th Cir. 1993)

VRATIL, DISTRICT JUDGE:

C. OPINIONS AND EXPERT TESTIMONY

Judy Louise Brown Markum appeals her conviction for one count of conspiracy to commit arson and mail fraud....

The evidence in this case was as follows:

Markum and her co-defendant, Jackie Mullins, experienced severe financial difficulties as early as January, 1987. The property insurance on Markum's residence had lapsed for non-payment of premiums and the utilities were disconnected for non-payment on June 4, 1987. As a result, Markum vacated the residence and moved into her mother's home.

Mullins owned and operated Show Business Video and also lived with his mother. Mullins' video business did not fare well in the summer of 1987 and suppliers placed it on C.O.D. status. During this time, Markum and Mullins had little or no income. In September of 1987, however, they jointly obtained a $45,000 loan secured by a mortgage on Markum's home and the inventory of Mullins' video business. Markum and Mullins used the loan proceeds to pay off the first mortgage on Markum's home and to reinstate its property insurance. They deposited the remaining cash, totaling $21,000, in the video store business account.

On May 28, 1988, nine months after Markum and Mullins had reinsured the Markum home, fire destroyed the property. Markum had vacated the home some eleven months earlier and the house was apparently vacant at the time it burned. It had minimal furnishings, the lawn was grown up in weeds, at least one window was broken, and a rototiller and lawn mower occupied the kitchen. According to the first witness at the scene, the fire at that point consisted of two unconnected blazes: a large fire in the kitchen and a smaller fire in a back bedroom.

The fire department extinguished the blaze and, before leaving the scene, inspected the attic for heat buildup and (as a precautionary measure) doused it with water. This effort, in total, consumed 1,100 gallons of water. About an hour after the firefighters returned to the station, however, they received a second alarm on the Markum house. Fire chief Buck Pearson testified that when he and the firefighters returned, the Markum house was "totally involved, top to bottom, north, south, ... totally engulfed in flames." Only the foundation survived the second fire. Chief Pearson testified that he had seen fires rekindle, but never in such a short time or so completely. He testified that a quick and devastating rekindling is extremely rare because a house is soaked with water in the process of extinguishing the original fire. Chief Pearson therefore concluded that the second fire was "suspicious," and testified that, in his opinion, the second fire was a completely separate fire and not a rekindling of the first blaze.

Markum and Mullins were each at the residence between the time of the first and second fire....

....

II. *Expert Testimony*

The trial court's decision to admit expert testimony is reviewable for abuse of discretion.... If appellant failed to object at trial or objected on grounds not now asserted as error, review is for plain error only....

At trial, Markum objected to the introduction of Chief Pearson's expert opinion concerning the cause of the second fire, as follows:

> I would object to that under Rule 704(a). I don't think it would be a necessary opinion to aid this Jury in the proper understanding of the facts of this case....

Chief Pearson's testimony was not objectionable under Rule 704(a). Markum's only other objection, at trial, was that the testimony was not necessary to aid the jury in its understanding of the facts. This objection implicates Rule 702, which reads as follows:

> If scientific, technical, or other specialized knowledge will assist the trier of fact to understand the evidence or to determine a fact in issue, a witness qualified as an expert by knowledge, skill, experience, training, or education, many [sic] testify thereto in the form of an opinion or otherwise.

Under the standard for Rule 702 announced in *Daubert v. Merrell Dow Pharmaceuticals, Inc.,* ___ U.S. ___, 113 S. Ct. 2786, 125 L.Ed.2d 469, the trial court must determine whether the expert is proposing to testify to (1) scientific, technical, or other specialized knowledge that (2) will assist the trier of fact to understand or determine a fact in issue. *Id.* at ___, 113 S. Ct. at 2796. Whether the expert testimony will assist the trier of fact goes primarily to relevance. *Id.* at ___, 113 S. Ct. at 2795.

The very fact that the fire departments have specialized arson investigation units argues that arson is an area of technical and specialized knowledge beyond the ken of the average juror. Whether the second fire was the result of arson was a factual question highly relevant to the case and properly addressed by expert testimony. Chief Pearson did not opine that Markum set the fire, but only that someone deliberately set it....

... District courts have broad discretion in determining the competency of expert witnesses.... Experience alone can qualify a witness to give expert testimony....

Chief Pearson worked as a firefighter and Fire Chief for 29 years. In addition to observing and extinguishing fires throughout that period, he attended arson schools and received arson investigation training. The trial court found that Chief Pearson possessed the experience and training necessary to testify as an expert on the issue whether the second fire was a natural rekindling of the first fire or was deliberately set. That finding was not clearly erroneous.

....

C. OPINIONS AND EXPERT TESTIMONY

IN RE AIR DISASTER AT LOCKERBIE SCOTLAND ON DECEMBER 21, 1988

37 F.3d 804 (2d Cir. 1994)

CARDAMONE, CIRCUIT JUDGE:

Pan American World Airways, Inc. (Pan Am) and Alert Management Systems, Inc. (Alert) (collectively Pan Am ...) appeal from final judgments entered on September 9, 1992 in the United States District Court for the Eastern District of New York (Platt, C.J.) in three cases arising out of the Pan Am Flight 103 terrorist bombing that occurred over Lockerbie, Scotland in December 1988....

The dangers of a bomb hidden inside radios packed in interline bags were well known to Pan Am and the airline industry. These two incidents led to the adoption of a Federal Aviation Administration (FAA) regulation at issue in this case, Air Carrier Standard Security Program or ACSSP XV.C.1.(a) (A. 4194)....

....

A single jury trial was conducted before Chief Judge Platt to try the liability issues common to the passenger cases. The parties agreed that the case was governed by the Warsaw Convention, formally named the Convention for the Unification of Certain Rules Relating to International Transportation by Air, done at Warsaw, Oct. 12, 1929, (citation omitted). Although the Warsaw Convention generally limits a carrier's liability for damages to $75,000 per passenger, Article 25 permits recovery of unlimited compensatory damages provided the carrier's "wilful misconduct" caused the damages. An earlier decision of this Circuit established that punitive damages may not be collected under the Warsaw Convention. *In re Air Disaster at Lockerbie, Scotland on December 21, 1988* (*"Lockerbie I"*), 928 F.2d 1267 (2d Cir.), *cert. denied*, ___ U.S. ___, 112 S. Ct. 331, 116 L.Ed.2d 272 (1991).

On July 10, 1992 the jury found that the defendants engaged in wilful misconduct that led to this fatal crash. The trial's liability phase centered on Pan Am's alleged noncompliance with FAA directives concerning baggage inspection, particularly with regard to unaccompanied baggage that might contain explosives. Additional proof was introduced regarding other alleged misconduct on the air carrier's part. Plaintiffs contended that the bomb entered the flight on an unaccompanied bag that Pan Am, through its wilful misconduct, failed to inspect and detect. Under plaintiffs' theory — detailed by several expert witnesses — the bomb was hidden inside a radio-cassette player packed in a bronze Samsonite suitcase. The suitcase supposedly traveled from Malta to Frankfurt on Air Malta Flight 180. There, the experts posited, it was transferred to the first leg of Flight 103 from Frankfurt to London, where it was then placed on Flight 103 bound for New York.

....

Appellants' first objection is to the testimony of plaintiffs' expert witnesses, Rodney Wallis and Billie Vincent. Wallis and Vincent gave their opinions relying on evidence adduced at trial, at times displaying for purposes of reference trial transcripts on a projection screen. Based on this testimony, for example, Wallis opined that Pan Am was operating under a commercial rather than security priority and that training requirements had been violated. [JA 2689-90] Vincent stated — again based on other record testimony — that Pan Am had committed acts that violated ACSSP XV C.1.(a) [JA 2860].

....

... It is of some significance that neither Wallis nor Vincent was giving the type of summary testimony that appears on a chart or graph.

The trial judge, therefore, properly ruled on the summary testimony under the federal rules governing expert testimony rather than under Rule 1006. Under those rules, expert testimony may be based on other testimony or evidence obtained at trial. See Fed.R.Evid. 703 ("The facts or data in the particular case upon which an expert bases an opinion or inference may be those perceived by or made known to the expert at or before the hearing."). No error occurred from the format of testimony summarizing the trial record or from the use of transparencies to highlight portions of the trial transcripts to which the witnesses referred when they were on the witness stand.

Wallis' and Vincent's summaries of testimony in the record did not, as appellants assert, improperly impinge on the jury's functions. Pan Am avers that in assessing other witnesses' testimony, Wallis and Vincent made credibility judgments that are properly reserved to the jury. They rely for this contention on *United States v. Scop*, 846 F.2d 135, 142, modified, 856 F.2d 5 (2d Cir. 1988). There, it was said in dicta that one witness may not offer an opinion based on his or her assessment of the accuracy of another witness, where that other witness' credibility is to be determined by the trier of fact. *Id*. Even were *Scop*'s discussion of this point binding on us — and it is not — *Scop* does not, in any event, control the outcome of the present case.

Wallis' and Vincent's testimonies were not improper simply because they were based on the testimony of others. Precedent has long acknowledged the acceptability of expert testimony based on the trial record.... No doubt remains under the federal rules that an expert may testify based on facts elicited at trial. *See* Fed.R.Evid. 703. The rules also provide, "testimony in the form of an opinion or inference otherwise admissible is not objectionable because it embraces an ultimate issue to be decided by the trier of fact." Fed.R.Evid. 704(a). The credibility of a witness represents just such an ultimate issue normally decided by the jury.

Nor are we troubled by Vincent's testimony that he thought appellants engaged in "fraud" and "deceit," because it was clear from the content of this direct and cross-examination that he used those terms in a non-legal sense.... Neither do questions arise as to the propriety of testimony given by Wallis, because appellants highlight no specific statement by him containing a legal conclusion as to a specific ACSSP violation. Additionally, because Wallis had an extensive background in aviation security it was not an abuse of the trial court's discretion to permit him to testify regarding causation.

C. OPINIONS AND EXPERT TESTIMONY

....

We agree that Vincent's statement as to his belief that Pan Am violated the ACSSP is dubious.... While an expert witness may testify as to an ultimate fact issue the jury will decide, see Fed.R.Evid. 704, the general rule is that an expert may not testify as to what the law is, because such testimony would impinge on the trial court's function.... Permitting an expert to give a legal conclusion may implicitly provide a legal standard to the jury.... Thus, expert testimony expressing a legal conclusion should ordinarily be excluded because such testimony is not the way in which a legal standard should be communicated to the jury. Vincent's testimony that he had been lead to the conclusion "that Pan Am did indeed violate the ACSSP" ... embodied a legal conclusion that crossed the fine line between a permissible conclusion as to an ultimate issue of fact and an impermissible legal conclusion.

....

The judgments ... are affirmed.

FRYE v. UNITED STATES

293 F. 1013 (D.C. Cir. 1923)

VAN ORSDEL, ASSOCIATE JUSTICE:

Appellant, defendant below, was convicted of the crime of murder in the second degree, and from the judgment prosecutes this appeal.

A single assignment of error is presented for our consideration. In the course of the trial counsel for defendant offered an expert witness to testify to the result of a deception test made upon defendant. The test is described as the systolic blood pressure deception test. It is asserted that blood pressure is influenced by change in the emotions of the witness, and that the systolic blood pressure rises are brought about by nervous impulses sent to the sympathetic branch of the autonomic nervous system. Scientific experiments, it is claimed, have demonstrated that fear, rage, and pain always produce a rise of systolic blood pressure, and that conscious deception or falsehood, concealment of facts, or guilt of crime, accompanied by fear of detection when the person is under examination, raises the systolic blood pressure in a curve, which corresponds exactly to the struggle going on in the subject's mind, between fear and attempted control of that fear, as the examination touches the vital points in respect of which he is attempting to deceive the examiner.

....

Prior to the trial defendant was subjected to this deception test, and counsel offered the scientist who conducted the test as an expert to testify to the results obtained. The offer was objected to by counsel for the government, and the court sustained the objection. Counsel for defendant then offered to have the proffered witness conduct a test in the presence of the jury. This also was denied.

Counsel for defendant, in their able presentation of the novel question involved, correctly state in their brief that no cases directly in point have been found. The broad ground, however, upon which they plant their case, is succinctly stated in their brief as follows:

> "The rule is that the opinions of experts or skilled witnesses are admissible in evidence in those cases in which the matter of inquiry is such that inexperienced persons are unlikely to prove capable of forming a correct judgment upon it, for the reason that the subject-matter so far partakes of a science, art or trade as to require a previous habit or experience or study in it, in order to acquire a knowledge of it. When the question involved does not lie within the range of common experience or common knowledge, but requires special experience or special knowledge, then the opinions of witnesses skilled in that particular science, art or trade to which the question relates are admissible in evidence."

Numerous cases are cited in support of this rule. Just when a scientific principle or discovery crosses the line between the experimental and demonstrable stages is difficult to define. Somewhere in this twilight zone the evidential force of the principle must be recognized, and while courts will go a long way in admitting expert testimony deduced from a well-recognized scientific principle or discovery, the thing from which the deduction is made must be sufficiently established to have gained general acceptance in the particular field in which it belongs.

We think the systolic blood pressure deception test has not yet gained such standing and scientific recognition among physiological and psychological authorities as would justify the courts in admitting expert testimony deduced from the discovery, development, and experiments thus far made.

The judgment is affirmed.

UNITED STATES v. DOWNING

753 F.2d 1224 (3d Cir. 1985)

BECKER, CIRCUIT JUDGE:

Appellant, John W. Downing, was indicted for mail fraud, ... wire fraud, ... and interstate transportation of stolen property. All counts of the indictment arose from a scheme to defraud numerous vendors conducted in 1978 and 1979 by a group of individuals calling themselves the Universal League of Clergy (U.L.C.) ....

....

The government's case against the appellant consisted primarily of the testimony of twelve eyewitnesses who, with varying degrees of confidence, testified that appellant was the man they knew as Reverend Claymore. These witnesses testified on the basis of their personal observations of Reverend Claymore for periods ranging from 5 to 45 minutes during the course of business dealings that later were discovered to be fraudulent. Appellant contended at trial that these eyewitnesses were mistaken and that their testimony was unreliable

C. OPINIONS AND EXPERT TESTIMONY 81

because of the short period of time in which the witnesses had to view Claymore, the innocuous circumstances of their meetings with him, and the substantial lapse of time between their meetings and the subsequent identifications.

In an effort to overcome the substantial weight of twelve eyewitness identifications in the jury's mind, appellant's counsel, at the beginning of the trial, inquired whether the court would permit expert testimony on the unreliability of eyewitness testimony.... The district court deferred ruling on the motion and requested that appellant's counsel inform it during a break in the proceedings as to the substance of the proposed expert testimony, and as to any federal cases that have held such testimony to be admissible....

... [T]he district court articulated two reasons for refusing to permit appellant's expert witness to testify: (1) the witness would usurp the "function of the jury"; and (2) there was additional evidence "such as fingerprints [and] handwriting." We note at the outset, and the government concedes, that the court was in error as to the second: no fingerprint or handwriting evidence was offered against appellant; rather, the government's case rested almost exclusively on the eyewitness identifications.

The first ground for the court's decision does not proceed from a similar misapprehension of the record, but the court's reasoning in this regard does lack clarity. Initially, it would appear that the court was concerned that the expert witness would testify as to the "ultimate issue of fact." ... Were this so, the first ground of decision would be erroneous. As the advisory committee's note on Rule 704 points out, the basic approach to opinion testimony in the federal rules is one of helpfulness. "In order to render this approach fully effective and to allay any doubt on the subject, the so called 'ultimate issue' rule is specifically abolished by [Rule 704]." ... The rule rejects as "empty rhetoric" the notion that some testimony is inadmissible because it usurps the "province of the jury."
...

In light of this clear mandate of Fed. R. Evid. 704, it appears rather that the district court based its ruling on an interpretation of Fed. R. Evid. 702, in effect concluding that the expert testimony concerning the reliability of eyewitness identifications is never admissible in federal courts because such testimony concerns a matter of common experience that the jury is itself presumed to posses. Under this approach, an expert's testimony on the reliability of eyewitnesses can never meet the test for admissibility of expert testimony contained in Fed. R. Evid. 702.

> If scientific, technical, or other specialized knowledge will assist the trier of fact to understand the evidence or to determine a fact in issue, a witness qualified as an expert by knowledge, skill, experience, training, or education, may testify thereto in the form of an opinion or otherwise.

This rule invests trial courts with the broad discretion to admit expert testimony over the objection that it would improperly invade the province of the jury. Under Rule 702, "an expert can be employed if his testimony will be helpful to the trier of fact in understanding evidence that is simply difficult [though] not beyond ordinary understanding." ...

....

[The court concluded that] under certain circumstances expert testimony on the reliability of eyewitness identifications can assist the jury in reaching a correct decision and therefore may meet the helpfulness requirement of Rule 702....

....

III.

The conclusion that expert testimony on the perception of eyewitnesses, at least in certain cases, meets the helpfulness standard of Rule 702 does not end our analysis. On remand, the district court will still have to decide whether to admit the specific testimony proffered in this case. This exercise of the district court's discretion will be shaped by the policies of Fed. R. Evid. 702, as it impinges on the court's assessment of the scientific evidence for the proffered testimony, and by the policies of Fed. R. Evid. 403....

....

Because the general acceptance standard set out in *Frye* was the dominant view within the federal courts at the time the Federal Rules of Evidence were considered and adopted, one might expect that the rules themselves would make some pronouncement about the continuing vitality of the standard. Neither the text of the Federal Rules of Evidence nor the accompanying notes of the advisory committee, however, explicitly set forth the appropriate standard by which the admissibility of novel scientific evidence is to be established. Although the commentators agree that this legislative silence is significant, they disagree about its meaning. Professors Saltzburg and Redden, for example, have stated, "[i]t would be odd if the Advisory Committee and the Congress intended to overrule the vast majority of cases excluding such evidence as lie detectors without explicitly stating so." ...

The opposing view, espoused by Judge Weinstein, Professor Berger, and others, maintains that "[T]he silence of the rule [702] and its drafters should be regarded as tantamount to an abandonment of the general acceptance standard." (Citations omitted.) Arguing that *Frye* is inconsistent with the policies animating the Federal Rules of Evidence, this view focuses in particular on the broad scope of relevance in the federal rules. Fed. R. Evid. 401 specifically defines relevant evidence as "evidence having any tendency to make the existence of any fact that is of consequence to the determination of the action more probable or less probable than it would be without the evidence." Moreover, Fed. R. Evid. 402 provides that "[a]ll relevant evidence is admissible except as otherwise provided by the Constitution of the United States, by Act of Congress, by these rules, or by other rules prescribed by the Supreme Court pursuant to statutory authority." Thus, because the mere relevance of novel scientific evidence does not hinge on its "general acceptance" in the scientific community, Rules 401 and 402, taken together, arguably create an admissibility of novel scientific evidence....

C. OPINIONS AND EXPERT TESTIMONY

Notwithstanding the appeal of this analysis, the notes of the advisory committee make clear that Rule 402 is limited by Fed.R.Evid. 403 and by the rules contained in Article VII of the Federal Rules of Evidence, including Rule 702. The touchstone of Rule 702, as was noted above, is the helpfulness of the expert testimony, i.e., whether it "will assist the trier of fact to understand the evidence or to determine a fact in issue." ... Thus, the rules themselves contain a counterweight to a simple relevancy analysis.

Although we believe that "helpfulness" necessarily implies a quantum of reliability beyond that required to meet a standard of bare logical relevance ... it also seems clear to us that some scientific evidence can assist the trier of fact in reaching an accurate determination of facts in issue even though the principles underlying the evidence have not become "generally accepted" in the field to which they belong. Moreover, we can assume that the drafters of the Federal Rules of Evidence were aware that the *Frye* test was a judicial creation, and we find nothing in the language of the rules to suggest a disapproval of such interstitial judicial rulemaking. Therefore, although the codification of the rules of evidence may counsel in favor of a re-examination of the general acceptance standard, on balance we conclude that the Federal Rules of Evidence neither incorporate nor repudiate it....

....

... [T]he *Frye* test suffers from serious flaws. The test has proved to be too malleable to provide the method for orderly and uniform decision-making envisioned by some of its proponents. Moreover, in its pristine form the general acceptance standard reflects a conservative approach to the admissibility of scientific evidence that is at odds with the spirit, if not the precise language, of the Federal Rules of Evidence. For these reasons, we conclude that "general acceptance in the particular field to which [a scientific technique] belongs" ... should be rejected as an independent controlling standard of admissibility. Accordingly, we hold that a particular degree of acceptance of a scientific technique within the scientific community is neither a necessary nor a sufficient condition for admissibility; it is, however, one factor that a district court normally should consider in deciding whether to admit evidence based upon the technique.

IV.

The language of Fed.R.Evid. 702, the spirit of the Federal Rules of Evidence in general, and the experience with the *Frye* test suggest the appropriateness of a more flexible approach to the admissibility of novel scientific evidence. In our view, Rule 702 requires that a district court ruling upon the admission of (novel) scientific evidence, i.e., evidence whose scientific fundaments are not suitable candidates for judicial notice, conduct a preliminary inquiry focusing on (1) the soundness and reliability of the process or technique used in generating the evidence, (2) the possibility that admitting the evidence would overwhelm, confuse, or mislead the jury, and (3) the proffered connection between the scientific research or test result to be presented, and particular disputed factual issues in the case.

In establishing the reliability of novel scientific evidence as one criterion of its admissibility under Rule 702, we join a growing number of courts that have focused on reliability as a critical element of admissibility....

....

The reliability inquiry that we envision is flexible and may turn on a number of considerations, in contrast to the process of scientific "nose-counting" that would appear to be compelled by a careful reading of *Frye*. Unlike the *Frye* standard, the reliability assessment does not require, although it does permit, explicit identification of a relevant scientific community and an express determination of a particular degree of acceptance within that community. The district court in assessing reliability may examine a variety of factors in addition to scientific acceptance....

Where a form of scientific expertise has no established "track record" in litigation, the court may look to other factors that may bear on the reliability of the evidence.... For instance, a court assessing reliability may consider the "novelty" of the new technique, that is, its relationship to more established modes of scientific analysis.... The existence of a specialized literature dealing with the technique is another factor. Both of these factors bear on the likelihood that the scientific basis of the new technique has been exposed to critical scientific scrutiny....

The frequency with which a technique leads to erroneous results will be another important component of reliability.... In addition to the rate of error, the court might examine the type of error generated by a technique.... Finally, the district may take judicial notice of expert testimony that has been offered in earlier cases to support or dispute the merits of a particular scientific procedure. Undoubtedly, other factors could be added to the list.

....

The trial court must then balance its assessment of the reliability of a novel scientific technique against the danger that the evidence, even though reliable, might nonetheless confuse or mislead the finder of fact, and decide whether the evidence should be admitted. We decline to specify the foundational showing required for admissibility in traditional burden of proof terms ... because the balancing analysis incorporates important policy elements ... which render the determination something more than a fact-finding.... Therefore, we will review district court decisions ... by an abuse of discretion standard.

....

Having generally set out the appropriate inquiry, we now turn to the facts of this case. Unfortunately the district court never addressed the reliability question because it essentially — and erroneously — concluded that expert evidence of this type could never assist the trier of fact. From the facts available on the record and otherwise, it would appear that the scientific basis for the expert evidence in question is sufficiently reliable to satisfy Rule 702....

C. OPINIONS AND EXPERT TESTIMONY

....

For the reasons set forth above, we must vacate the judgment of conviction entered against the appellant....

DAUBERT v. MERRELL DOW PHARMACEUTICALS, INC.
113 S. Ct. 2786 (1993)

JUSTICE BLACKMUN delivered the opinion of the Court:

In this case we are called upon to determine the standard for admitting expert scientific testimony in a federal trial.

I

Petitioners Jason Daubert and Eric Schuller are minor children born with serious birth defects. They and their parents sued respondent in California state court, alleging that the birth defects had been caused by the mothers' ingestion of Bendectin, a prescription anti-nausea drug marketed by respondent. Respondent removed the suits to federal court on diversity grounds.

After extensive discovery, respondent moved for summary judgment, contending that Bendectin does not cause birth defects in humans and that petitioners would be unable to come forward with any admissible evidence that it does. In support of its motion, respondent submitted an affidavit of Steven H. Lamm, physician and epidemiologist, who is a well-credentialed expert on the risks from exposure to various chemical substances.... Doctor Lamm stated that he had reviewed all the literature on Bendectin and human birth defects — more than 30 published studies involving over 130,000 patients. No study had found Bendectin to be a human teratogen (i.e., a substance capable of causing malformations in fetuses). On the basis of this review, Doctor Lamm concluded that maternal use of Bendectin during the first trimester of pregnancy has not been shown to be a risk factor for human birth defects.

Petitioners did not (and do not) contest this characterization of the published record regarding Bendectin. Instead, they responded to respondent's motion with the testimony of eight experts of their own, each of whom also possessed impressive credentials. These experts had concluded that Bendectin can cause birth defects. Their conclusions were based upon "in vitro" (test tube) and "in vivo" (live) animal studies that found a link between Bendectin and malformations; pharmacological studies of the chemical structure of Bendectin that purported to show similarities between the structure of the drug and that of other substances known to cause birth defects; and the "reanalysis" of previously published epidemiological (human statistical) studies.

The District Court granted respondent's motion for summary judgment. The court stated that scientific evidence is admissible only if the principle upon which it is based " 'sufficiently established to have general acceptance in the field to which it belongs.' " (Citations omitted.) The court concluded that petitioners' evidence did not meet this standard. Given the vast body of epidemiological data

concerning Bendectin, the court held, expert opinion which is not based on epidemiological evidence is not admissible to establish causation. Thus, the animal-cell studies, live animal studies, and chemical structure analysis on which petitioners had relied could not raise by themselves a reasonably disputable jury issue regarding causation. Petitioners' epidemiological analysis, based as they were on recalculations of data in previously published studies that had found no causal link between the drug and birth defects, were ruled to be inadmissible because they had not been published or subjected to peer review....
....

We granted certiorari, ___ U.S. ___, 113 S. Ct. 320, 121 L.Ed.2d 240 (1992), in light of sharp divisions among the courts regarding the proper standard for the admission of expert testimony....

II

A

In the 70 years since its formulation in the *Frye* case, the "general acceptance" test has been the dominant standard for determining the admissibility of novel scientific evidence at trial.... Although under increasing attack of late, the rule continues to be followed by a majority of courts, including the Ninth Circuit.

The *Frye* test has its origin in a short and citation-free 1923 decision concerning the admissibility of evidence derived from a systolic blood pressure deception test, a crude precursor to the polygraph machine. In what has become a famous (perhaps infamous) passage, the then Court of Appeals for the District of Columbia described the device and its operation and declared:

> "Just when a scientific principle or discovery crosses the line between the experimental and demonstrable stages is difficult to define. Somewhere in this twilight zone the evidential force of the principle must be recognized, and while courts will go a long way in admitting expert testimony deduced from a well-recognized scientific principle or discovery, *the thing from which the deduction is made must be sufficiently established to have gained general acceptance in the particular field in which it belongs.*" 54 App.D.C. at 47, 293 F. at 1014 (emphasis added).

Because the deception test had "not yet gained such standing and scientific recognition among physiological and psychological authorities as would justify the courts in admitting expert testimony deduced from the discovery, development, and experiments thus far made," evidence of its results was ruled inadmissible. *Ibid.*

The merits of the *Frye* test have been much debated, and scholarship on its proper scope and application is legion. Petitioners' primary attack, however, is not on the content but on the continuing authority of the rule. They contend that

C. OPINIONS AND EXPERT TESTIMONY

the *Frye* test was superseded by the adoption of the Federal Rules of Evidence.... We agree.

We interpret the legislatively-enacted Federal Rules of Evidence as we would any statute.... Rule 402 provides the baseline:

> "All relevant evidence is admissible, except as otherwise provided by the Constitution of the United States, by Act of Congress, by these rules, or by other rules prescribed by the Supreme Court pursuant to statutory authority. Evidence which is not relevant is not admissible."

"Relevant evidence" is defined as that which has "any tendency to make the existence of any fact that is of consequence to the determination of the action more probable or less probable than it would be without the evidence." Rule 401. The rule's basic standard of relevance thus is a liberal one.

Frye, of course, predated the Rules by half a century. In *United States v. Abel*, 469 U.S. 45, 105 S.Ct. 465, 83 L.Ed.2d 450 (1984), we considered the pertinence of background common law in interpreting the Rules of Evidence. We noted that the Rules occupy the field, ... but, quoting Professor Cleary, the Reporter, explained that the common law nevertheless could serve as an aid to their application:

> "In principle, under the Federal Rules no common law of evidence remains. 'All relevant evidence is admissible, except as otherwise provided....' In reality, of course, the body of common law knowledge continues to exist, though in the somewhat altered form of a source of guidance in the exercise of delegated powers." *Id.* at 51-52, 105 S. Ct. at 469.

We found the common-law precept at issue in the *Able* case entirely consistent with Rule 402's general requirement of admissibility, and considered it unlikely that the drafters had intended to change the rule.... In *Bourjaily v. United States*, 483 U.S. 171, 107 S.Ct. 2775, 97 L.Ed.2d 144 (1987), on the other hand, the Court was unable to find a particular common-law doctrine in the Rules, and so held it superseded.

Here there is a specific Rule that speaks to the contested issue. Rule 702, governing expert testimony, provides:

> "If scientific, technical, or other specialized knowledge will assist the trier of fact to understand the evidence or to determine a fact in issue, a witness qualified as an expert by knowledge, skill, experience, training, or education, may testify thereto in the form of an opinion or otherwise."

Nothing in the text of this Rule established "general acceptance" as an absolute prerequisite to admissibility. Nor does respondent present any clear indication that Rule 702 or the Rules as a whole were intended to incorporate a "general acceptance" standard. The drafting history makes no mention of *Frye*, and a rigid "general acceptance" requirement would be at odds with the "liberal thrust" of the Federal Rules and their "general approach of relaxing traditional barriers to 'opinion' testimony.'' *Beechcraft Aircraft Corp. v. Rainey*, 488 U.S. at 169, 109 S.Ct. at 450) (citing Rules 701 to 705). Given the Rules' permissive backdrop and their inclusion of a specific rule on expert testimony that does not mention ''general acceptance,'' the assertion that the Rules somehow assimilated *Frye* is unconvincing. *Frye* made ''general acceptance'' the exclusive test for admitting expert scientific testimony. That austere standard, absent from and incompatible with the Federal Rules of Evidence, should not be applied in federal trials.

....

The primary locus of this obligation is Rule 702, which clearly contemplates some degree of regulation of the subjects and theories about which an expert may testify. *"If scientific*, technical or other specialized *knowledge will assist the trier of fact* to understand the evidence or to determine a fact in issue'' an expert ''may testify *thereto*.'' The subject of an expert's testimony must be ''scientific ....knowledge.'' The adjective ''scientific'' implies a grounding in the methods and procedures of science. Similarly, the word ''knowledge'' connotes more than the subjective belief or unsupported speculation. The term ''applies to any body of known facts or accepted as truths on good grounds.'' Webster's Third International Dictionary 1252 (1986). Of course, it would be unreasonable to conclude that the subject of scientific testimony must be known to a certainty; arguably, there are no certainties in science.... But, in order to qualify as ''scientific knowledge,'' an inference or assertion must be derived by the scientific method. Proposed testimony must be supported by appropriate validation — i.e., ''good grounds,'' based on what is known. In short, the requirement that an expert's testimony pertain to ''scientific knowledge'' establishes a standard of evidentiary reliability.

Rule 702 further requires that the evidence or testimony ''assist the trier of fact to understand the evidence or to determine a fact in issue.'' This condition goes primarily to relevance. ''Expert testimony which does not relate to any issue in the case is not relevant and, ergo, non-helpful.'' 3 Weinstein & Berger ¶ 702[02], p. 702-18.... Rule 702's ''helpfulness'' standard requires a valid scientific connection to the pertinent inquiry as a precondition to admissibility.

....

Faced with a proffer of expert scientific testimony, then, the trial judge must determine at the outset, pursuant to Rule 104(a), whether the expert is proposing to testify to (1) scientific knowledge that (2) will assist the trier of fact to understand or determine a fact in issue. This entails a preliminary assessment of whether the reasoning or methodology underlying the testimony is scientifically valid and of whether that reasoning or methodology properly can be applied to the facts in issue. We are confident that federal judges possess the capacity to undertake this review. Many factors will bear on the inquiry, and we do not presume to set out a definitive checklist or test. But some general observations are appropriate.

C. OPINIONS AND EXPERT TESTIMONY

Ordinarily, a key question to be answered in determining whether a theory or technique is scientific knowledge that will assist the trier of fact will be whether it can be (and has been) tested. "Scientific methodology today is based on generating hypotheses and testing them to see if they can be falsified; indeed, this methodology is what distinguishes science from other fields of human inquiry." (Citation omitted.)

Another pertinent consideration is whether the theory or technique has been subjected to peer review and publication. Publication (which is but one element of peer review) is not a sine qua non of admissibility; it does not necessarily correlate with reliability ... and in some instances well-grounded but innovative theories will not have been published. Some propositions, moreover, are too particular, too new, or of too limited interest to be published. But submission to the scrutiny of the scientific community is a component of "good science," in part because it increases the likelihood that substantive flaws in methodology will be detected.... The fact of publication (or lack thereof) in a peer-reviewed journal thus will be a relevant, though not dispositive, consideration in assessing the scientific validity of a particular technique or methodology on which an opinion is premised.

Additionally, in the case of a particular scientific technique, the court ordinarily should consider the known or potential rate of error ... and the existence and maintenance of standards controlling the technique's operation....

Finally, "general acceptance" can yet have a bearing on the inquiry. A "reliability assessment does not require, although it does permit, explicit identification of a relevant scientific community and an express determination of a particular degree of acceptance within that community." (Citation omitted.) Widespread acceptance can be an important factor in ruling particular evidence admissible, and "a known technique that has been able to attract only minimal support within the community" ... may properly be viewed with skepticism.

The inquiry envisioned by Rule 702 is, we emphasize, a flexible one. Its overarching subject is the scientific validity — and thus the evidentiary relevance and reliability — of the principles that underlie a proposed submission. The focus, of course, must be solely on principles and methodology, not on the conclusions that they generate.

....

III

We conclude by briefly addressing what appear to be two underlying concerns of the parties and amici in this case. Respondent expresses apprehension that abandonment of "general acceptance" as the exclusive requirement for admission will result in a "free-for-all" in which befuddled juries are confounded by absurd and irrational pseudoscientific assertions. In this regard respondent seems to us to be overly pessimistic about the capabilities of the jury, and of the adversary system generally. Vigorous cross-examination, presentation of contrary evidence, and careful instruction on the burden of proof are the traditional and appropriate means of attacking shaky but admissible evidence.... Additionally, in the event the trial court concludes that the scintilla of evidence presented supporting a position is insufficient to allow a reasonable juror to conclude that the position more likely than not is true, the court remains free to direct a judgment, Fed.Rule Civ.Proc. 50(a), and likewise to grant summary judgment, Fed.Rule Civ.Proc. 56.... These conventional devices, rather than wholesale exclusion under an uncompromising "general acceptance" test, are the appropriate safeguards where the basis of scientific testimony meets the standards of Rule 702.

....

IV

To summarize: "general acceptance" is not a necessary precondition to the admissibility of scientific evidence under the Federal Rules of Evidence, but the Rules of Evidence — especially Rule 702 — do assign to the trial judge the task of ensuring that an expert's testimony both rests on a reliable foundation and is relevant to the task at hand. Pertinent evidence based on scientifically valid principles will satisfy those demands.

The inquiries of the District Court and the Court of Appeals focused almost exclusively on "general acceptance," as gauged by publication and the decisions of other courts. Accordingly, the judgment of the Court of Appeals is vacated and the case is remanded for further proceedings consistent with this opinion.

It is so ordered.

....

UNITED STATES v. RINCON

28 F.3d 921 (9th Cir.),
cert. denied, 115 S. Ct. 605 (1994)

T.G. NELSON, CIRCUIT JUDGE:

I. *Overview*

Hugo Rincon (Rincon) was convicted on two counts of unarmed bank robbery. On Rincon's first appeal to this court, he contended that the district court erred in refusing to admit expert testimony regarding the reliability of eyewitness identification. We affirmed the district court's exclusion of that expert testimony in *United States v. Rincon (Rincon I)*, 984 F.2d 1003 (9th Cir.1993). After the Supreme Court's recent decision in *Daubert v. Merrell Dow Pharmaceuticals, Inc.,* 509 U.S. ___, 113 S.Ct. 2786, 125 L.Ed.2d 469 (1993), regarding the admissibility of expert testimony, the Court remanded this case and asked us to reexamine that issue in light of *Daubert*. We remanded to the district court for reconsideration. The district court upheld its earlier decision to exclude the expert testimony. We affirm.

C. OPINIONS AND EXPERT TESTIMONY

....

III. *Expert Testimony*

We review for abuse of discretion the district court's decision regarding the admissibility of expert testimony on the reliability of eyewitness identifications....

In *Daubert,* the Supreme Court held that Fed.R.Evid. 702 supersedes the general acceptance standard established in *Frye.* 509 U.S. at ___, 113 S.Ct. at 2793-94. It noted, however, that notwithstanding its holding, the Federal Rules of Evidence still place limits on the admissibility of scientific evidence. *Id.* at ___, 113 S.Ct. at 2794-95. "Nor is the trial judge disabled from screening such evidence. To the contrary, under the Rules the trial judge must ensure that any and all scientific testimony or evidence admitted is not only relevant, but reliable." *Id.* at ___, 113 S.Ct. at 2795....

On remand, the district court excluded the expert testimony on eyewitness identification, ruling that:

1. The proposed testimony invades the province of the jury (i.e., it does not assist the trier of fact);
2. No showing has been made that the testimony relates to an area that is recognized as a science; and
3. The testimony is likely to confuse the jury.

Moreover, the district court stated that "the proposed expert eyewitness identification testimony is being offered by the defense more in the role of an advocate and not as a scientifically valid opinion." We conclude that the district court did not abuse its discretion in excluding Dr. Pezdek's expert testimony because Rincon's proffer failed to satisfy the admissibility standard established in *Daubert.*

A. *Scientific Knowledge*

"[I]n order to qualify as 'scientific knowledge,' an inference or assertion must be derived by the scientific method. Proposed testimony must be supported by appropriate validation — i.e., 'good grounds,' based on what is known." *Id.* at ___, 113 S.Ct. at 2795.... *Daubert* set forth several factors which the district court may consider in determining whether a theory or technique constitutes "scientific knowledge," including: (1) whether the theory or technique can be or has been tested; (2) whether the theory or technique has been subjected to peer review and publication; (3) the known or potential rate of error; and (4) the particular degree of acceptance within the scientific community. *Id.* at ___, 113 S.Ct. at 2796-97. This list is not exhaustive. Nor did the Court "presume to set out a definitive checklist or test." *Id.* at ___, 113 S.Ct. at 2796.

The first inquiry, then, under *Daubert* is whether the proposed testimony of Dr. Pezdek was on a "scientific" subject. On remand, the district court denied Rincon's motion on three grounds, one of which was that "no showing has been made that the testimony relates to an area that is recognized as a science."

In the initial motion, Rincon asserted that Dr. Pezdek held a Ph.D. in psychology from the University of Massachusetts at Amherst, and was a full professor at the Claremont Graduate School of Psychology. She would testify that there are three phases of eyewitness identification: perception and encoding; storage and retention (memory); and retrieval. In turn, the perception and encoding phase are affected by the factors of stress, duration of exposure, cross-racial identification, and availability of facial features (whether or not the face is partially obscured). The storage and retrieval stages are affected by time delay and suggestibility.

....

... However, none of the research was submitted or described so that the district court could determine if the studies were indeed scientific on the basis the Court explained in *Daubert*: "whether the reasoning or methodology underlying the testimony is scientifically valid...." *Daubert* at ___, 113 S.Ct. at 2796.

On remand, Rincon supplemented the record with a copy of an article entitled *The "General Acceptance" of Psychological Research on Eyewitness Testimony*. The article described a survey of sixty-three experts on eyewitness testimony relating to their views of the scientific acceptance of research on a number of topics, including those that Dr. Pezdek would testify to ....

However, while the article identified the research on some of the topics, it did not discuss the research in sufficient detail that the district court could determine if the research was scientifically valid. In the argument before the district court, counsel for Rincon told the court that Dr. Pezdek could testify about the studies that had been done on the various topics. However, he again did not offer or describe the studies themselves. The district court's determination that Rincon had not shown the proposed testimony related to a scientific subject is supported by the record.

B. *Assist Trier of Fact*

Even when a theory or methodology satisfies the "scientific knowledge" requirement, in order to be admissible, expert testimony must also "assist the trier of fact to understand or to determine a fact in issue."...

The expert testimony Rincon offered was no doubt relevant to his defense....

In this case, the district court found that Dr. Pezdek's testimony would not assist the trier of fact and that it would likely confuse or mislead the jury.... We decline to disturb the district court's ruling.

Even though the factors about which Dr. Pezdek was to testify may have been informative, the district court conveyed that same information by providing a comprehensive jury instruction to guide the jury's deliberations....

The district court gave the jury in this case a comprehensive instruction on eyewitness identifications. The instruction addressed many of the factors about which Dr. Pezdek would have testified. The district court instructed the jury to consider whether: (1) the eyewitness had the capacity and adequate opportunity to observe the offender based upon the length of time for observation as well as the conditions of observation; (2) the identification was the product of the eyewitness's own recollection or was the result of subsequent influence or suggestiveness; (3) the eyewitness has made inconsistent identifications; and (4) the eyewitness was credible. The instruction also pointed out the danger of a showup versus the reliability of a lineup with similar individuals from which the eyewitness must choose. Finally, it permitted the jury to consider, as a factor bearing upon the reliability of the eyewitness testimony, the length of time which may have elapsed between the occurrence of the crime and the eyewitness's identification.

As Rincon's article indicates, "it remains to be seen whether experts can enhance jurors' ability to distinguish accurate from inaccurate eyewitnesses, or whether the dangers of such testimony outweigh its probative value; *e.g.,* whether jurors become not more or less skeptical, but more or less *accurate* in their judgments of eyewitness testimony." In any event, the article is inconclusive as to the effect such evidence has on a jury. Given the powerful nature of expert testimony, coupled with its potential to mislead the jury, we cannot say that the district court erred in concluding that the proffered evidence would not assist the trier of fact and that it was likely to mislead the jury.

Notwithstanding our conclusion, we emphasize that the result we reach in this case is based upon an individualized inquiry, rather that strict application of the past rule concerning expert testimony on the reliability of eyewitness identification.... Our conclusion does not preclude the admission of such testimony when the proffering party satisfies the standard established in *Daubert* by showing that the expert opinion is based upon "scientific knowledge" which is both reliable and helpful to the jury in any given case. *See Daubert,* 509 U.S. at ___, 113 S.Ct. at 2796. District courts must strike the appropriate balance between admitting reliable, helpful expert testimony and excluding misleading or confusing testimony to achieve the flexible approach outlined in *Daubert. See id.* at ___, 113 S.Ct. at 2798-99. The district court struck such a balance in this case.

....

Affirmed.

CARROLL v. MORGAN

17 F.3d 787 (5th Cir. 1994)

DAVIS, CIRCUIT JUDGE:

In this medical malpractice action alleging wrongful death of plaintiff-appellant's brother, the jury rendered a take nothing verdict in favor of the defendant doctor. Finding no reversible error, we affirm.

I.

On July 10, 1987, Dr. John D. Morgan, a physician specializing in internal medicine, examined 30-year-old Michael Eugene Carroll. Dr. Morgan had previously diagnosed Carroll in 1977 as having aortic stenosis and, in 1980, Dr. Charles Lewis surgically replaced Carroll's aortic valve.

During the July 10, 1987 examination, Carroll reported dizziness, shortness of breath, inability to walk or stand, numbness in his legs, and chest pain. Dr. Morgan discovered a previously undetected heart murmur and diagnosed a "leaking aortic valve." Dr. Morgan referred Carroll to Vocational Rehabilitation to arrange funding for cardiological evaluation and testified that he advised Carroll not to return to work. On July 17, 1987, seven days after Dr. Morgan examined Carroll but before Carroll's cardiological evaluation, Carroll died of congestive heart failure while operating heavy equipment at his place of employment.

James Carroll, the decedent's brother and estate administrator, brought this medical malpractice suit against Dr. Morgan for the wrongful death of his brother. The plaintiff alleged that his brother died of bacterial endocarditis, a condition which Dr. Morgan should have detected and treated without delay on July 10, 1987. The plaintiff maintained that Dr. Morgan was negligent in failing to refer his brother for immediate cardiological evaluation and that this negligence caused his brother's death.

....

II.

A. *Dr. Bennett's Testimony*

The appellant argues that the district court erred in a number of evidentiary rulings relating to the testimony of Dr. Ken Bennett, the defendant's expert cardiologist. First, the appellant challenges the admissibility of Dr. Bennett's testimony because Bennett failed to base his testimony on "a well-founded methodology" or on "generally accepted principles within the medical profession." Specifically, the appellant argues that Dr. Bennett's testimony should have been excluded because Dr. Bennett refused to recognize any medical textbooks or journal articles as authoritative on endocarditis.

When the plaintiff asked Dr. Bennett about several textbooks and medical journals, Dr. Bennett responded that the publications included contributions from numerous authors; Dr. Bennett testified that he was therefore unwilling to recognize the materials in toto as authoritative and that he would not cite one particular source as the exclusive authority on endocarditis. The trial judge interpreted Dr. Bennett's testimony not as a categorical denouncement of widely recognized authorities on endocarditis, but rather as a reluctance to accept as authoritative the materials in their entirety and to accept one particular source as the exclusive authority on endocarditis.

A trial judge's decision to admit expert testimony will not be disturbed absent an abuse of discretion.... In this case, the trial judge did not abuse his wide discretion in allowing Dr. Bennett to testify as an expert in the field of cardiology. Moreover, the plaintiff does not allege that Dr. Bennett relied on a

C. OPINIONS AND EXPERT TESTIMONY

particularly objectionable or unconventional scientific theory or methodology. *See Daubert v. Merrell Dow Pharmaceuticals, Inc.*, ___ U.S. ___, ___-___, 113 S.Ct. 2786, 2796-97, 125 L.Ed. 2d 469, 485, 37 Fed Rules Evid Serv 1 (1993) (holding that expert scientific testimony must be "ground[ed] in the methods and procedures of science" and based on "more than a subjective belief or unsupported speculation").

Because the district court did not abuse its discretion in interpreting Dr. Bennett's testimony with respect to the textbooks and journals, Dr. Bennett was qualified under *Daubert* to give an expert opinion on the standard of medical care owed to Carroll. His testimony was based on thirty years of experience as a practicing, board-certified cardiologist, on his review, among other things, of Carroll's medical records and the coroner's records, and on a broad spectrum of published materials. His testimony was therefore "ground[ed] in the methods and procedures of science" and was not mere "unsupported speculation." *See id.* ___ U.S. ___, 113 S.Ct. 2786, 125 L.Ed.2d at 482. That Bennett refused to base his testimony on a single medical textbook or journal article does not warrant wholesale exclusion of his testimony. In short, the trial judge did not commit manifest error in refusing to exclude Dr. Bennett's testimony on this ground.

The plaintiff argues next that the district court violated the teachings of *Daubert* in allowing Dr. Bennett to testify as to the cause of Carroll's death. Essentially, the plaintiff argues that Dr. Bennett was not qualified to testify as to Carroll's cause of death because Dr. Bennett is not a pathologist.

Daubert does not support plaintiff's position that the subject of Carroll's cause of death falls within the exclusive confines of pathology. The district court did not abuse its discretion in allowing Dr. Bennett, an expert cardiologist, to give an opinion on the relationship between Mr. Carroll's heart problems and his death.... The plaintiff's argument that three testifying pathologists disagreed with Dr. Bennett's opinion as to the cause of Carroll's death does not disqualify Bennett as an expert; the conflict among the expert testimony was grist for the jury.

....

For the foregoing reasons, the judgment of the district court is affirmed.

ENGEBRETSEN v. FAIRCHILD AIRCRAFT CORP.

21 F.3d 721 (6th Cir. 1994)

KENNEDY, CIRCUIT JUDGE:

Plaintiff David Engebretsen appeals the judgment entered after a jury verdict for defendant Fairchild Aircraft Corporation in this airplane products liability action. On appeal, plaintiff first argues that the District Court erred in denying his motion for judgment as a matter of law. Further, plaintiff argues that the District Court erroneously denied his motion for a new trial because of the admission of two reports by defendant's expert witnesses that contained inadmissible and prejudicial hearsay; the admission of expert testimony regarding post-incident tests; and the District Court's refusal to admit certain government reports offered by plaintiff. For the reasons stated below, we affirm.

I.

This case concerns an emergency landing of a Metro III aircraft manufactured by defendant. Plaintiff, a captain for Comair, alleges that, while attempting to land the plane, he sustained a back injury as a result of the plane's allegedly defective Stall Avoidance System ("SAS"). During the incident in question, plaintiff and First Officer Sean Belcher were flying a Metro III aircraft, a small plane with a capacity for eighteen passengers and two crew members. The Metro III has a flight control known as the elevator, which controls the pitch attitude of the aircraft. The elevator or pitch trim system is used to adjust the elevator and thereby relieve some of the pressure felt by the pilot on the control column or "yoke." The plane is also equipped with an SAS. The SAS senses an impending stall and serves to warn the pilot of the stall and attempts to avoid the stall by causing a forward or nose-down pressure on the control yoke.

....

Unable to fully control the rate of descent, plaintiff had to maintain a high speed in order to reach the runway. He managed to land the plane at 155 knots, approximately fifty-percent faster than normal landing speed. The forward pressure continued on the yoke until all the SAS circuit breakers were pulled. Plaintiff taxied the plane to the gate and the passengers deplaned. Although not then apparent, plaintiff later experienced back pain which he attributes to the incident. At the time of trial, plaintiff was on disability flight status due to his back injury.

....

We conclude that the District Court applied an incorrect legal standard on one of the grounds on which the court denied plaintiff's motion for a new trial. In particular, the District Court erroneously concluded that Federal Rules of Evidence 702 and 703 permit the admission, on direct examination, of testifying experts' opinions contained in written documents. Rules 702 & 703 provide:

Rule 702. Testimony by Experts

If scientific, technical, or other specialized knowledge will assist the trier of fact to understand the evidence or to determine a fact in issue, a witness qualified as an expert by knowledge, skill, experience, training, or education, may testify thereto in the form of an opinion or otherwise.

Rule 703. Bases of Opinion Testimony by Experts

The facts or data in the particular case upon which an expert bases an opinion or inference may be those perceived by or made known to the expert at or before the hearing. If of a type reasonably relied upon by experts in the particular field in forming opinions or inferences upon the subject, the facts or data need not be admissible in evidence.

C. OPINIONS AND EXPERT TESTIMONY

Fed. R. Evid. 702 & 703. Rule 702 permits the admission of expert opinion testimony not opinions contained in documents prepared out of court. *See* Fed. R. Evid. 702. Rule 703 allows a testifying expert to rely on materials, including inadmissible hearsay, in forming the basis of his opinion. Rules 702 and 703 do not, however, permit the admission of materials, relied on by an expert witness, for the truth of the matters they contain if the materials are otherwise inadmissible.... "Rule 703 merely permits such hearsay, or other inadmissible evidence, upon which an expert properly relies, to be admitted to explain the basis of the expert's opinion." *Id.* Moreover, such materials should not be admitted if the risk of prejudice substantially outweighs their probative value.... When inadmissible materials are admitted for explanatory purposes, the opposing party is entitled to a limiting instruction to the jury that the evidence may be considered "solely as a basis for the expert opinion and not as substantive evidence." ...

In concluding that the expert reports were properly admitted, the trial court reasoned that the experts could have referred to the exhibits during direct examination and therefore defendant could properly move for their admission at a later time. As discussed above, however, Rules 702 and 703 carve out a narrow exception to the rule against the admission of hearsay. Heaslip and Morgan were entitled to testify as to their opinion, and rely on inadmissible evidence. Neither their written opinions nor the materials on which they relied were admissible under Rules 702 and 703. Thus, the District Court's conclusion that Rules 702 and 703 permit the admission of the reports was erroneous.

....

UNITED STATES v. PICCINONNA

885 F.2d 1529 (11th Cir. 1989)

FAY, CIRCUIT JUDGE:

....

... Julio Piccinonna appeals his conviction on two counts of knowingly making false material statements to a Grand Jury in violation of Title IV of the Organized Crime Control Act of 1970. Piccinonna argues that the trial judge erred in refusing to admit the testimony of his polygraph expert and the examinations results....

I. *Background*

Julio Piccinonna has been in the waste disposal business in South Florida for over twenty-five years. In 1983, a Grand Jury conducted hearings to investigate antitrust violations in the garbage business. The government believed that South Florida firms in the waste disposal business had agreed not to compete for each other's accounts, and to compensate one another when one firm did not adhere to the agreement and took an account from another firm.

....

Prior to trial, Piccinonna requested that the Government stipulate to the admission into evidence of the result of a polygraph test which would be administered subsequently. The Government refused to stipulate to the admission of any testimony regarding the polygraph test or its results. Despite the Government's refusal, George B. Slattery, a licensed polygraph examiner, tested Piccinonna on November 25, 1985. Piccinonna asserted that the expert's report left no doubt that he did not lie when he testified before the Grand Jury.... On November 27, 1985, Piccinonna filed a motion with the district court requesting a hearing on the admission of the polygraph testimony. On January 6, 1986, the district court held a hearing on the defendant's motions. Due to the per se rule, which holds polygraph evidence inadmissible in this circuit, the trial judge refused to admit the evidence. The judge noted, however, that the Eleventh Circuit may wish to reconsider the issue of the admissibility of polygraph evidence since these tests have become much more widely used, particularly by the Government....

....

II. *The Per Se Rule*

In federal courts, the admissibility of expert testimony concerning scientific tests or findings is governed by Rule 702 of the Federal Rules of Evidence. Rule 702 provides:

> If scientific, technical, or other specialized knowledge will assist the trier of fact to understand the evidence or to determine a fact in issue, a witness qualified as an expert by knowledge, skill, experience, training or education, may testify thereto in the form of an opinion or otherwise.

Fed.R.Evid. 702. Under this rule, to admit expert testimony the trial judge must determine that the expert testimony will be relevant and will be helpful to the trier of fact. In addition, courts require the proponent of the testimony to show that the principle or technique is generally accepted in the scientific community....

....

... [W]e believe it is no longer accurate to state categorically that polygraph testing lacks general acceptance for use in all circumstances. For this reason, we find it appropriate to reexamine the per se exclusionary rule and institute a rule more in keeping with the progress made in the polygraph field.

III. *Differing Approaches to Polygraph Admissibility*

Courts excluding polygraph evidence typically rely on three grounds: 1) the unreliability of the polygraph test, 2) the lack of standardization of polygraph procedure, and 3) undue impact on the jury. Proponents of admitting polygraph evidence have attempted to rebut these concerns. With regard to unreliability, proponents stress the significant advances made in the field of polygraphy. Professor McCormick argues that the fears of unreliability "are not sufficient to

C. OPINIONS AND EXPERT TESTIMONY 99

warrant a rigid exclusionary rule. A great deal of lay testimony routinely admitted is at least as unreliable and inaccurate, and other forms of scientific evidence involve risks of instrumental or judgmental error." (Citation omitted.) Further, proponents argue that the lack of standardization is being addressed and will progressively be resolved as the polygraph establishes itself as a valid scientific test.... Finally, proponents argue that there is no evidence that jurors are unduly influenced by polygraph evidence.... In fact, several studies refute the proposition that jurors are likely to give disproportionate weight to polygraph evidence.

In the wake of new empirical evidence and scholarly opinion which have undercut many of the traditional arguments against admission of polygraph evidence, a substantial number of courts have revisited the admissibility question. Three roughly identifiable approaches to the problem have emerged. First, the traditional approach holds polygraph evidence inadmissible when offered by either party, either as substantive evidence or as relating to the credibility of a witness.... Second, a significant number of jurisdictions permit the trial court, in its discretion, to receive polygraph evidence if the parties stipulate to the evidence's admissibility before the administration of the test and if certain other conditions are met. Finally, some courts permit the trial judge to admit polygraph evidence even in the absence of a stipulation, but only when special circumstances exist. In these jurisdictions, the issue is within the sound discretion of the trial judge.

....

The common thread running through the various approaches taken by the courts which have modified the per se rule is a recognition that while wholesale exclusion under Rule 702 is unwarranted, there must be carefully constructed limitations placed upon the use of polygraph evidence in court. Absent a stipulation by the parties, we are unable to locate any case in which a court has allowed polygraph expert testimony offered as substantive proof of the truth or falsity of the statements made during the polygraph examination. The myriad of "special circumstances" and conditions that have been held to constitute appropriate scenarios for use of polygraph evidence are necessarily rough estimates by the courts of when and where the danger of unfair prejudice due to the admission of the evidence is least significant.

IV. *Principles for Admissibility*

There is no question that in recent years polygraph testing has gained increasingly widespread acceptance as a useful and reliable scientific tool. Because of the advances that have been achieved in the field which have led to the greater use of polygraph examination, coupled with a lack of evidence that juries are unduly swayed by polygraph evidence, we agree with those courts which have found that a per se rule disallowing polygraph evidence is no longer warranted. Of course, polygraphy is a developing and inexact science, and we continue to believe it inappropriate to allow the admission of polygraph evidence in all situations in which more proven types of expert testimony are allowed. However, as Justice Potter Stewart wrote, "any rule that impedes the discovery of truth in a court of law impedes as well the doing of justice." (Citation omitted.) Thus, we believe the best approach in this area is one which balances the need to admit all relevant and reliable evidence against the danger that the admission of the evidence for a given purpose will be unfairly prejudicial. Accordingly we outline two instances where polygraph evidence may be admitted at trial, which we believe achieve the necessary balance.

A. *Stipulation*

The first rule governing admissibility of polygraph evidence is one easily applied. Polygraph expert testimony will be admissible in this circuit when both parties stipulate in advance as to the circumstances of the test and as to the scope of its admissibility. The stipulation as to circumstances must indicate that the parties agree on material matters such as the manner in which the test is conducted, the nature of the questions asked, and the identity of the examiner administering the test. The stipulation as to scope of admissibility must indicate the purpose or purposes for which the evidence will be introduced. Where the parties agree to both of these conditions in advance of the polygraph test, evidence of the test results is admissible.

B. *Impeachment or Corroboration*

The second situation in which polygraph evidence may be admitted is when used to impeach or corroborate the testimony of a witness at trial. Admission of polygraph evidence for these purposes is subject to three preliminary conditions. First, the party planning to use the evidence at trial must provide adequate notice to the opposing party that the expert testimony will be offered. Second, polygraph expert testimony by a party will be admissible only if the opposing party was given reasonable opportunity to have [his] own polygraph expert administer a test covering substantially the same questions. Failure to provide adequate notice or reasonable opportunity for the opposing side to administer its own test is proper grounds for exclusion of the evidence.

Finally, whether used to corroborate or impeach, the admissibility of the polygraph administrator's testimony will be governed by the Federal Rules of Evidence for the admissibility of corroboration or impeachment testimony. For example, Rule 608 limits the use of opinion or reputation evidence to establish the credibility of a witness in the following way: "[E]vidence of truthful character is admissible only after the character of the witness for truthfulness has been attacked by opinion or reputation evidence or otherwise." Thus, evidence that a witness passed a polygraph examination, used to corroborate that witness's in-court testimony, would not be admissible under Rule 608 unless or until the credibility of that witness were first attacked. Even where the above three conditions are met, admission of polygraph evidence for impeachment or corroboration purposes is left entirely to the discretion of the trial judge.

C. OPINIONS AND EXPERT TESTIMONY

....

Thus under the Federal Rules of Evidence governing the admissibility of expert testimony, the trial court may exclude polygraph expert testimony because 1) the polygraph examiner's qualifications are unacceptable; 2) the test procedure was unfairly prejudicial or the test was poorly administered; or 3) the questions were irrelevant or improper. The trial judge has wide discretion in this area, and rulings on admissibility will not be reversed unless a clear abuse of discretion is shown....

....

V. *Conclusion*

We neither expect nor hope that today's holding will be the final word within our circuit on this increasingly important issue. The advent of new and developing technologies calls for flexibility within the legal system so that the ultimate ends of justice may be served. It is unwise to hold fast to a familiar rule when the basis for that rule ceases to be persuasive. We believe that the science of polygraphy has progressed to a level of acceptance sufficient to allow the use of polygraph evidence in limited circumstances where the danger of unfair prejudice is minimized. We proceed with caution in this area because the reliability of polygraph testing remains a subject of intense scholarly debate. As the field of polygraph testing continues to progress, it may become necessary to reexamine the rules regarding the admissibility of polygraph evidence.

The judgment of conviction is *Vacated* ....

2. OPINIONS AND EXPERT TESTIMONY PROBLEMS

1. "In My Opinion"

Janie, known for her opinions on everything, was an eyewitness to a carjacking in a shopping center parking lot. Two men are charged with the crime and Janie testifies at trial. Which of the following testimony would be proper?

a. Janie: "I'd estimate that the men were both about six feet tall and weighed 175 pounds."
b. Janie: "One of the men, the guy who went to the passenger side of the car, smelled of alcohol."
c. Janie: "That same guy looked quite angry, like he had just stepped on a tack."
d. Janie: "They both looked like vicious killers."
e. Janie: "They drove away at about 80 miles per hour after knocking the driver, who looked like a teenage boy, violently to the ground; those two guys are carjackers as sure as I'm sitting here!"
f. Janie: "After they left, I smelled burnt rubber from the tires. They were obviously in quite a hurry to get away."

2. Daughter of Ms. Jean Dixon

In a murder trial in which the defense is mistaken identity, the defendant calls to the witness stand a psychic, Akilah, who claims she saw a metaphysical image of the murderer and it was not the defendant. Permissible? Why?

3. Sister-in-Law

Andi, a surgeon, is sued for malpractice after a routine gall bladder operation went awry. At trial, Dr. Andi called her sister, Dr. Natsu, an internist, to testify on her behalf. Natsu is asked whether, in her expert opinion, Andi acted with the requisite standard of care during the operation.

    a. Is this question permissible? Why?
    b. Could Dr. Natsu testify if her opinion was based largely on the hearsay statements of other doctors? Please explain.

4. Cops

Sgt. Darryl Johnson of New York's lower east side has been an undercover police officer attached to the narcotics division for twelve years. During that time, he has participated in several thousand drug arrests, many of which concerned cocaine trafficking. Could Sgt. Johnson properly testify in a cocaine distribution case as an expert? For example, could Johnson testify that the amount of crack cocaine seized from a defendant's residence indicated that the drugs were intended for distribution and not personal use, that drug traffickers regularly take payment in ten or twenty dollar bills, and that scales, razor blades, and cellular phones were commonly part of drug transactions? Please explain.

5. The Legacy of Daubert

Explain whether any of the following experts would be allowed to testify under either *Frye* or *Daubert*.

    a. DPT. Li, a two year old child, died after suffering a brain seizure. The seizure occurred five days after she was given a DPT vaccine (pertussis). Li's parents brought suit claiming the vaccination caused the seizure. Dr. Randi Palmer, an epidemiologist, testified for the plaintiff. Dr. Palmer said a study indicated that DPT vaccines could cause seizures up to a week after administration. The study covered seven cases of children who had been vaccinated. Dr. Palmer observed that there were 1,182 cases of serious neurological illness in children between the ages of two and three years of age during the previous year. No prior neurological testing had been done on the seven children before they were vaccinated. The results of this study had not been duplicated in any subsequent controlled study. Dr. Palmer further observed that when animals were given pertussis, some developed brain damage. Should Dr. Palmer be permitted to testify? Why?

b. Pest Control. The Smyths filed suit against Ralph's Pest Control because of family health problems they claim were caused by Ralph's commercial termiticide (involving the "tenting" and fumigating of the Smyths' house). The plaintiffs' expert, Dr. Marjorie Palmetto, utilized an experimental test not generally accepted by the scientific community to conclude that while other potential causes still remained, the Smyths' illnesses could be traced to Ralph's tenting. Should Dr. Palmetto be permitted to testify? Why?

c. Acne 10. Plaintiff, Polly, used a special topical acne medication during pregnancy. After her child was born with birth defects, she and her husband brought suit, claiming that the medication caused the defects. The plaintiffs' expert, Dr. Rhonda Vanderstern, a highly respected dermatologist, testified that in her expert opinion, the dosage of the medication was sufficient to cause the defects. Dr. Vanderstern based her opinion on a study that had not been subject to peer testing. Dr. Vanderstern could not provide any published material that supported her conclusions. (She did point to several tests administered on animals, however, that generally supported her conclusions.) Should Dr. Vanderstern be permitted to testify? Why?

D. THE IMPEACHMENT OF WITNESSES

In accordance with the bulk of judicial authority, the inquiry is strictly limited to character for veracity, rather than allowing evidence as to character generally.

Fed. R. Evid. 608(a) Advisory Committee's Note

[T]he present rule generally bars evidence of specific instances of conduct of a witness for the purpose of attacking or supporting his credibility. There are, however, two exceptions: (1) specific instances are provable when they have been the subject of criminal conviction, and (2) specific instances may be inquired into on cross-examination of the principal witness or of a witness giving an opinion of his character for truthfulness.

Fed. R. Evid. 608(b) Advisory Committee's Note

1. IMPEACHMENT CASES

UNITED STATES v. SWANSON

9 F.3d 1354 (8th Cir. 1993)

MAGILL, CIRCUIT JUDGE:

Wade R. Swanson (Swanson) appeals a jury verdict and district court order sentencing him to 168 months' imprisonment under 21 U.S.C. § 841 for conspiracy to manufacture and distribute marijuana and 18 U.S.C. § 1956 for money laundering. On appeal, Swanson seeks reversal for a series of evidentiary rulings as well as allegations of prosecutorial misconduct. We affirm.

I. *Background*

On February 7, 1991, officers executed a search warrant at the Rush City Farm (the Farm) and discovered one of the largest and most sophisticated indoor marijuana growing operations ever uncovered by enforcement officials in Minnesota. The officers seized approximately 638 marijuana plants, sophisticated indoor growing equipment, and financial records and tax statements in the names of Brad Johnson (Johnson) and Wade Swanson....

....

II. *Discussion*

A. *Admission of Swanson's Prior Guilty Plea*

Swanson first seeks reversal of his conviction because the trial court admitted evidence of a guilty plea by Swanson in connection with a 1987 felony menacing incident (1987 Incident) in Colorado. Swanson argues, for the first time on appeal, that evidence of the 1987 Incident was inadmissible because his guilty plea does not qualify as "conviction" as required by Federal Rule of Evidence 609(a).

Whether evidence of a prior conviction should be admitted is left to the discretion of the trial court. *United States v. Reeves*, 730 F.2d 1189, 1196 (8th Cir. 1984). A court should admit evidence of a conviction under Rule 609(a)(1) if the court determines that "the probative value of admitting this evidence outweighs the prejudicial effect to the defendant." Fed. R. Evid. 609(a)(1). An appellate court will only overturn a trial court's decision of what evidence to admit if the trial court abuses its discretion. *United States v. Rogers*, 939 F.2d 591, 594 (8th Cir.), *cert. denied*, 116 L. Ed. 2d 632, 112 S.Ct. 609 (1991)....

At trial, Swanson argued that the 1987 Incident was inadmissible because the Colorado district court previously had dismissed the case against him. Swanson argued that the dismissal of the case after his probationary period was equivalent to a pardon, annulment or other procedure that precludes admission of evidence under Rule 609(c). Tr. Vol. VI at 4, 8-9, 14; see Fed. R. Evid. 609(c). The trial court properly held that it could not exclude evidence of the 1987 Incident based on Rule 609(c) because Swanson did not provide any evidence that the dismissal of the case was based on a finding of innocence or rehabilitation. *See* Fed. R. Evid. 609(c); *cf. Brown v. Frey*, 889 F.2d 159, 171 (8th Cir. 1989) (holding that evidence of conviction properly excluded where convicted party received pardon "based on rehabilitation")....

....

We need not decide whether Swanson's guilty plea, two-year probation, suspended sentence, and subsequent dismissal of the case qualify as a conviction for purposes of Rule 609(a). [4] Even if the 1987 Incident does not qualify as a conviction, its admission into evidence on cross-examination did not constitute plain error. We believe that no substantial rights were prejudiced by the admission of the evidence, and in light of the evidence presented at trial we cannot say that admission of the 1987 Incident resulted in a miscarriage of justice....

UNITED STATES v. BRACKEEN

969 F.2d 827 (9th Cir. 1992)

PER CURIAM:

This court has convened en banc to determine whether bank robbery necessarily involves "dishonesty," as that term is used in Federal Rule of Evidence 609(a)(2). The question arises in the context of whether a witness can be impeached by evidence of prior convictions.... We now conclude that for purposes of Rule 609(a)(2) bank robbery is not per se a crime of "dishonesty."

Facts and Proceedings Below

Robert Nello Brackeen robbed three different banks, one bank a day on each of three separate days in July 1990. In the first robbery, Brackeen and an accomplice, Jermaine Moore, presented a threatening note to a teller....

Brackeen was charged in a single indictment with one count of aiding and abetting an armed bank robbery, in violation of 18 U.S.C. §§ 2, 2113(a), 2113(d) (1988), and two counts of unarmed bank robbery, in violation of 18 U.S.C. § 2113(a). On September 24, 1990, Brackeen pleaded guilty to both unarmed bank robberies. On October 2, 1990, Brackeen went to trial on count one of the indictment, aiding and abetting Moore in the armed bank robbery. He claimed he did not know Moore had a gun.

On the second day of the two-day trial, Brackeen indicated he would testify, and objected before taking the stand to the use for impeachment of his guilty pleas to the two unarmed bank robberies. The court reserved its ruling on the objection until after Brackeen testified. Brackeen was the sole defense witness. On cross-examination, the court allowed impeachment with the guilty pleas.

The trial court's basis for admitting the prior guilty pleas as impeachment evidence was Federal Rule of Evidence 609(a)(2), which allows impeachment of a defendant by any crime involving "dishonesty or false statement." The court expressly refused to admit the pleas under Rule 609(a)(1), which allows impeachment using any felony "if the court determines that the probative value of admitting this evidence outweighs its prejudicial effect to the accused...." The court stated, "I'm going to base my ruling on Rule 609(a)(2) that this is a crime

---

[4] We note, without deciding the issue, that this court has held that "use of convictions for which a suspended sentence were received is permissible for impeachment purposes." ...

involving dishonesty and the government has an absolute right to use it to impeach him." ...

Brackeen appeals, claiming the impeachment was improper because ... (2) the guilty pleas were to bank robbery, a crime that does not involve "dishonesty or false statement" as required by Rule 609(a)(2)....

Analysis

Rule 609 provides in part:

Rule 609. Impeachment by Evidence of Conviction of Crime
(a) General rule. For the purpose of attacking the credibility of a witness,
(1) evidence that a witness other than an accused has been convicted of a crime shall be admitted, subject to Rule 403, if the crime was punishable by death or imprisonment in excess of one year under the law under which the witness was convicted, and evidence that an accused has been convicted of such a crime shall be admitted if the court determines that the probative value of admitting this evidence outweighs its prejudicial effect to the accused; and
(2) evidence that any witness has been convicted of a crime shall be admitted if it involved dishonesty or false statement, regardless of the punishment. Fed.R.Evid. 609.

Brackeen's bank robberies did not involve any "false statement[s]," *id.*, and were not "actually committed by fraudulent or deceitful means." *United States v. Glenn*, 667 F.2d 1269, 1273 (9th Cir. 1982). Accordingly, the only issue in this case is whether bank robbery is per se a crime of "dishonesty" under Rule 609, regardless of the means by which it is perpetrated. Our circuit has not spoken with one voice on this question.... We now ... adopt the holding in *Glenn*: bank robbery is not per se a crime of "dishonesty" under Federal Rule of Evidence 609(a)(2).

Our first step in interpreting any statute or rule is to consider the plain meaning of the provision in question....

Unfortunately, "dishonesty" has more than one meaning. In the dictionary, and in everyday use, "dishonesty" has two meanings, one of which includes, and one of which excludes, crimes such as bank robbery. In its broader meaning, "dishonesty" is defined as a breach of trust, a "lack of ... probity or integrity in principle," "lack of fairness," or a "disposition to ... betray." Webster's Third New International Dictionary 650 (1986 unabridged ed.). This dictionary states, under the heading "synonyms," that "dishonest may apply to any breach of honesty or trust, as lying, deceiving, cheating, stealing, or defrauding." *Id.* Bank robbery fits within this definition of "dishonesty" because it is a betrayal of principles of fairness and probity, a breach of community trust, like stealing.

In its narrower meaning, however, "dishonesty" is defined as deceitful behavior, a "disposition to defraud ... [or] deceive," *id.*, or a "[d]isposition to lie, cheat, or defraud," Black's Law Dictionary 421 (5th ed. 1979). Bank robbery does not fit within this definition of "dishonesty" because it is a crime of violent, not deceitful, taking. Everyday usage mirrors the dictionary: we use "dishonesty" narrowly to refer to a liar, and broadly to refer to a thief.

Fortunately, we are not operating in a vacuum: while nothing in the text of Rule 609 indicates precisely what Congress meant when it used the term "dishonesty," we find guidance in the legislative history of the rule....

The legislative history of Rule 609 makes clear that Congress used the term "dishonesty" in the narrower sense, to mean only those crimes which involve deceit. The House Conference Committee Report on Rule 609 states:

> By the phrase "dishonesty and false statement" the Conference means crimes such as perjury or subornation of perjury, false statement, criminal fraud, embezzlement, or false pretense, or any other offense in the nature of crimen falsi, the commission of which involves some element of deceit, untruthfulness, or falsification bearing on the accused's propensity to testify truthfully....

Bank robbery is not "in the nature of crimen falsi." Black's Law Dictionary defines "crimen falsi" as follows: "[The] term generally refers to crimes in the nature of perjury or subornation of perjury, false statement, criminal fraud, embezzlement, false pretense, or any other offense which involves some element of deceitfulness, untruthfulness, or falsification bearing on witness' propensity to testify truthfully." Black's Law Dictionary 335 (5th ed. 1979)....

We think the legislative history of this provision shows that Congress intended to limit the term to prior convictions involving some element of deceit, untruthfulness, or falsification which would tend to show that an accused would be likely to testify untruthfully....

....

Conclusion

Congress intended Rule 609(a)(2) to apply only to those crimes that factually or by definition entail some element of misrepresentation or deceit, and not to "'those crimes which, bad though they are, do not carry with them a tinge of falsification.'" *Glenn*, 667 F.2d at 1273 (quoting *United States v. Ortega*, 561 F.2d 803, 806 (9th Cir.1977)). We must follow Congress' intent. *See Green*, 490 U.S. at 508, 109 S.Ct. at 1984 ("Our task in deciding this case ... is not to fashion the rule we deem desirable but to identify the rule that Congress fashioned."). Brackeen's conviction is *Reversed*, and the case is *Remanded* for a new trial.

2. IMPEACHMENT PROBLEMS

1. "Betty Sue"

Astrid was charged with counterfeiting. Betty Sue testified as an eyewitness for the prosecution in its case in chief.

a. Can the prosecutor ask Betty Sue on direct examination:
   1. "Were you convicted of armed robbery in 1990?"
   2. "Do you know, Betty Sue, that Astrid was previously convicted of counterfeiting in 1991?"
b. Can Betty Sue be impeached with the following?
   1. "Isn't it true, Betty Sue, that you observed Astrid for just under one minute, and not 'around ten minutes' as you just testified?"
   2. "You've hated Astrid since she was promoted ahead of you when you worked together at the Department of the Treasury, isn't that right?"
   3. "Betty Sue, you've been convicted of shoplifting, correct?"
   4. "You've also been convicted of aggravated battery?"
   5. "You've also spanked your child?"
   6. "In fact, Betty Sue, you have a form of attention deficit disorder, true?"
   7. "Betty Sue, didn't you say in your deposition that you weren't sure of the denomination of the bill Astrid used to purchase her groceries, when you just testified that you were positive she used a twenty dollar bill?"
c. If Astrid testifies that she did not pass a counterfeit bill as charged, can the prosecution, in rebuttal,
   1. Call Melissa to testify that Astrid is known in the community for being a liar?
   2. Call Mistral to testify that Astrid filed a false Sears credit card application?

2. Cliff and Norm

Officer Cliff arrested Norm at Sammy's Pool Hall after Norm battered another patron with a pool cue. At trial, Officer Cliff testifies.

a. Officer Cliff is asked on direct examination whether Norm has a reputation in the community for being violent. Permissible?
b. On cross examination of Officer Cliff, he is asked whether he had arrested Norm on two previous occasions. Permissible?
c. If Officer Cliff denies arresting Norm on two other occasions, can a different witness be brought in on rebuttal to testify that she saw Cliff arrest Norm twice before?
d. Can Cliff be asked on cross examination, "Isn't it true that you were indicted by a grand jury for embezzlement?"

3. Dr. Doctor

Dr. Artis Polaski testified as an expert witness for the plaintiff on the cause of death of a person who died suddenly after returning from a construction job on a Caribbean island.

D. THE IMPEACHMENT OF WITNESSES

a. On cross examination of Dr. Polaski, can the opposing counsel, Sarah, ask Dr. Polaski, "Your conclusion about the meaning of decedent's symptoms disagrees with Dr. Von Hayes in her treatise, *Tropical Diseases and Their Treatment*, isn't that right?"

b. Also on cross examination, can Sarah ask Dr. Polaski, "You now testify that you reviewed the records twice prior to reaching your conclusions?" [Yes.] "Yet in your deposition that was taken six months ago, you did not mention that you reviewed any records at all in reaching your conclusion in response to the question 'What did you do to prepare for reaching a conclusion on the cause of death?'"

c. If Dr. Polaski is asked about and denies having been convicted of filing a false income tax statement, can Sarah offer a certified copy of the conviction in evidence?

4. Perjury

Paulette is prosecuted for perjury. She testifies, claiming she told the truth when she testified in the previous trial concerning allegations her boyfriend was a major trafficker in narcotics. In rebuttal, can the prosecution call Paulette's estranged brother to testify that Paulette has a reputation in the community for being untruthful? Explain.

VII. HEARSAY

The factors to be considered in evaluating the testimony of a witness are perception, memory, and narration....

In order to encourage the witness to do his best with respect to each of these factors, and to expose any inaccuracies which may enter in, the Anglo-American tradition has evolved three conditions under which witnesses will ideally be required to testify: (1) under oath, (2) in the personal presence of the trier of fact, (3) subject to cross-examination.

....

Emphasis on the basis of the hearsay rule today tends to center upon the condition of cross-examination ... a "vital feature" of the Anglo-American system.

Common sense tells that much evidence which is not given under the three [ideal] conditions may be inherently superior to much that is. Moreover, when the choice is between evidence which is less than best and no evidence at all, only clear folly would dictate an across-the-board policy of doing without....

The approach to hearsay in these rules is that of the common law, i.e., a general rule excluding hearsay, with exceptions under which evidence is not required to be excluded even though hearsay....

Fed. R. Evid. 801 Advisory Committee's Note ("Introductory Note: The Hearsay Problem")

A. NON-HEARSAY

"Hearsay" is a statement, other than one made by the declarant while testifying at the trial or hearing, offered in evidence to prove the truth of the matter asserted.

Fed. R. Evid. 801(c)

1. NON-HEARSAY CASES

UNITED STATES v. EMMONS
24 F.3d 1210 (10th Cir. 1994)

SHADUR, SENIOR DISTRICT JUDGE:

After a jury trial, Kansas farmer Roger Emmons ("Roger") was found guilty of each of the four drug-related counts in a superseding indictment.... One of

Roger's two codefendants, Jack Rivard ("Rivard"), entered a guilty plea before trial, while the other codefendant, Roger's brother Daryl Emmons ("Daryl"), went to trial jointly with Roger. Roger raises four issues on this appeal, charging the district court with errors in:

....
2. admitting an item of evidence that Roger characterizes as hearsay;
....

We reject each of Roger's arguments and affirm his conviction.

In April 1992 informant Lynette Hines ("Hines") told Wichita Police detectives Bruce Watts ("Watts") and John Stinson ("Stinson") that "Jack Rivard was possibly involved in the growing of marijuana and possibly growing it at a house in Wichita." After Rivard denied the detectives' request to search his home, he moved to Greenwood County, Kansas, where he took up residence on property owned by Roger.

Some time during the following month, Watts and Stinson passed Hines' tip along to Special Agent Rickey Atteberry ("Atteberry") of the Kansas Bureau of Investigation ("KBI"). Atteberry decided to visit Rivard's property along with Watts, Stinson and Hines. There they saw over 100 marijuana plants, the majority of which were protectively enclosed within wire screens.

....
Later that night (July 9) KBI Special Agent Ray Lundin ("Lundin") submitted an application to a Greenwood County judge for a search warrant for Roger's residence and garage. In the space calling for the particular description of the objects of the search, Lundin referred to his attached sworn affidavit, as did the warrant promptly issued by the judge. Upon executing the warrant the agents located and seized a hand-drawn map found in Roger's kitchen, which Atteberry testified at trial corresponded to the configuration of the marijuana patches, along with various items in the garage consistent with the cultivation of marijuana (though also useable for legitimate purposes): watering buckets, wire screening, an unopened 12-pound bag of Miracle Gro brand plant food and quantities of lime (a chemical used to treat the ground when growing marijuana).

....
Roger next urges that the district court erred in admitting into evidence the hand-drawn sketch seized from Roger's kitchen during the July 9 search of his residence. That one-page drawing marks out 13 different locations identified by letters, each with a number as well. There was also a key in the corner of the map, showing a star as the symbol for "lime" (there were six locations so marked on the map itself) and a "+" as the symbol for urea (shown on one location).

Evidentiary rulings are generally committed to the discretion of the trial judge and are reviewed only for an abuse of that discretion.... And such deference to the trial judge is heightened when (as here) we review rulings as to the admissibility of what is claimed to be hearsay evidence.

A. NON-HEARSAY

Roger contends that the alleged map should have been excluded as inadmissible hearsay. But the evidence was not offered "to prove the truth of the matter asserted" (Fed. R. Evid. 801(c)) — that marijuana was indeed growing on Roger's property. After all, the agents had found the drugs on the property, so there was no need to rely on the map to establish that. Instead the map was plainly admissible for the non-hearsay purpose of demonstrating that Roger had knowledge of the location and quantity of the marijuana plants and of the efforts to treat the ground for their cultivation.... Roger has not shown that the trial court's decision was an abuse of discretion.

....

WRIGHT v. DOE DEM. TATHAM

7 AD. & E. 313 (1837)

BOSANQUET, J.:

In support of the affirmative three letters were tendered in evidence upon which the following questions arose: first, whether letters addressed to the testator by persons well acquainted with him, and since deceased, which letters were found among the testator's papers after his death, but do not appear to be recognized in any way by the testator, are admissible in proof of his capacity? Secondly, if not admissible without some recognition of them by the testator, whether any of the letters set forth on the record is shewn to have been recognized by the testator?

First, the letters cannot be admissible unless they are relevant to the matter in issue, which matter is the capacity of the testator. The contents of the letters have no direct relation to the testator's state of mind, but may be taken to shew the opinion of the writers that the person addressed was of competent understanding. If the writers of these letters were produced as witnesses and examined upon oath, their opinion would be receivable in evidence, because the grounds of their knowledge and the credibility of their testimony might be ascertained by cross-examination; but I know of no rule by which the opinion, however clearly expressed, of a person, whoever well informed, is receivable in evidence, unless it be given in the course of legal examination.

That the three letters were each of them written by the persons whose names they bear, and sent, at some time before they were found, to the testator's house, no doubt are facts, and those facts are proved on oath; and the letters are without a doubt admissible on an issue in which the fact of sending such letters by those persons, and within that limit of time, is relevant to the matter in dispute; as, for instance, on a feigned issue to try the question whether such letters were sent to the testator's house, or on any issue in which it is the material question whether such letters or any of them had been sent. Verbal declarations of the same parties are also facts, and in like manner admissible under the same circumstances; and so would letters or declarations to third persons upon the like supposition.

But the question is, whether the contents of these letters are evidence of the fact to be proved upon this issue, — that is, the actual existence of the qualities which the testator is, in those letters, by implication, stated to possess; and those letters may be considered in this respect to be on the same footing as if they had contained a direct and positive statement that he was competent. For this purpose they are mere hearsay evidence, statements of the writers, not on oath, of the truth of the matter in question, with this addition, that they have acted upon the statements on the faith of their being true, by their sending the letters to the testator. That an acting cannot give a sufficient sanction for the truth of the statement is perfectly plain; for it is clear that, if the same statements had been made by parol or in writing to a third person, that would have been insufficient; and this is conceded by the learned counsel for the plaintiff in error. Yet in both cases there has been an acting on the belief of the truth, by making the statement, or writing and sending a letter to a third person; and what difference can it possibly make that this is an acting of the same nature by writing and sending the letter to the testator? It is admitted, and most properly, that you have no right to use in evidence the fact of writing, and sending a letter to a third person containing a statement of competence, on the ground that it affords an inference that such an act would not have been done unless the statement was true, or believed to be true, although such an inference no doubt would be raised in the conduct of the ordinary affairs of life, if the statement were made by a man of veracity. But it cannot be raised in a judicial inquiry; and, if such an argument were admissible, it would lead to the indiscriminate admission of hearsay evidence of all manner of facts.

The conclusion at which I have arrived is, that proof of a particular fact, which is not of itself a matter in issue, but which is relevant only as implying a statement or opinion of a third person on the matter in issue is inadmissible in all cases where such a statement or opinion not on oath would be of itself inadmissible; and, therefore, in this case the letters which are offered only to prove the competence of the testator, that is the truth of the implied statements therein contained, were properly rejected, as the mere statement or opinion of the writer would certainly have been inadmissible....

UNITED STATES v. ALOSA

14 F.3d 693 (1st Cir. 1994)

BOUDIN, CIRCUIT JUDGE:

On April 9, 1992, law enforcement agents armed with a search warrant entered the home of Pasquale and Lisa Alosa in Loudon, New Hampshire. The search uncovered substantial amounts of marijuana, marijuana plants, a basement "garden" for growing them, scales, plastic bags, two loaded handguns, and 16 other unloaded firearms. Also found were two different collections of papers which, for simplicity, have been referred to as ledgers. A man named Robb Hamilton was also present on the premises and was later implicated.

Both Alosas and Hamilton were later named in an indictment that ... charged Pasquale and Lisa in four counts.

....

... [T]he second string to [Pasquale's] bow on appeal is a claim that the court erred in admitting the drug ledgers. One set of papers had been found inside a stove in the kitchen; the other set was in the living room. They contained entries concerning various transactions, including amounts and customer names. The government not only introduced the ledgers but, over objection, offered expert handwriting and print evidence that associated both ledgers in some degree with Lisa and one of them with Hamilton.

Pasquale's brief says that it was error to admit the ledgers because the government failed to offer evidence, independent of the ledgers, to show that they qualified as co-conspirator statements made in furtherance of the conspiracy. Under Fed.R.Evid. 801(d)(2)(E), a statement avoids hearsay objections if the trial judge finds by a preponderance of the evidence that an out-of-court statement was made by a co-conspirator and was made in furtherance of the conspiracy. *See Bourjaily v. United States*, 483 U.S. 171, 107 S.Ct. 2775, 97 L.Ed.2d 144 (1987). It may lessen the confusion that surrounds drug ledger evidence to point out that what needs to be proved for admissibility depends upon the use to be made of the evidence.

First, if records manifestly are or are shown by other evidence to be drug records, they are admissible "real evidence" tending to make it more likely that a drug business was being conducted, *see United States v. Tejada*, 886 F.2d 483, 487 (1st Cir.1989), and for this use there is ordinarily no hearsay problem to be overcome. Rather, the records help to show "the character and use of the place where the notebooks were found," *United States v. Wilson*, 532 F.2d 641, 645 (8th Cir. 1976), just like drugs, scales and guns. Here, the nature of the ledgers was indicated not only by the type of entry — which would have been sufficient — but also by expert testimony from a DEA agent who gave his opinion that the records related to drug transactions.[3]

Second, in this case the ledgers served the further purpose of helping to prove the existence of a conspiracy. Pasquale's own involvement in drugs was established by his pleas and much other evidence, but relatively little direct evidence in his trial showed active participation by Lisa in the business (her own admissions to the police were not made known to Pasquale's jury). Most of the drugs and related items were found either in Pasquale's areas of the house or in

---

[3] Using the entries to show the character of the ledgers as drug records does, of course, present some of the risks of hearsay; but under the modern definition of hearsay, such a use does not render the entries hearsay because the entries are not being used to prove the truth of the matter asserted in the entries (e.g., that a specific transaction took place on a particular date). *See* Fed.R.Evid. 801(c) (hearsay is an out of court statement offered "to prove the truth of the matter asserted"); 2 John W. Strong et al., McCormick on Evidence § 250, at 112 (1992) (collecting cases).

common areas. But the ledgers, once they were tied to Lisa by handwriting and print evidence, made the inference of conspiracy easy. Once again this use of the ledgers presented no hearsay problem in this case. The "truth" of individual statements in the ledgers is beside the point; all that matters is that the ledgers are drug records to which Lisa may be linked by other evidence. Nor is there a hearsay problem posed by testimony from a handwriting or print expert that connected Lisa to the ledgers. Thus, for the most important use of the ledgers in this case — to help show more than one participant and thus a conspiracy — there was no need for a preliminary finding of likely conspiracy nor any need to satisfy Rule 801(d)(2)(E).

Third, when it made its proffer in support of the ledgers, the government reserved the right to use the ledgers to show not only the fact of conspiracy but also, by relying on specific entries, the dimensions of the conspiracy. To the extent that the prosecutor wanted to argue that an individual entry was "true" — say, one showing a specific sale of a specific amount to a specific person — then some hearsay exception or exclusion did need to be satisfied. Here, Rule 801(d)(2)(E) was invoked. In admitting the evidence, the district court expressly found by a preponderance of the evidence that the ledgers were made by conspirators in furtherance of the conspiracy. These findings were amply supported by admissible non-hearsay evidence.[4] Lisa's presence in the home, with a marijuana garden in the cellar and drugs and paraphernalia throughout, was highly suggestive. The notion that "presence" at a crime does not equal guilt is not a ban on common sense inferences: the evidence of pervasive drug production and dealing in Lisa's home was material evidence that made her involvement more plausible. Once she was linked to the drug ledgers — a linkage that also did not happen to depend on hearsay — the trial judge could easily conclude that a conspiracy had been shown and admit the ledgers for the truth of the statements contained within them.

Not only did the evidence of joint drug dealing between husband and wife satisfy Rule 801(d)(2)(E) — which requires only a probability or likelihood of conspiracy — but the evidence amply satisfied the higher standard of proof beyond a reasonable doubt required for conviction....

2. NON-HEARSAY PROBLEMS

1. Is It Hearsay?

State whether the following are hearsay. Assume all statements are made out of court unless otherwise indicated. Determine only whether all of the elements of hearsay are met, not whether the item will be admissible.

---

[4] Actually, Fed.R.Evid. 104(a) permits the judge to consider the hearsay statements for their truth in making the admissibility findings, see Bourjaily, 483 U.S. at 178-80, 107 S.Ct. at 2780-81, although this court has recently joined other circuits in holding that there must be some evidence of conspiracy independent of the hearsay statements themselves.

A. NON-HEARSAY

a. To show that a bird named Crackers is owned by Sounia, Crackers' statements when she is in the same room with Sounia, "That's my Sounia! Caw! That's my Sounia!"
b. On the issue of whether Mary liked Lee, the fact that Mary hugged Lee upon seeing him.
c. On the issue of whether Mary liked Lee, the fact that Mary chose Lee last for her team in a moot court competition.
d. On the issue of whether Mary liked Lee, Mary's statement, "I like Lee."
e. On the question of who robbed the laundromat at gunpoint, witness Paul's deposition statement, "Larry robbed the laundromat."
f. To prove that Theresa and Sal are married, testimony by Roseanne that they said "I do" when asked by the priest whether they would take each other as lawfully wedded husband and wife.
g. To prove that Cassandra stabbed her husband DeWayne, the fact that Cassandra was seen fleeing their house at 4:15 p.m., 5 minutes before the police arrived at the house to investigate loud noises at the house.
h. On the issue of whether Beowulf died as a result of the accident, Beowulf's statement immediately after the accident, "The red Jeep Laredo just hit me and knocked me over."
i. To show that Jeanette committed a murder, the fact that she attempted to poison a prospective witness after she (Jeanette) had been charged with the crime.
j. To prove that Percival died of accidental causes, the autopsy report indicating such.
k. To prove that Steve is Patrick's father, testimony that Steve often referred to Patrick as "my son."
l. On the issue of whether Riddick had struck Lennox, Riddick's statement, "I boxed his ears but good."
m. To show that Louis Lightfeather committed the robbery of the convenience store, his written confession.
n. To show that Belinda went to the store with Aretha, the overheard question, "Why did Belinda go to the store with Aretha?"
o. To show that the road turns sharply, Otis' statement, "hey, watch out, that road turns sharply!"
p. To show that the driver of the car was negligent in running off of the road at the turn, Otis' statement, "hey, watch out, that road turns sharply!"
q. To impeach Grover, a witness in the case, Grover is asked on cross examination, "Didn't you say at the time of the incident that you were not home at all that night, unlike your testimony today?"
r. On the issue of whether the new model of the four-wheel-drive vehicle, the Laramie Cruiser, was safe, a Consumer Reports article declaring it to be "extraordinarily safe."

s. On the issue of whether the accused committed burglary, evidence that the defendant twice attempted to escape the jurisdiction after being arrested for the crime.
t. On the question of whether the Jaguar XJ12 convertible was a gift or loan from Ronald Crump, Crump's statement, "Here are the keys to the Jaguar; you can use it for a year as a birthday present."
u. On the issue of whether a newspaper article had defamed the Mayor, a statement by the reporter the day after the article had been published to the effect that "Yeah, I said some not-so-nice things about the Mayor in that article."

B. STATUTORY "NOT-HEARSAY" CASES (SPECIAL PRIOR STATEMENTS OF WITNESSES AND ADMISSIONS OF A PARTY-OPPONENT)

Considerable controversy has attended the question whether a prior out-of-court statement by a person now available for cross-examination concerning it, under oath and in the presence of the trier of fact, should be classed as hearsay.... The bulk of the case law has been against allowing prior statements of witnesses to be used generally as substantive evidence....

The position taken by the Advisory Committee ... requires in each instance, as a general safeguard, that the declarant actually testify as a witness, and it [the rule] then enumerates three situations in which the statement is excepted from the category of hearsay....

....

Admissions by a party-opponent are excluded from the category of hearsay on the theory that their admissibility in evidence is the result of the adversary system rather than satisfaction of the conditions of the hearsay rule.

Fed. R. Evid. 801(d)(2) Advisory Committee's Note

1. STATUTORY "NOT-HEARSAY" CASES

UNITED STATES v. ODOM
13 F.3d 949 (6th Cir.),
cert. denied, 115 S. Ct. 116 (1994)

JOINER, SENIOR DISTRICT JUDGE:
Defendants Gary Odom, Leonard Johnson and Terrance Bulger appeal their convictions and sentences for cocaine distribution and firearm offenses, challenging the admission of a co-conspirator's grand jury testimony.... For the reasons stated, we affirm all defendants' convictions and the sentences of Johnson and Odom.

B. STATUTORY "NOT-HEARSAY" CASES

I. *Arrests*

On November 2, 1991, Memphis law enforcement officers executed a search warrant at a local motel, finding five men in possession of 995 grams of cocaine and four firearms. The occupants of the room, Leonard Johnson, Myron Johnson, Chancee Allen, Gilbert Smith and Carl Warner, were arrested. Myron Johnson agreed to assist the police, telling them that the knew where two and one-half kilograms of cocaine were stored. He led the police to Allen's apartment in Nashville, where the officers found Todd Hoffman and 2385 grams of cocaine, a .30 caliber pistol and a triple beam scale....

Hoffman initially cooperated with the police, and agreed to testify before the grand jury....

II. *Hoffman's Grand Jury Testimony*

All three defendants challenge the admission of Hoffman's grand jury testimony. Defendants argue that Hoffman's testimony constituted hearsay, and was admitted in violation of their Fifth and Sixth Amendment rights to due process and to confront the witnesses against them.

Federal Rule of Evidence 801(c) defines hearsay as an out-of-court statement offered to prove the truth of the matter asserted. Rule 801(d) excepts from this general definition certain categories of statements, specifically providing that a statement is not hearsay if the "declarant testifies at the trial or hearing and is subject to cross-examination concerning the statement, and the statement is (A) inconsistent with the declarant's testimony, and was given under oath subject to the penalty of perjury at a trial, hearing, or other proceeding, or in a deposition[.]" Fed. R. Evid. 801(d)(1)(A). In *United States v. Distler*, 671 F.2d 954, 959 [7 Fed Rules Evid Serv 1380] (6th Cir.), *cert. denied*, 454 U.S. 827 (1981), this court stated that the admission, as substantive evidence, of grand jury testimony that meets the requirements of Fed.R. Evid. 801(d)(1)(A) does not run afoul of the Constitution. Thus, if the admission of Hoffman's grand jury testimony met the requirements of Rule 801(d)(1)(A), defendants have no legitimate basis on which to challenge its admission as substantive evidence of their guilt.

There is no question but that Hoffman was present at trial and subject to cross-examination, and that his grand jury testimony was given under oath, subject to the penalty of perjury. Defendants contend that, because the prosecutor did not elicit trial testimony inconsistent with Hoffman's grand jury testimony, the grand jury testimony was inadmissible under Rule 801(d)(1)(A).

During the government's direct examination of Hoffman, the prosecutor asked:

"Q. And Mr. Hoffman, did you appear before the grand jury in this matter regarding Terrance Bulger?
"A. Yes, I did.
"Q. Did you testify before the grand jury?
"A. Yes. I falsely testified.

"Q. Were you represented by counsel?
"A. Yes, I was.
"Q. And did you tell the grand jury that Terrance Bulger is the source of cocaine?
"A. Yes I lied to tell the grand jury that.
"Q. Did you tell the grand jury that Gary Odom was involved with you in the cocaine business?
"A. Yes, sir. Another lie. But I did tell them that.
"Q. And did you tell the grand jury that Terrance Bulger became involved in the distribution of cocaine in the summer — "

At this point, defense counsel objected on the grounds that the prosecutor was asking Hoffman to repeat "perjured testimony," and because the prosecutor had not laid a foundation for impeachment. The court overruled these objections. Hoffman testified on cross-examination to facts inconsistent with his grand jury testimony. Hoffman stated that Bulger knew nothing about his drug dealings, and that he had recanted his testimony about Odom because he was destroying Odom's life. At the conclusion of Hoffman's trial testimony, the court admitted as substantive evidence the transcript of Hoffman's grand jury testimony and the transcript of the recantation hearing.

Contrary to defendants' assertions, the admissibility of Hoffman's grand jury testimony does not hinge on whether the prosecutor elicited inconsistent trial testimony. Hoffman testified on cross-examination, prior to the admission of his grand jury testimony, to facts inconsistent with his grand jury testimony. It is immaterial whether the prosecutor or defense counsel elicits the foundation for the testimony, so long as the requirements of Rule 801(d)(1)(A) are satisfied. They were satisfied in this case, and the admission of Hoffman's grand jury testimony as substantive evidence was proper.

In addition, when a witness testifies at trial and labels his prior testimony as false, a sufficient inconsistency is shown to permit the admission of prior testimony (footnote omitted). The witness twice stated at trial that the grand jury testimony was a lie before it was published to the jury. This is a sufficient inconsistency to satisfy Fed.R. Evid. 801(d)(1)(A). To be sure, the better (and arguably more effective) method is for the proponent of the testimony to elicit a response from the witness that contradicts his prior testimony. In this case, however, this line of questions was unnecessary in light of the witness' immediate statement when asked whether he testified before the grand jury: "Yes. I falsely testified." This laid the required foundation for the admission of the grand jury testimony.

. . . .

LIPPAY v. CHRISTOS
996 F.2d 1490 (3d Cir. 1993)

GREENBERG, CIRCUIT JUDGE:

I. *Factual and Procedural Background*

Appellant Dean C. Christos appeals from a district court order entered July 31, 1992, denying his motion for judgment as a matter of law or, in the alternative, for a new trial, as well as from a judgment of February 14, 1992, entered on a jury verdict for $150,000 in favor of the appellee Richard M. Lippay. Lippay brought this action under 42 U.S.C. § 1983 claiming that Christos violated his Fourth and Fourteenth Amendment rights by initiating criminal proceedings against him maliciously and without probable cause and by unlawfully causing his arrest....

Because we conclude that the district court should not have permitted introduction of the hearsay testimony and that this error prejudiced Christos, we will vacate the order denying Christos' motion for a judgment as a matter of law and will remand the matter to the district court to reconsider that motion without the hearsay testimony. In the event that the court again denies that motion, the district court will grant a new trial limited to the Fourth Amendment seizure claim....

The germane facts as developed at the trial are as follows. In November 1986, the Bureau of Narcotics Investigation of the Pennsylvania Attorney General's Office initiated an investigation into suspected drug sales in Haddock's Bar, located in Coal Township, Northumberland County, Pennsylvania. In this investigation, Christos, an undercover agent for the bureau, worked with an informant, Darryl Philbin. Lippay was not an initial target of the investigation....

....

Philbin picked out Lippay in the photograph as the person from whom he had purchased drugs on August 5, 1987, even though in the yearbook photograph Lippay did not have a beard and was not wearing glasses. Later that same day, while Christos was working undercover at Haddocks's, he heard someone ask Dick how was everything on the school board. Subsequently, Marlin Haddock, the bar owner, informed Philbin that Dick was Richard Lippay....

Based upon all this information, Christos filed criminal complaints against Lippay in Northumberland and Lehigh Counties. The courts issued arrest warrants on which Lippay was arrested on February 27, 1989. But both sets of charges were dismissed without trial. At a preliminary hearing in Northumberland County, Philbin testified that at that time he could not positively identify Lippay as the person from whom he made the drug purchases, in part because at the hearing Lippay looked different from Dick as he did not have a beard and was not wearing glasses. Consequently, the district justice dismissed the charges....

Despite the fact that the charges were dismissed in both prosecutions, the Pennsylvania Department of Corrections terminated Lippay from his job as a corrections officer, and he resigned from the school board.

Lippay filed suit against Christos in the United States District Court for the Middle District of Pennsylvania on January 7, 1991. His complaint asserted three claims under 42 U.S.C. § 1983: (1) that Christos' filing of the complaints, which led to Lippay's subsequent arrest on the warrants, effectuated an unreasonable seizure of Lippay's person in violation of the Fourth Amendment; (2) that Christos, by causing the warrants to be issued and Lippay to be arrested, maliciously prosecuted Lippay thus depriving him of due process in violation of the Fourteenth Amendment; and (3) that Christos violated Lippay's equal protection rights under the Fourteenth Amendment.

The case was tried before a jury from February 10 through February 14, 1992. During the trial, Lippay's mother testified that Philbin had stated to her in a conversation on September 21, 1990, that he told "his superiors all along" that he could not identify her son, but that they nevertheless brought the charges. According to Mrs. Lippay, Philbin, in the same conversation, said that he and Christos had been "set up" and led to believe that Lippay was involved in drug dealing. Christos objected to this testimony on hearsay grounds, but the district court admitted it under Fed.R.Evid. 801(d)(2)(D) — as an admission against interest made by an agent of a party-opponent.[4] In his testimony Philbin confirmed that he had a conversation with Lippay's mother, but denied making any of these comments. Furthermore, Philbin testified that he did not warn Christos prior to Lippay's arrest that he was uncertain as to his identification.

....

III. *Discussion*

A. *Hearsay Testimony*

Christos first contends that the district court erred by permitting Lippay's mother to testify that Philbin told the investigators with whom he worked that he could not identify Lippay as the individual who sold him narcotics. The district court allowed the testimony as an admission by a party-opponent's agent pursuant to Fed.R.Evid. 801(d)(2)(D)[7] over Christos' objection.[8]

---

[4] The district court overruled Christos' objection without explaining its basis for the ruling. But the court indicated that the evidence was admissible under Rule 801(d)(2)(D) in its memorandum opinion of July 31, 1992, denying Christos' motion for a judgment as a matter of law or for a new trial.

[7] Lippay also argued that Philbin's alleged statement was admissible for substantive purposes as a prior inconsistent statement under Rule 801(d)(1)(A). However, because Philbin did not make the statement under oath at a proceeding or a deposition, the district court correctly ruled that it was not admissible under that rule. Similarly, the statement was not admissible under Rule 804(b)(3), which makes admissible any "statement which ... so far tended to subject [the declarant] to ... criminal liability ... that a reasonable person in the declarant's position would not have made the statement unless believing it to be true." It is clear that Philbin's statements were not sufficiently self-incriminating to fall within the rule, for the proffered testimony discloses only that Philbin had doubts regarding Lippay's guilt and that he informed the officers of the doubts. But inasmuch as Philbin did not testify against Lippay at one of the criminal proceedings and could not identify him at the other, nothing suggests that he committed perjury, falsified evidence, or committed any other crime in connection with Lippay's prosecution.

B. STATUTORY "NOT-HEARSAY" CASES

Rule 801(d)(2)(D) provides:

A statement is not hearsay if —
(2) The statement is offered against a party and is ...
(D) a statement by the party's agent on servant concerning a matter within the scope of the agency or employment, made during the existence of the relationship.

As the proponent of the evidence, Lippay had the burden to demonstrate that Philbin made this statement within the scope of an agency relationship with Christos.... Because the Federal Rules of Evidence do not define "agent" or "servant," we believe that Congress intended Rule 801(d)(2)(D) "to describe the traditional master-servant relationship as understood by common law agency doctrine." *Boren v. Sable*, 887 F.2d 1032, 1038 (10th Cir. 1989). Furthermore, given Congress' intent that the Federal Rules of Evidence have uniform nationwide application, we apply federal common law rules of agency, rather than relying on the agency law of the forum in determining whether Philbin's statement comes within the Rule. *Id.*

Although recognizing that "Philbin was not an employee of the Commonwealth," the district court ruled that Rule 801(d)(2)(D) still applied because Philbin "worked with Pennsylvania drug enforcement agents on a regular basis, was still working with them at the time he made the statement in question to Phyllis Lippay, and was compensated for his work." Christos argues that Philbin's alleged statement does not fit within the rule because, as an informer, Philbin was not Christos' agent.

The question of whether Philbin's alleged statement to Mrs. Lippay comes within Rule 801(d)(2)(D) raises a novel issue. We recognize that several courts have held that statements by police officers are not admissible on an admissions theory as substantive evidence against the sovereign in a criminal prosecution.... Furthermore, one district court has applied this principle to a government informer testifying in a criminal trial, holding that his prior, inconsistent statements did not, "by virtue of his status as a government informant, [fall]

Thus, Philbin's statements were not against his penal interest. *See United States v. Pena*, 527 F.2d 1356, 1361 (5th Cir. 1976) (holding that prior statement of informant who did not falsify testimony did not fall within the rule where he stated that he wanted to "set up" defendant to get even with him), *cert. denied*, 426 U.S. 949, 96 S.Ct. 3168, 49 L.Ed.2d 1185 (1976).

Philbin's statement was not admissible under Rule 801(d)(2)(E), which permits the admission by a co-conspirator of a party during the course and in furtherance of the conspiracy. There has been no showing that Philbin engaged in a conspiracy with Christos to frame Lippay. Thus, the only arguable bases for admission are Rules 801(d)(2)(D) and 613(b), which we consider below.

[8] While Lippay argues that Christos waived his objection on this issue during Lippay's offer of proof, we are satisfied from our review of the record that Christos objected on the ground of hearsay at the time of the testimony. Furthermore, the district court noted in its opinion denying Christos' motion for a new trial that although "defendant's counsel objected somewhat belatedly to the admission of this testimony, [he] nevertheless preserved his objection on the record."

within the scope of the Rule" 801(d)(2)(D). *See United States v. Finley*, 708 F.Supp. 906, 910 (N.D.Ill. 1989); *see also United States v. Pena*, 527 F.2d 1356, 1361 (5th Cir. 1976) (refusing to decide whether informant should be considered an "agent" of the DEA for purposes of Rule 801(d)(2)(D), because the statements were made after the informant's relationship with the government had ended), *cert. denied*, 426 U.S. 949, 96 S.Ct. 3168, 49 L.Ed.2d 1185 (1976). But, to our knowledge, no federal court ever has decided whether a government informant's statements may be used as vicarious admissions under Rule 801(d)(2)(D) against a government agent in a civil trial.

Inasmuch as Lippay seeks to use the statement against Christos instead of against the Commonwealth, the most analogous cases concern the admission of extra-judicial statements by corporate employees for use in civil suits against their superiors, as distinguished from the corporations themselves. These statements are admissible under Rule 801(d)(2)(D) if the factors which normally make up an agency relationship are present as between the employee and superior. *See United States v. Young*, 736 F.2d 565, 567 (10th Cir. 1983) (per curiam) ("[W]hen such a statement is offered against another corporate employee, instead of the corporation, proper admission under Rule 801(d)(2)(D) will necessarily depend on the nature of the relationship between the declarant and the defendant.") ...

Applying the principles of these cases to the facts before us, we conclude that Philbin was not Christos' agent for the purposes of Rule 801(d)(2)(D). These cases indicate that the federal courts will not impute the statements of a declarant to a party-opponent who is merely the declarant's co-employee. Instead, an agency relationship is established only where the party-opponent personally "directed [the declarant's] work, on *a continuing basis.*"(empasis added) ...

Based on this case law, we find that Christos lacked the continuous supervisory control over Philbin that would create an agency relationship for the purposes of Rule 801(d)(2)(D). We find no evidence establishing that Christos acted as Philbin's supervisor on a regular basis. Indeed, Philbin testified that he *never* considered the agents with whom he worked to be his superiors. Even Philbin's relationship with the Bureaus of Narcotics Investigation was tenuous as the bureau neither paid him a regular salary nor recognized him as an employee. Instead, the bureau made occasional payments to Philbin for the time he spent setting up drug purchases. Therefore, Philbin seems to have functioned as a sort of independent contractor to the bureau. *See Merrick v. Farmers Ins. Group*, 892 F.2d at 1440 (holding that establishing that declarant was merely an independent contractor to defendant does not suffice to show agency relationship for the purposes of Rule 801(d)(2)(D)).

Thus, to the extent that he can be considered to have worked at the bureau, Philbin acted more as Christos' "partner" than as his subordinate. Although Christos supervised some discrete aspects of Philbin's activities — *i.e.,* giving him the money to make drug purchases and searching him before and after transactions — this does not mean that he functioned as his supervisor in the context of an employer-employee relationship within Rule 801(d)(2)(D)....

We recognize that there may be situations where a police officer and informer will have an agency relationship. Thus, we will apply a case-by-case analysis to determine whether the officer had a sufficiently continuous supervisory relationship with the informer to establish agency. Therefore, all that we hold today is that in the circumstances of this case because the informant, Philbin, lacked the status of an employee regularly controlled by Christos, Philbin's statement was not saved from being hearsay by Rule 801(d)(2)(D), [9] thus, the district court should not have permitted Mrs. Lippay to testify as to what Philbin told her.

....

BOURJAILY v. UNITED STATES

483 U.S. 171 (1987)

CHIEF JUSTICE REHNQUIST delivered the opinion of the Court:

Federal Rules of Evidence 801(d)(2)(E) provides: "A statement is not hearsay if ... [t]he statement is offered against a party and is ... a statement by a coconspirator of a party during the course and in furtherance of the conspiracy." We granted certiorari to answer three questions regarding the admission of statements under Rule 801(d)(2)(E): (1) whether the court must determine by independent evidence that the conspiracy existed and that the defendant and the declarant were members of this conspiracy; (2) the quantum of proof on which such determinations must be based; and (3) whether a court must in each case examine the circumstances of such a statement to determine its reliability. 479 U.S. 881, 107 S.Ct. 268, 93 L.Ed.2d 246 (1986).

....

Before admitting a co-conspirator's statement over an objection that it does not qualify under Rule 801(d)(2)(E), a court must be satisfied that the statement actually falls within the definition of the Rule. There must be evidence that there was a conspiracy involving the declarant and the nonoffering party, and that the statement was made "during the course and in furtherance of the conspiracy." Federal Rule of Evidence 104(a) provides: "Preliminary questions concerning ... the admissibility of evidence shall be determined by the court." Petitioner and the Government agree that the existence of a conspiracy and petitioner's involvement in it are preliminary questions of fact that, under Rule 104, must be

---

[9] We recognize that Lippay sought to introduce Philbin's alleged statement to demonstrate that Christos heard and understood Philbin's warnings, not to prove that what Philbin told Christos was allegedly true. But, "the fact that the alleged statement of" Philbin to Christos or other police officers "was nonhearsay, does not render admissible the alleged statement of" Philbin to Mrs. Lippay, about which she testified. *See Boren v. Sable*, 887 F.2d at 1035.

resolved by the court. The Federal Rules, however, nowhere define the standard of proof the court must observe in resolving these questions.

We are therefore guided by our prior decisions regarding admissibility determinations that hinge on preliminary factual questions. We have traditionally required that these matters be established by a preponderance of proof. Evidence is placed before the jury when it satisfies the technical requirements of the evidentiary Rules, which embody certain legal and policy determinations. The inquiry made by a court concerned with these matters is not whether the proponent of the evidence wins or loses his case on the merits, but whether the evidentiary Rules have been satisfied. Thus, the evidentiary standard is unrelated to the burden of proof on the substantive issues, be it a criminal case ... or a civil case. The preponderance standard ensures that before admitting evidence, the court will have found it more likely than not that the technical issues and policy concerns addressed by the Federal Rules of Evidence have been afforded due consideration. As in *Lego v. Twomey*, 404 U.S. 477, 488, 92 S.Ct. 619, 626, 30 L.Ed.2d 618 (1972), we find "nothing to suggest that admissibility rulings have been unreliable or otherwise wanting in quality because not based on some higher standard." We think that our previous decisions in the area resolve the matter.... Therefore, we hold that when the preliminary facts relevant to Rule 801(d)(2)(E) are disputed, the offering party must prove them by a preponderance of the evidence.[1] ...

Petitioner argues that in determining whether a conspiracy exists and whether the defendant was a member of it, the court must look only to independent evidence — that is, evidence other than the statements sought to be admitted....

Petitioner concedes that Rule 104, on its face, appears to allow the court to make the preliminary factual determinations relevant to Rule 801(d)(2)(E) by considering any evidence it wishes, unhindered by considerations of admissibility. Brief for Petitioner 27. That would seem to many to be the end of the matter. Congress has decided that courts may consider hearsay in making these factual determinations. Out-of-court statements made by anyone, including putative co-conspirators, are often hearsay. Even if they are, they may be considered, *Glasser* and the boot-strapping rule notwithstanding. But petitioner nevertheless argues that the bootstrapping rule, as most Courts of Appeals have construed it, survived this apparently unequivocal change in the law unscathed and that Rule 104, as applied to the admission of co-conspirator's statements, does not mean what it says. We disagree.

---

[1] We intimate no view on the proper standard of proof for questions falling under Federal Rule of Evidence 104(b) (conditional relevancy). We also decline to address the circumstances in which the burden of coming forward to show that the proffered evidence is inadmissible is appropriately placed on the nonoffering party.... Finally, we do not express an opinion on the proper order of proof that trial courts should follow in concluding that the preponderance standard has been satisfied in an ongoing trial.

B. STATUTORY "NOT-HEARSAY" CASES

Petitioner claims that Congress evidenced no intent to disturb the bootstrapping rule, which was embedded in the previous approach, and we should not find that Congress altered the rule without affirmative evidence so indicating. It would be extra-ordinary to require legislative history to *confirm* the plain meaning of Rule 104. The Rule on its face allows the trial judge to consider any evidence whatsoever, bound only by the rules of privilege. We think that the Rule is sufficiently clear that to the extent that it is inconsistent with petitioner's interpretation of *Glasser* and *Nixon*, the Rule prevails. (Footnote omitted.)

Nor do we agree with petitioner that this construction of Rule 104(a) will allow courts to admit hearsay statements without any credible proof of the conspiracy, thus fundamentally changing the nature of the co-conspirator exception. Petitioner starts with the proposition that co-conspirators' out-of-court statements are deemed unreliable and are inadmissible, at least until a conspiracy is shown. Since these statements are unreliable, petitioner contends that they should not form any part of the basis for establishing a conspiracy, the very antecedent that renders them admissible.

Petitioner's theory ignores two simple facts of evidentiary life. First, out-of-court statements are only presumed unreliable. The presumption may be rebutted by appropriate proof.... Second, individual pieces of evidence, insufficient in themselves to prove a point, may in cumulation prove it. The sum of an evidentiary presentation may well be greater than its constituent parts. Taken together, these two propositions demonstrate that a piece of evidence, unreliable in isolation, may become quite probative when corroborated by other evidence. A per se rule barring consideration of these hearsay statements during preliminary factfinding is not therefore required. Even if out-of-court declarations by co-conspirators are presumptively unreliable, trial courts must be permitted to evaluate these statements for their evidentiary worth as revealed the particular circumstances of the case. Courts often act as factfinders, and there is no reason to believe that courts are any less able to properly recognize the probative value of evidence in this particular area. The party opposing admission has an adequate incentive to point out the shortcomings in such evidence before the trial court finds the preliminary facts. If the opposing party is unsuccessful in keeping the evidence from the factfinder, he still has the opportunity to attack the probative value of the evidence as it relates to the substantive issue in the case....

We think that there is little doubt that a co-conspirator's statements could themselves be probative of the existence of a conspiracy and the participation of both the defendant and the declarant in the conspiracy. Petitioner's case presents a paradigm. The out-of-court statements of Lonardo indicated that Lonardo was involved in a conspiracy with a "friend." The statements indicated that the friend had agreed with Lonardo to buy a kilogram of cocaine and to distribute it. The statements also revealed that the friend would be at the hotel parking lot, in his car, and would accept the cocaine from Greathouse's car after Greathouse gave Lonardo the keys. Each one of Lonardo's statements may itself be unreliable, but taken as a whole, the entire conversation between Lonardo and Greathouse was

corroborated by independent evidence. The friend, who turned out to be petitioner, showed up at the prearranged spot at the prearranged time. He picked up the cocaine, and a significant sum of money was found in his car. On these facts, the trial court concluded, in our view correctly, that the Government had established the existence of a conspiracy and petitioner's participation in it....
. . . .

We also reject any suggestion that admission of these statements against petitioner violated his rights under the Confrontation Clause of the Sixth Amendment. That Clause provides: "In all criminal prosecutions, the accused shall enjoy the right ... to be confronted with the witnesses against him." At petitioner's trial, Lonardo exercised his right not to testify. Petitioner argued that Lonardo's unavailability rendered the admission of his out-of-court statements unconstitutional since petitioner had no opportunity to confront Lonardo as to these statements. The Court of Appeals held that the requirements for admission under Rule 801(d)(2)(E) are identical to the requirements of the Confrontation Clause, and since the statements were admissible under the Rule, there was no constitutional problem. We agree.

While a literal interpretation of the Confrontation Clause could bar the use of any out-of-court statements when the declarant is unavailable, this Court has rejected that view as "unintended and too extreme." *Ohio v. Roberts*, 448 U.S. 56, 63, 100 S.Ct. 2531, 2537, 65 L.Ed.2d 597 (1980). Rather, we have attempted to harmonize the goal of the Clause — placing limits on the kind of evidence that may be received against a defendant — with a societal interest in accurate factfinding, which may require consideration of out-of-court statements. To accommodate these competing interests, the Court has, as a general matter only, required the prosecution to demonstrate both the unavailability of the declarant and the "indicia of reliability" surrounding the out-of-court declaration. *Id.*, at 65-66, 100 S.Ct. at 2538-2539. Last Term in *United States v. Inadi*, 475 U.S. 387, 106 S.Ct. 1121, 89 L.Ed.2d 390 (1986), we held that the first of these two generalized inquiries, unavailability, was not required when the hearsay statement is the out-of-court declaration of a co-conspirator. Today, we conclude that the second inquiry, independent indicia of reliability, is also not mandated by the Constitution.

The Court's decision in *Ohio v. Roberts* laid down only "a general approach to the problem" of reconciling hearsay exceptions with the Confrontation Clause. See 448 U.S., at 65, 100 S.Ct. at 2538. In fact, *Roberts* itself limits the requirement that a court make a separate inquiry into the reliability of an out-of-court statement. Because "'hearsay rules and the Confrontation Clause are generally designed to protect similar values,' *California v. Green*, 399 U.S. [149, 155, 90 S.Ct. 1930, 1933, 26 L.Ed.2d 489 (1970)], and 'stem from the same roots,' *Dutton v. Evans*, 400 U.S. 74, 86, 91 S.Ct. 210, 218, 27 L.Ed.2d 213 (1970)," *id.*, at 66, 100 S.Ct., at 2539, we concluded in *Roberts* that no independent inquiry into reliability is required when the evidence "falls within a firmly rooted hearsay exception." *Ibid.* We think that the co-conspirator

B. STATUTORY "NOT-HEARSAY" CASES

exception to the hearsay rule is firmly enough rooted in our jurisprudence that, under this Court's holding in *Roberts*, a court need not independently inquire into the reliability of such statements.... The admissibility of co-conspirators' statements was first established in this Court over a century and a half ago in *United States v. Gooding*, 12 Wheat. 460, 6 L.Ed. 693 (1827) (interpreting statements of co-conspirator as *res gestae* and thus admissible against defendant), and the Court has repeatedly reaffirmed the exception as accepted practice. In fact, two of the most prominent approvals of the rule came in cases that petitioner maintains are still vital today, *Glasser v. United States*, 315 U.S. 60, 62 S.Ct. 457, 86 L.Ed. 680 (1942), and *United States v. Nixon*, 418 U.S. 683, 94 S.Ct. 3090, 41 L.Ed.2d 1039 (1974). To the extent that these cases have not been superseded by the Federal Rules of Evidence, they demonstrate that the co-conspirator rule exception to the hearsay rule is steeped in our jurisprudence. In *Delaney v. United States*, 263 U.S. 586, 590, 44 S.Ct. 206, 207, 68 L.Ed. 462 (1924), the Court rejected the very challenge petitioner brings today, holding that there can be no separate Confrontation Clause challenge to the admission of a co-conspirator's out-of-court statement. In so ruling, the Court relied on established precedent holding such statements competent evidence. We think that these cases demonstrate that co-conspirators' statements, when made in the course and in furtherance of the conspiracy, have a long tradition of being outside the compass of the general hearsay exclusion. Accordingly, we hold that the Confrontation Clause does not require a court to embark on an independent inquiry into the reliability of statements that satisfy the requirements of Rule 801(d)(2)(E)....

....

2. STATUTORY "NOT-HEARSAY" PROBLEMS

1. Bribery

Mayor Maitland is prosecuted for taking a bribe from several contractors through their attorney, Gabe. At his trial, Maitland testifies he didn't take any bribe and he wasn't even in the same room with Gabe at any time on the evening in question.

   a. On cross examination, can defendant Maitland be asked "Didn't you state in your deposition that 'I was with Gabe only a short time that evening'?" If this question is permissible, will the statement be admissible only to impeach Maitland or for the truth of its contents as well? Why?

   b. On cross examination, counsel inferred that Maitland recently manufactured his assertion that he did not spend any time with Gabe that evening. On redirect examination, Maitland is asked, "What, if anything, did you do later that evening after the party?" Maitland answers, "I told my wife that that crook Gabe was at the party and I only yelled hello and exchanged the usual pleasantries briefly from the adjacent room." Is this answer permissible? Why?

c. Maitland is also asked on redirect, "Who, if anyone, was with Gabe?" Maitland answered: "When I saw them, I told my friend Steve, 'Hey, that's my opponent's campaign manager, Ted Souvlos, with Gabe! Strange.'" Admissible? Explain.

2. Dognappers

Midnight Blue, a black labrador retriever, was stolen from his doghouse by several professional dognappers. Two months after the theft, a neighbor, Mr. Rogers, positively identified the dognappers in a lineup. At the dognappers' trial, Mr. Rogers testified for the prosecution. Can he be asked about his identification of the dognappers at the lineup?

3. Translator

The Arturo Gonzalez Mortgage Broker Company, with its headquarters in Mexico City but branches in New York and San Antonio, was charged with numerous violations of securities regulations. A translator for the president of the company stated at a news conference, "President Gonzalez is confident that the company will be cleared of all charges. He has fired the disloyal member of the board of trustees, Mr. Perdido, who set him up on the financial transactions in question." Are the statements by the translator admissible against the President and the company? Explain.

4. Free Agent

A disputed issue at trial was whether Barry was acting as the agent of employer Giant Bread at the time the Giant Bread truck Barry was driving crashed. The truck barrelled into the living room of the MacKenzie family, along with 10,000 loaves of Giant Bread. Luckily, no one was hurt. Several hours after the accident, Barry told the police officer preparing an accident investigation report, "I am the agent of Giant Bread and the accident was all my fault. The bread shifted and I turned around to look. Boom, there I was in their living room. I was much better at my other job." Are Barry's statements admissible against Giant Bread in a subsequent action brought by the MacKenzies against the company? Why?

5. Just a Guess

Margaret was the Chief Operating Officer for Lorton's Limo Service. After being informed that car No. 8 was in an accident for the third time that month, Margaret threw up her hands and exclaimed for everyone in the office to hear, "Car No. 8 is Willie's car, and I'll bet the accident was our fault because he was probably drinking again." Are Margaret's statements admissible at trial in an action against Lorton's Limo Service? Why?

6. Confession

Catarina and Bob engaged in an elaborate plan to kill Catarina's husband, but were caught before they could carry it out. As the police put the handcuffs on them, Bob blurted out, "Dear, I didn't think this plan of ours about your *$#@(% husband had any holes in it; these cops must have been very, very lucky to catch us."

a. Are Bob's statements admissible against Bob in a later trial for conspiracy to commit murder? Why?
b. If Catarina is tried separately, are Bob's statements admissible against Catarina? Explain.

C. HEARSAY EXCEPTIONS

1. HEARSAY EXCEPTION CASES

MUTUAL LIFE INSURANCE CO. v. HILLMON
145 U.S. 285 (1892)

MR. JUSTICE GRAY delivered the opinion of the Court:

On July 13, 1880, Sallie E. Hillmon, a citizen of Kansas, brought an action against the Mutual Life Insurance Company, a corporation of New York, on a policy of insurance, dated December 10, 1878, on the life of her husband, John W. Hillmon, in the sum of $10,000, payable to her within sixty days after notice and proof of his death. On the same day the plaintiff brought two other actions, the one against the New York Life Insurance Company, a corporation of New York, on two similar policies of life insurance, dated respectively November 30, 1878, and December 10, 1878, for the sum of $5,000 each; and the other against the Connecticut Mutual Life Insurance Company, a corporation of Connecticut, on a similar policy, dated March 4, 1879, for the sum of $5,000.

In each case, the declaration alleged that Hillmon died on March 17, 1879, during the continuance of the policy, but that the defendant, though duly notified of the fact, had refused to pay the amount of the policy, or any part thereof; and the answer denied the death of Hillmon, and alleged that he, together with John H. Brown and divers other persons, on or before November 30, 1878, conspiring to defraud the defendant, procured the issue of all the policies, and afterwards, in March and April, 1879, falsely pretended and represented that Hillmon was dead, and that a dead body which they had procured was his, whereas in reality he was alive and in hiding....

At the trial the plaintiff introduced evidence tending to show that on or about March 5, 1879, Hillmon and Brown left Wichita in the State of Kansas, and travelled together through Southern Kansas in search of a site for a cattle ranch; that on the night of March 18, while they were in camp at a place called Crooked Creek, Hillmon was killed by the accidental discharge of a gun; that Brown at once notified persons living in the neighborhood; and that the body was thereupon taken to a neighboring town, where, after an inquest, it was buried. The defendants introduced evidence tending to show that the body found in the camp at Crooked Creek on the night of March 18 was not the body of Hillmon, but was the body of one Frederick Adolph Walters. Upon the question whose body this was, there was much conflicting evidence, including photographs and descriptions of the corpse, and of the marks and scars upon it, and testimony to its likeness to Hillmon and to Walters.

The defendants introduced testimony that Walters left his home at Fort Madison in the State of Iowa in March, 1878, and was afterwards in Kansas in 1878, and in January and February, 1879; that during that time his family frequently received letters from him, the last of which was written from Wichita; and that he had not been heard from since March 1879. The defendants also offered the following evidence:

Elizabeth Rieffenach testified that she was a sister of Frederick Adolph Walters, and lived at Fort Madison; and thereupon, as shown by the bill of exceptions, the following proceedings took place:

"Witness further testified that she had received a letter written from Wichita, Kansas about the 4th or 5th day of March 1879, by her brother Frederick Adolph; that the letter was dated at Wichita, and was in the handwriting of her brother; that she had searched for the letter, but could not find the same, it being lost; that she remembered and could state the contents of the letter."

"Thereupon the defendants' counsel asked the questions: 'State the contents of that letter.' To which the plaintiff objected, on the ground that the same is incompetent, irrelevant, and hearsay. The objection was sustained, and the defendants duly excepted. The following is the letter as stated by witness:

"Wichita, Kansas,

"March 4th or 5th or 3d or 4th — I don't know — 1879.

"Dear sister and all: I now in my usual style drop you a few lines to let you know that I expect to leave Wichita on or about March the 5th, with a certain Mr. Hillmon, a sheeptrader, for Colorado or parts unknown to me. I expect to see the country now. News are of no interest to you, as you are not acquainted here. I will close with compliments to all inquiring friends. Love to all.

"I am truly your brother,
Fred. Adolph Walters."

....

The evidence that Walters was at Wichita on or before March 5, and had not been heard from since, together with the evidence to identify as his the body found at Crooked Creek on March 18, tended to show that he went from Wichita to Crooked Creek between those dates. Evidence that just before March 5 he had the intention of leaving Wichita with Hillmon would tend to ... show that he went from Wichitato Crooked Creek with Hillmon. Letters from him to his family and his betrothed were the natural, if not the only attainable, evidence of his intention....

....

The existence of a particular intention in a certain person at a certain time being a material fact to be proved, evidence that he expressed that intention at that time is as direct evidence of the fact, as his own testimony that he then had that intention would be. After his death there can hardly be any other way of proving it; and while he is still alive, his own memory of his state of mind at a former time is no more likely to be clear and true than a bystander's recollection of what he then said, and is less trustworthy than letters written by him at the very time and under circumstances precluding suspicion of misrepresentation.

The letters in question were competent, not as narratives of facts communicated to the writer by others, nor yet as proof that he actually went away from Wichita, but as evidence that, shortly before the time when other evidence tended to show that he went away, he had the intention of going, and of going with Hillmon, which made it more probable both that he did go and that he went with Hillmon, than if there had been no proof of such intention. In view of the mass of conflicting testimony introduced upon the question whether it was the body of Walters that was found in Hillmon's camp, this evidence might properly influence the jury in determining that question.

The rule applicable to this case has been thus stated by this court: "Wherever the bodily or mental feelings of an individual are material to be proved, the usual expressions of such feelings are original and competent evidence. Those expressions are the natural reflexes of what it might be impossible to show by other testimony. If there be such other testimony, this may be necessary to set the facts thus developed in their true light, and to find them their proper effect. As independent explanatory or corroborative evidence, it is often indispensable to the due administration of justice. Such declarations are regarded as verbal acts, and are as competent as any other testimony, when relevant to the issue. Their truth or falsity is an inquiry for the jury." *Insurance Co. v. Mosley*, 8 Wall. 397, 404, 405.

Upon principle and authority, therefore, we are of opinion that the two letters were competent evidence of the intention of Walters at the time of writing them, which was material fact bearing upon the question in controversy; and that for the exclusion of these letters, as well as for the undue restriction of the defendants' challenges, the verdicts must be set aside, and a new trial had....

SHEPARD v. UNITED STATES

290 U.S. 96 (1933)

MR. JUSTICE CARDOZO delivered the opinion of the Court:

The petitioner, Charles A. Shepard, a major in the medical corps of the United States army, has been convicted of the murder of his wife, Zenana Shepard, at Fort Riley, Kansas, a United States military reservation. The jury having qualified their verdict by adding thereto the words "without capital punishment" (18 U.S.C. § 567), the defendant was sentenced to imprisonment for life. The judgment of the United States District Court has been affirmed by the Circuit Court of Appeals for the Tenth Circuit, one of the judges of that court dissenting. 62 F. (2d) 683; 64 F. (2d) 641. A writ of certiorari brings the case here.

The crime is charged to have been committed by poisoning the victim with bichloride of mercury. The defendant was in love with another woman, and wished to make her his wife. There is circumstantial evidence to sustain a finding by the jury that to win himself his freedom he turned to poison and murder. Even so, guilt was contested and conflicting inferences are possible. The defendant asks us to hold that by the acceptance of incompetent evidence the scales were weighted to his prejudice and in the end to his undoing.

The evidence complained of was offered by the Government in rebuttal when the trial was nearly over. On May 22, 1929, there was a conversation in the absence of the defendant between Mrs. Shepard, then ill in bed, and Clara Brown, her nurse. The patient asked the nurse to go to the closet in the defendant's room and bring a bottle of whisky that would be found upon a shelf. When the bottle was produced, she said that this was the liquor she had taken just before collapsing. She asked whether enough was left to make a test for the presence of poison, insisting that the smell and taste were strange. And then she added the words "Dr. Shepard has poisoned me."

....

1. Upon the hearing in this court the Government finds its main prop in the position that what was said by Mrs. Shepard was admissible as a dying declaration. This is manifestly the theory upon which it was offered and received. The prop, however, is a broken reed. To make out a dying declaration the declarant must have spoken without hope of recovery and in the shadow of impending death. The record furnishes no proof of that indispensable condition. So, indeed, it was ruled by all the judges of the court below, though the majority held the view that the testimony was competent for quite another purpose, which will be considered later on.

We have said that the declarant was not shown to have spoken without hope of recovery and in the shadow of impending death. Her illness began on May 20. She was found in a state of collapse, delirious, in pain, the pupils of her eyes dilated, and the retina suffused with blood. The conversation with the nurse occurred two days later. At that time her mind had cleared up, and her speech was rational and orderly. There was as yet no thought by any of her physicians that she was dangerously ill, still less that her case was hopeless. To all seeming she had greatly improved, and was moving forward to recovery. There had been no diagnosis of poison as the cause of her distress. Not till about a week afterwards was there a relapse, accompanied by an infection of the mouth, renewed congestion of the eyes, and later hemorrhages of the bowels. Death followed on June 15.

C. HEARSAY EXCEPTIONS

Nothing in the condition of the patient on May 22 gives fair support of the conclusion that hope had then been lost.... Despair of recovery may indeed be gathered from the circumstances if the facts support the inference.... What is decisive is the state of mind. Even so, the state of mind must be exhibited in the evidence, not left to conjecture. The patient must have spoken with the consciousness of a swift and certain doom.

What was said by this patient was not spoken in that mood. There was no warning to her in the circumstances that her words would be repeated and accepted as those of a dying wife, charging murder to her husband, and charging it deliberately and solemnly as a fact within her knowledge. To the focus of that responsibility her mind was never brought. She spoke as one ill, giving voice to the beliefs and perhaps the conjectures of the moment. The liquor was to be tested, to see whether her beliefs were sound. She did not speak as one dying, announcing to the survivors a definite conviction, a legacy of knowledge on which the world might act when she had gone.

....

Reversed.

PALMER v. HOFFMAN

318 U.S. 109 (1943)

MR. JUSTICE DOUGLAS delivered the opinion of the Court:

This case arose out of a grade crossing accident which occurred in Massachusetts. Diversity of citizenship brought it to the federal District Court in New York....

I.

The accident occurred on the night of December 25, 1940. On December 27, 1940, the engineer of the train, who died before the trial, made a statement at a freight office of petitioners where he was interviewed by an assistant superintendent of the road and by a representative of the Massachusetts Public Utilities Commission. *See* Mass. Gen. L. (1932) c. 159, § 29. This statement was offered in evidence by petitioners under the Act of June 20, 1936, 49 Stat. 1561, 28 U.S.C. § 695.[1] They offered to prove (in the language of the Act) that the

---

[1] "In any court of the United States and in any court established by Act of Congress, any writing or record, whether in the form of an entry in a book or otherwise, made as a memorandum or record of any act, transaction, occurrence, or event, shall be admissible as evidence of said act, transaction, occurrence, or event, if it shall appear that it was made in the regular course of any business, and that it was the regular course of such business to make such memorandum or record at the time of such act, transaction, occurrence, or event or within a reasonable time thereafter. All other circumstances of the making of such writing or record, including lack of personal knowledge by the entrant to maker, may be shown to affect its weight, but they shall not affect its

statement was signed in the regular course of business, it being the regular course of such business to make such a statement. Respondent's objection to its introduction was sustained....

We agree with the majority view below that it was properly excluded.

We may assume that if the statement was made "in the regular course" of business, it would satisfy the other provisions of the Act. But we do not think that it was made "in the regular course" of business within the meaning of the Act. The business of the petitioners is the railroad business. That business like other enterprises entails the keeping of numerous books and records essential to its conduct or useful in its efficient operation. Though such books and records were considered reliable and trustworthy for major decisions in the industrial and business world, their use in litigation was greatly circumscribed or hedged about by the hearsay rule — restrictions which greatly increased the time and cost of making the proof where those who made the records were numerous. 5 Wigmore, Evidence (3d ed., 1940) § 1530. It was that problem which started the movement towards adoption of legislation embodying the principles of the present Act.... And the legislative history of the Act indicates the same purpose....

In short, it is manifest that in this case those reports are not for the systematic conduct of the enterprise as a railroad business. Unlike payrolls, accounts receivable, accounts payable, bills of lading and the like, these reports are calculated for use essentially in the court, not in the business. Their primary utility is in litigating, not in railroading.

It is, of course, not for us to take these reports out of the Act if Congress has put them in. But there is nothing in the background of the law on which this Act was built or in its legislative history which suggests for a moment that the business of preparing cases for trial should be included....

The several hundred years of history behind the Act ... indicate the nature of the reforms which it was designed to effect. It should of course be liberally interpreted so as to do away with the anachronistic rules which gave rise to its need and at which it was aimed. But "regular course" of business must find its meaning in the inherent nature of the business in question and in the methods systematically employed for the conduct of the business as a business....

....

Affirmed.

BEECH AIRCRAFT CORP. v. RAINEY
488 U.S. 153 (1988)

JUSTICE BRENNAN delivered the opinion of the Court:

---

admissibility. The term 'business' shall include business, profession, occupation, and calling of every kind.''

C. HEARSAY EXCEPTIONS 137

In this action we address a longstanding conflict among the Federal Courts of Appeals over whether Federal Rule of Evidence 803(8)(C), which provides an exception to the hearsay rule for public investigatory reports containing "factual findings," extends to conclusions and opinions contained in such reports. We also consider whether, on the facts of this litigation, the trial court abused its discretion in refusing to admit, on cross-examination, testimony intended to provide a more complete picture of a document about which the witness had testified on direct....

Controversy over what "public records and reports" are made not excludable by Rule 803(8)(C) has divided the federal courts from the beginning. In the present litigation, the Court of Appeals followed the "narrow" interpretation of *Smith v. Ithaca Corp., supra*, at 220-223, which held that the term "factual findings" did not encompass "opinions" or "conclusions." Courts of appeal other than those of the Fifth and Eleventh Circuits, however, have generally adopted a broader interpretation. For example, the Court of Appeals for the Sixth Circuit, in *Baker v. Elcona Homes Corp.*, 588 F.2d 551, 557-558 (1978), *cert. denied*, 441 U.S. 933 (1979), held that "factual findings admissible under Rule 803(8)(C) may be those which are made by the preparer of the report from disputed evidence ...." The other courts of appeals that have squarely confronted the issue have also adopted the broader interpretation. We agree and hold that factually based conclusions or opinions are not on that account excluded from the scope of Rule 803(8)(C)....

The Advisory Committee's comments are notable, first, in that they contain no mention of any dichotomy between statements of "fact" and "opinions" or "conclusions." What was on the Committee's mind was simply whether what it called "evaluative reports" should be admissible. Illustrating the previous division among the courts on this subject, the Committee cited numerous cases in which the admissibility of such reports had been both sustained and denied. It also took note of various federal statutes that made certain kinds of evaluative reports admissible in evidence. What is striking about all of these examples is that these were *reports that stated conclusions*.... The Committee's concern was clearly whether reports of this kind should be admissible. Nowhere in its comments is there the slightest indication that it even considered the solution of admitting only "factual" statements from such reports. Rather the Committee referred throughout to "reports," without such differentiation regarding the statements they contained. What the Committee referred to in the Rule's language as "reports ... setting forth ... factual findings" is surely nothing more or less than what in its commentary it called "evaluative reports." Its solution as to their admissibility is clearly stated in the final paragraph of its report on this Rule. That solution consists of two principles: First, the "rule ... assumes admissibility in the first instance ...." Second, it provides "ample provision for escape if sufficient negative factors are present."

That "provision for escape" is contained in the final clause of the Rule: evaluative reports are admissible "unless the sources of information or other circumstances indicate lack of trustworthiness." This trustworthiness inquiry — and not an arbitrary distinction between "fact" and "opinion" — was the Committee's primary safeguard against the admission of unreliable evidence, and it is important to note that it applies to all elements of the report. Thus, a trial judge has the discretion, and indeed the obligation, to exclude an entire report or portion thereof — whether narrow "factual" statements or broader "conclusions" — that she determined to be untrustworthy. Moreover, safeguards built in to other portions of the Federal Rules, such as those dealing with relevance and prejudice, provide the court with additional means of scrutinizing and, where appropriate, excluding evaluative reports or portions of them. And of course it goes without saying that the admission of a report containing "conclusions" is subject to the ultimate safeguard — the opponent's right to present evidence tending to contradict or diminish the weight of those conclusions.

Our conclusion that neither the language of the Rule nor the intent of its framers calls for a distinction between "fact" and "opinion" is strengthened by the analytical difficulty of drawing such a line....

....

We hold, therefore, that portions of investigatory reports otherwise admissible under Rule 803(8)(C) are not inadmissible merely because they state a conclusion or opinion. As long as the conclusion is based on a factual investigation and satisfies the Rule's trustworthiness requirement, it should be admissible along with other portions of the report....

DALLAS COUNTY v. COMMERCIAL UNION ASSURANCE CO.

286 F.2d 388 (5th Cir. 1961)

WISDOM, CIRCUIT JUDGE:

This appeal presents a single question — the admissibility in evidence of a newspaper to show that the Dallas County Courthouse in Selma, Alabama was damaged by fire in 1901. We hold that the newspaper was admissible, and affirm the judgment below.

On a bright, sunny morning, July 7, 1957, the clock tower of the Dallas County Clubhouse at Selma, Alabama, commenced to lean, made loud cracking and popping noises, then fell, and telescoped into the courtroom. Fortunately, the collapse of the tower took place on a Sunday morning; no one was injured, but damage to the courthouse exceeded $100,000. An examination of the tower debris showed the presence of charcoal and charred timbers. The State Toxicologist, called in by Dallas County, reported the char was evidence that lightning struck the courthouse. Later, several residents of Selma reported that a bolt of lightning struck the courthouse July 2, 1957. On this information, Dallas County concluded that a lightning bolt had hit the building causing the collapse of the clock tower five days later. Dallas County carried insurance for loss to its courthouse caused by fire or lightning. The insurers' engineers and investigators found that the courthouse collapsed of its own weight. They

C. HEARSAY EXCEPTIONS

reported that the courthouse had not been struck by lightning; that lightning could not have caused the collapse of the tower; that the collapse of the tower was caused by structural weaknesses attributable to a faulty design, poor construction, gradual deterioration of the structure, and overloading brought about by remodelling and the recent installation of an air-conditioning system, part of which was constructed over the courtroom trusses. In their opinion, the char was the result of a fire in the courthouse tower and roof that must have occurred many, many years before July 2, 1957. The insurers denied liability.

The County sued its insurers in the Circuit Court of Dallas County....
....

During the trial the defendants introduced a copy of the Morning Times of Selma for June 9, 1901. This issue carried an unsigned article describing a fire that occurred at two in the morning of June 9, 1901, while the courtroom was still under construction. The article stated, in part: "The unfinished dome of the County's new courthouse was in flames at the top, and ... soon fell in. The fire was soon under control and the main building was saved...." The insurers do not contend that the collapse of the tower resulted from unsound charred timbers used in the repair of the building after the fire; they offered the newspaper account to show there had been a fire long before 1957 that would account for charred timber in the clock tower....

The plaintiff objected that the newspaper article was hearsay; that it was not a business record nor an ancient document, nor was it admissible under any recognized exception to the hearsay doctrine. The trial judge admitted the newspaper as part of the records of the Selma Times-Journal....

In the Anglo-American adversary system of law, courts usually will not admit evidence unless its accuracy and trustworthiness may be tested by cross-examination. Here, therefore, the plaintiff argues that the newspaper should not be admitted: "You cannot cross-examine a newspaper."[1] ...

---

[1] This argument, a familiar one, rests on a misunderstanding of the origin and the nature of the hearsay rule. The rule is not an ancient principle of English law recognized at Runnymede. And, gone is its odor of sanctity.

Wigmore is often quoted for the statement that "cross-examination is beyond any doubt the greatest legal engine ever invented for the discovery of the truth." 5 Wigmore § 1367 (3rd ed.). In over 1200 pages devoted to the hearsay rule, however, he makes it very clear that: "[T]he rule aims to insist on testing all statements by cross-examination, *if they can be*.... No one could defend a rule which pronounced that all statements thus untested are worthless; for all historical truth is based on un-cross-examined assertions; and every day's experience of life gives denial to such an exaggeration. What the Hearsay Rule implies — and with profound verity — is that all testimonial assertions *ought to be* tested by cross-examination, as the best attainable measure; and it should not be burdened with the pedantic implication that they must be rejected as worthless if the test is unavailable." 1 Wigmore § 8c. In this connection see Falknor, The Hearsay Rule and Its Exceptions, 2 UCLA L.Rev. 43 (1954).

In The Introductory Note to Chapter VI, Hearsay Evidence, American Law Institute, Model Code of Evidence (1942), Edmund M. Morgan, Reporter, it is pointed out that "the hearsay rule is the child of the adversary system." The Note continues: "During the first centuries of the jury

We hold, that in matters of local interest, when the fact in question is of such a public nature it would be generally known throughout the community, and when the questioned fact occurred so long ago the testimony of an eye-witness would probably be less trustworthy than a contemporary newspaper account, a federal court, under Rule 43(a), may relax the exclusionary rules to the extent of admitting the newspaper article in evidence. We do not characterize this newspaper as a "business record", nor as an "ancient document", nor as any other readily identifiable and happily tagged species of hearsay exception. It is admissible because it is necessary and trustworthy, relevant and material, and its admission is within the trial judge's exercise of discretion in holding the hearing within reasonable bounds.

Judgement is affirmed.

UNITED STATES v. SALERNO

112 S. Ct. 2503 (1992)

JUSTICE THOMAS delivered the opinion of the Court:

Federal Rule of Evidence 804(b)(1) states an exception to the hearsay rule that allows a court, in certain circumstances, to admit the former testimony of an unavailable witness. We must decide in this case whether the Rule permits a

---

system, the jury based its decision upon what the jurors themselves knew of the matter in dispute and what they learned through the words of their fathers and through such words of these persons whom they are bound to trust as worthy.... Until the end of the sixteenth century hearsay was received without question.... The opportunity for cross-examination is not a necessary element of the jury system, while it is the very heart of the adversary system.... As the judges began their attempts to rationalize the results of the decisions dealing with evidence, they first relied upon the general notion that a party was obliged to produce the best evidence available, but no more. Had they applied this generally, hearsay would have been received whenever better evidence could not be obtained. Therefore the judges discovered a special sort of necessity in ... exceptional cases ... [making] the admissible hearsay less unreliable than hearsay in general.... [By 1840] it became the fashion to attribute the exclusion of hearsay to the incapacity of the jury to evaluate, and in the development of exceptions to the rule, courts have doubtless been influenced by this notion.... Modern text-writers and judges have purported to find for each exception some sort of necessity for resort to hearsay and some condition attending the making of the excepted statement which will enable the jury to put a fair value upon it and will thus serve as a substitute for cross-examination. A careful examination of the eighteen or nineteen classes of utterances, each of which is now recognized as an exception to the hearsay rule by some respectable authority, will reveal that in many of them the necessity resolves itself into mere convenience and the substitute for cross-examination is imperceptible.... In most of the exceptions, however, the adversary theory is disregarded. There is nothing in any of the situations to warrant depriving the adversary of an opportunity to cross-examine; but those rationalizing the results purport to find some substitute for cross-examination. In most instances one will look in vain for anything more than a situation in which an ordinary man making such a statement would positively desire to tell the truth; and in some the most that can be claimed is the absence of a motive to falsify." For the history of the rule see 5 Wigmore, Evidence, § 1364 (3rd ed.); 9 Holdsworth's History of English Law 214 (1926).

C. HEARSAY EXCEPTIONS

criminal defendant to introduce the grand jury testimony of a witness who asserts the Fifth Amendment privilege at trial.

The seven respondents, Anthony Salerno, Vincent DiNapoli, Louis DiNapoli, Nicholas Auletta, Edward Halloran, Alvin O. Chattin, and Aniello Migliore, allegedly took part in the activities of a criminal organization known as the Genovese Family of La Cosa Nostra (Family) in New York City....

According to the indictment and evidence later admitted at trial, the Family used its influence over labor unions and its control over the supply of concrete to rig bidding on large construction projects in Manhattan. The Family purportedly allocated contracts for these projects among a so-called "Club" of six concrete companies in exchange for a share of the proceeds.

Much of the case concerned the affairs of the Cedar Park Concrete Construction Corporation (Cedar Park). Two of the owners of the firm, Frederick DeMatteis and Pasquale Bruno, testified before the grand jury under a grant of immunity. In response to questions by the United States, they repeatedly stated that neither they nor Cedar Park had participated in the Club. At trial, however, the United States attempted to show that Cedar Park, in fact, had belonged to the Club by calling two contractors who had taken part in the scheme and by presenting intercepted conversations among the respondents....

To counter the United States evidence, the respondents subpoenaed DeMatteis and Bruno as witnesses in the hope that they would provide the same exculpatory testimony that they had presented to the grand jury. When both witnesses invoked their Fifth Amendment privilege against self-incrimination and refused to testify, the respondents asked the District Court to admit the transcripts of their grand jury testimony. Although this testimony constituted hearsay, see Rule 801(c), the respondents argued that it fell within the hearsay exception in Rule 804(b)(1) for former testimony of unavailable witnesses.

The District Court refused to admit the grand jury testimony....

The United States Court of Appeals for the Second Circuit reversed, holding that the District Court had erred in excluding DeMatteis and Bruno's grand jury testimony....

We must decide whether the Court of Appeals properly interpreted Rule 804(b)(1) in this case.

The parties agree that DeMatteis and Bruno were "unavailable" to the defense as witnesses, provided that they properly invoked the Fifth Amendment privilege and refused to testify. See Rule 804(a)(1). They also agree that DeMatteis and Bruno's grand jury testimony constituted "testimony given as ... witness[es] at another hearing." They disagree, however, about whether the "similar motive" requirement in the final clause of Rule 804(b)(1) should have prevented admission of the testimony in this case.

A

Nothing in the language of Rule 804(b)(1) suggests that a court may admit former testimony absent satisfaction of each of the Rule's elements. The United

States thus asserts that, unless it had a "similar motive," we must conclude that the District Court properly excluded DeMatteis and Bruno's testimony as hearsay. The respondents, in contrast, urge us not to read Rule 804(b)(1) in a "slavishly literal fashion." Brief for Respondents at 31. They contend that "adversarial fairness" prevents the United States from relying on the similar motive requirement in this case. We agree with the United States.

When Congress enacted the prohibition against admission of hearsay in Rule 802, it placed 24 exceptions in Rule 803 and 5 additional exceptions in Rule 804. Congress thus presumably made a careful judgment as to what hearsay may come into evidence and what may not. To respect its determination, we must enforce the words that it enacted. The respondents, as a result, had no right to introduce DeMatteis and Bruno's former testimony under Rule 804(b)(1) without showing a "similar motive". This Court cannot alter evidentiary rules merely because litigants might prefer different rules in a particular class of cases....

. . . .

We ... fail to see how we may create an exception to Rule 804(b)(1).... In this case, the language of Rule 804(b)(1) does not support the respondents. Indeed, the respondents specifically ask us to ignore it....

HORNE v. OWENS-CORNING FIBERGLAS CORP.

4 F.3d 276 (4th Cir. 1993)

Ervin, Chief Judge:

Linda P. Horne, together with her husband Benny Gerald Horne, initiated this products liability action against Owens-Corning Fiberglas Corporation ("Owens-Corning") and numerous other asbestos manufacturers, alleging that Benny Horne's exposure to insulation manufactured by Owens-Corning and containing asbestos caused him to contract lung cancer. After Benny Horne's death, Linda Horne ("Horne") proceeded with the action as executrix of his estate. At the close of the trial, the jury returned a verdict form finding Owens-Corning negligent, Benny Horne contributorily negligent, and Owens-Corning not willfully and wantonly negligent. Based on these findings, Horne could not recover. Horne now appeals the district court's admission of various pieces of evidence and the format of the jury verdict form. After reviewing these issues, we find Horne's appeal to be without merit and, accordingly, affirm....

Owens-Corning introduced, and the district court admitted, portions of the February 11, 1981, and March 27, 1981 depositions of Mr. W.G. Hazard, a former industrial hygienist for the Owens-Illinois Company, Owens-Corning's predecessor in ownership of Kaylo. The district court admitted the Hazard depositions pursuant to Rule 804(b)(1) of the Federal Rules of Evidence. Rule 804(b)(1) provides:

> (b) Hearsay exceptions. The following are not excluded by the hearsay rule if the declarant is unavailable as a witness:

C. HEARSAY EXCEPTIONS

> (1) Former testimony. Testimony given as a witness ... in a deposition taken in compliance with law in the course of the same or another proceeding, if the party against whom the testimony is now offered, or, in a civil action or proceeding, a predecessor in interest, had an opportunity and similar motive to develop the testimony by direct, cross, or redirect examination.

Fed. R. Evid. 804(b)(1). The Notes of the Advisory Committee following the rule raise the question "whether strict identity, or privity, should continue as a requirement with respect to the party against whom offered." *Id.* advisory committee notes. The notes suggest that "the rule departs to the extent of allowing substitution of one with the right and opportunity to develop the testimony with similar motive and interest." *Id.*

When reviewing the admissibility of evidence pursuant to Rule 804(b)(1), we have focused on the similarity of motives between the predecessor in interest and the one against whom the deposition is now offered to determine the scope of Rule 804(b)(1). In a situation in which the motives differ, the testimony may not be introduced. Our decision in *Lohrmann v. Pittsburgh Corning Corp.* demonstrates this limit to admissibility. *See Lohrmann*, 782 F.2d at 1160-61. In *Lohrmann* the prior action from which the deposition derived involved claims based on the hazardous effects upon the health of plant workers exposed to raw asbestos. *Id. at 1161.* The *Lohrmann* plaintiff sought to introduce the deposition against Pittsburgh Corning Corp., a manufacturer of asbestos not involved in the earlier litigation. *Id. at 1160.* The *Lohrmann* plaintiff was not a plant worker, but a pipe-fitter, who from time to time worked in close proximity to insulators and others using products containing processed asbestos. *Id. at 1161.* Cross-examination in the deposition would not have brought out the distinction between employees exposed to raw asbestos and those exposed to asbestos by-products and dust. *Id.* Therefore, we affirmed the district court's determination that the deposition did not present a similar opportunity and motive to develop testimony and should not be admitted against Pittsburgh Corning Corp. in the subsequent litigation. *Id.*

Horne challenges the admission of the Hazard depositions on two grounds. First, she claims that the court failed to determine the witness's unavailability. Second, she claims that the participants in the deposition did not share similar motives to develop testimony as she, preventing the testimony from being introduced against her now.

In this case the district court made the following finds regarding witness availability:

> *The Court:* Is he dead now?
> *Mr. Modesitt:* I am under the belief that he is dead. He is unavailable at any rate, but I think he's dead.
> *The Court:* How do you know he is unavailable? Well, I will be here about 8:15 and we will take this and anything else up that you have at that time.
> *Recess.*

Upon resuming proceedings the next day, neither party nor the court revisited the availability issue, and Horne did not renew her objection. Despite the absence of a finding as to availability, we see no merit in Horne's challenge on this basis. The record indicates that Owens-Corning represented that Hazard was dead, and Horne did not, nor does she now, contest the fact. Without some evidence of Hazard's availability, we cannot conclude that the district court's failure to make findings specifically as to unavailability represents an abuse of discretion. The court's admission of the Hazard deposition pursuant to Rule 804(b)(1) implicitly incorporates a finding of unavailability absent the introduction of evidence to the contrary.

As a second ground for challenging the Hazard depositions, Horne suggests that the claimants in the other asbestos litigation for which Hazard gave his depositions were not predecessors in interest to Horne. Horne's contention is based on a misapprehension of the law, not on valid distinctions between the litigants. Rather than pointing to factual and legal differences in the proceedings, such as those detailed in *Lohrmann*, Horne contends that the other claimants are not predecessors in interest because they have no relationship to Horne. Horne's argument relies on the need for some showing of privity. The *Lohrmann* holding makes clear that privity is not the gravamen of the analysis. Instead, the party against whom the deposition is offered must point up distinctions in her case not evident in the earlier litigation that would preclude similar motives of witness examination.

Horne offers no such distinctions; therefore, the district court's introduction of the deposition excerpts does not represent an abuse of discretion....

WILLIAMSON v. UNITED STATES

114 S. Ct. 2431 (1994)

JUSTICE O'CONNOR delivered the opinion of the Court, except as to Part II-C:

In this case we clarify the scope of the hearsay exception for statements against penal interest. Fed. Rule Evid. 804(b)(3).

I

A deputy sheriff stopped the rental car driven by Reginald Harris for weaving on the highway. Harris consented to a search of the car, which revealed 19 kilograms of cocaine in two suitcases in the trunk. Harris was promptly arrested.

Shortly after Harris' arrest, Special Agent Donald Walton of the Drug Enforcement Administration (DEA) interviewed him by telephone. During that conversation, Harris said that he got the cocaine from an unidentified Cuban in Fort Lauderdale; that the cocaine belonged to petitioner Williamson; and that it was to be delivered that night to a particular dumpster. Williamson was also connected to Harris by physical evidence. The luggage bore the initials of Williamson's sister, Williamson was listed as an additional driver on the car

C. HEARSAY EXCEPTIONS

rental agreement, and an envelope addressed to Williamson and a receipt with Williamson's girlfriend's address were found in the glove compartment.

Several hours later, Agent Walton spoke to Harris in person. During that interview, Harris said he had rented the car a few days earlier and had driven it to Fort Lauderdale to meet Williamson. According to Harris, he had gotten the cocaine from a Cuban who was Williamson's acquaintance, and the Cuban had put the cocaine in the car with a note telling Harris how to deliver the drugs. Harris repeated that he had been instructed to leave the drugs in a certain dumpster, to return in his car, and to leave without waiting for anyone to pick up the drugs.

Agent Walton then took steps to arrange a controlled delivery of the cocaine. But as Walton was preparing to leave the interview room, Harris "got out of [his] chair ... and ... took a half step toward [Walton] ... and ... said, ... 'I can't let you do that,' threw his hands up and said 'that's not true, I can't let you go up there for no reason.'" App.40. Harris told Walton he had lied about the Cuban, the note, and the dumpster. The real story, Harris said, was that he was transporting the cocaine to Atlanta for Williamson, and that Williamson was traveling in front of him in another rental car. Harris added that after his car was stopped, Williamson turned around and drove past the location of the stop, where he could see Harris' car with its trunk open. *Ibid.* Because Williamson had apparently seen the police searching the car, Harris explained that it would be impossible to make a controlled delivery. *Id.* at 41.

Harris told Walton that he had lied about the source of the drugs because he was afraid of Williamson. *Id.* at 61, 68; see also *id.*, at 30-31. Though Harris freely implicated himself, he did not want his story to be recorded, and he refused to sign a written version of the statement. *Id.* at 24-25. Walton testified that he had promised to report any cooperation by Harris to the Assistant United States Attorney. Walton said Harris was not promised any reward or other benefit for cooperating. *Id.* at 25-26.

Williamson was eventually convicted of possessing cocaine with intent to distribute, conspiring to possess cocaine with intent to distribute, and traveling interstate to promote the distribution of cocaine, 21 U.S.C. §§ 841(a)(1), 846; 18 U.S.C. § 1952. When called to testify at Williamson's trial, Harris refused, even though the prosecution gave him use immunity and the court ordered him to testify and eventually held him in contempt. The District Court then ruled that, under Rule 804(b)(3), Agent Walton could relate what Harris had said to him.... The Court of Appeals for the Eleventh Circuit affirmed without opinion....

A

The hearsay rule, Fed. Rule Evid. 802, is premised on the theory that out-of-court statements are subject to particular hazards. The declarant might be lying; he might have misperceived the events which he relates; he might have faulty memory; his words might be misunderstood or taken out of context by the listener. And the ways in which these dangers are minimized for in-court statements — the oath, the witness' awareness of the gravity of the proceedings, the jury's ability to observe the witness' demeanor, and, most importantly, the right of the opponent to cross-examine — are generally absent for things said out of court.

Nonetheless, the Federal Rules of Evidence also recognize that some kinds of out-of-court statements are less subject to these hearsay dangers, and therefore except them from the general rule that hearsay is inadmissible. One such category covers statements that are against the declarant's interest:

> "statement[s] which at the time of [their] making ... so far tended to subject the declarant to ... criminal liability ... that a reasonable person in the declarant's position would not have made the statement[s] unless believing [them] to be true." Fed. Rule Evid. 804(b)(3).

To decide whether Harris' confession is made admissible by Rule 804(b)(3), we must first determine what the Rule means by "statement," which Federal Rule of Evidence 801(a)(1) defines as "an oral or written assertion." One possible meaning, "a report or narrative," Webster's Third New International Dictionary 2229, defn. 2(a) (1961), connotes an extended declaration. Under this reading, Harris' entire confession — even if it contains both self-inculpatory and non-self-inculpatory parts — would be admissible so long as in the aggregate the confession sufficiently inculpates him. Another meaning of "statement," "a single declaration or remark," *ibid.*, defn. 2(b), would make Rule 804(b)(3) cover only those declarations or remarks within the confession that are individually self-inculpatory....

Although the text of the Rule does not directly resolve the matter, the principle behind the Rule, so far as it is discernible from the text, points clearly to the narrower reading. Rule 804(b)(3) is founded on the commonsense notion that reasonable people who are not especially honest tend not to make self-inculpatory statements unless they believe them to be true. This notion simply does not extend to the broader definition of "statement." The fact that a person is making a broadly self-inculpatory confession does not make more credible the confession's non-self-inculpatory parts. One of the most effective ways to lie is to mix falsehood with truth, especially truth that seems particularly persuasive because of its self-inculpatory nature.

In this respect, it is telling that the non-self-inculpatory things Harris said in his first settlement actually proved to be false, as Harris himself admitted during the second interrogation. And when part of the confession is actually self-exculpatory, the generalization on which Rule 804(b)(3) is founded becomes even less applicable. Self-exculpatory statements are exactly the ones which people are most likely to make even when they are false; and mere proximity to other, self-inculpatory, statements does not increase the plausibility of the self-exculpatory statements....

Nothing in the text of Rule 804(B)(3) or the general theory of the hearsay Rules suggests that admissibility should turn on whether a statement is collateral

C. HEARSAY EXCEPTIONS

to a self-inculpatory statement. The fact that a statement is self-inculpatory does make it more reliable; but the fact that a statement is collateral to a self-inculpatory statement says nothing at all about the collateral statement's reliability. We see no reason why collateral statements, even ones that are neutral as to interest, *post*, at 2443-44, should be treated any differently from other hearsay statements that are generally excluded....

In our view, the most faithful reading of Rule 804(b)(3) is that it does not allow admission of non-self-inculpatory statements, even if they are made with a broader narrative that is generally self-inculpatory. The district court may not just assume for purposes of Rule 804(b)(3) that a statement is self-inculpatory because it is part of a fuller confession, and this is especially true when the statement implicates someone else. "[T]he arrest statements of a codefendant have traditionally been viewed with special suspicion. Due to his strong motivation to implicate the defendant and to exonerate himself, a codefendant's statements about what the defendant said or did are less credible than ordinary hearsay evidence."...

JUSTICE KENNEDY suggest that the Advisory Committee Notes to Rules 804(b)(3) should be read as endorsing the position we reject — that an entire narrative, including non-self-inculpatory parts (but excluding the clearly self-serving parts, *post*, at 11), may be admissible if it is in the aggregate self-inculpatory. See *post*, at 2442. The Notes read, in relevant part:

> "[T]he third-party confession ... may include statements implicating [the accused], and under the general theory of declarations against interest they would be admissible as related statements ... by no means is it required that all statements implicating another person be excluded from the category of declarations against interest. Whether a statement is in fact against interest must be determined from the circumstances of each case. Thus a statement admitting guilt and implicating another person, made while in custody, may well be motivated by a desire to curry favor with the authorities and hence fail to qualify as against interest.... On the other hand, the same words spoken under different circumstances, *e.g.*, to an acquaintance, would have no difficulty in qualifying .... The balancing of self-serving against dissenting *[sic]* aspects of a declaration is discussed in McCormick § 256." 28 U.S.C.App., p. 790.

This language, however, is not particularly clear, and some of it — especially the Advisory Committee's endorsement of the position taken by Dean McCormick's treatise — points the other way:

> "A certain latitude as to contextual statements, neutral as to interest, giving meaning to the declaration against interest seems defensible, but bringing in self-serving statements contextually seems questionable.... Admitting the deserving parts of the declaration, and excluding the self-serving parts ... seems the most realistic method of adjusting admissibility to trustworthiness,

where the serving and deserving parts can be severed." *See* C. McCormick, Law of Evidence § 256, pp. 551-553 (1954) (footnotes omitted).

Without deciding exactly how much weight to give the Notes in this particular situation, we conclude that the policy expressed in the statutory text points clearly enough in one direction that it outweighs whatever force the Notes may have....

B

[W]hether a statement is self-inculpatory or not can only be determined by viewing it in context. Even statements that are on their face neutral may actually be against the declarant's interest. "I hid the gun in Joe's apartment" may not be a confession of a crime; but if it is likely to help the police find the murder weapon, then it is certainly self-inculpatory. "Sam and I went to Joe's house" might be against the declarant's interest if a reasonable person in the declarant's shoes would realize that being linked to Joe and Sam would implicate the declarant in Joe and Sam's conspiracy....

C

In this case, however, we cannot conclude that all that Harris said was properly admitted. Some of Harris' confession would clearly have been admissible under Rule 804(b)(3); for instance, when he said he knew there was cocaine in the suitcase, he essentially forfeited his only possible defense to a charge of cocaine possession, lack of knowledge. But other parts of his confession, especially the parts that implicated Williamson, did little to subject Harris himself to criminal liability....

Nothing in the record shows that the District Court or the Court of Appeals inquired whether each of the statements in Harris' confession was truly self-inculpatory. As we explained above, this can be a fact-intensive inquiry, which would require careful examination of all the circumstances surrounding the criminal activity involved; we therefore remand to the Court of Appeals to conduct this inquiry in the first instance.

The judgment of the Court of Appeals is vacated, and the case is remanded for further proceedings consistent with this opinion.

So ordered....

....

JUSTICE KENNEDY, with whom THE CHIEF JUSTICE and JUSTICE THOMAS join, concurring in the judgment:

....

The Court resolves the issue, as I understand its opinion, by adopting the extreme position that no collateral statements are admissible under Rule 804(b)(3). See *ante*, at 2435 (adopting "narrower reading" that "Rule 804(b)(3) cover[s] only those declarations or remarks within the confession that are individually self-inculpatory"); *ante*, at 2438 (GINSBURG, J., concurring in part

C. HEARSAY EXCEPTIONS

and concurring in judgment); but cf. *ante*, at 2438 (SCALIA, J., concurring). The Court reaches that conclusion by relying on the "principle behind the Rule" that reasonable people do not make statements against their interest unless they are telling the truth, *ante*, at 2435, and reasons that this policy "expressed in the statutory text," *ante*, at 2436, "simply does not extend" to collateral statements. *Ante*, at 2435. Though conceding that Congress can "make statements admissible based on their proximity to self-inculpatory statements," the Court says that it cannot "lightly assume that the ambiguous language means anything so inconsistent with the Rule's underlying theory." *Ante*, at 2435.

With respect, I must disagree with this analysis. All agree that the justification for admission of hearsay statements against interest was, as it still is, that reasonable people do not make those statements unless believing them to be true, but that has not resolved the long-running debate over the admissibility of collateral statements, as to which there is no clear consensus in the authorities. Indeed, to the extent the authorities come close to any consensus, they support admission of some collateral statements. *See supra*, at 2440-41. Given that the underlying principle for the hearsay exception has not resolved the debate over collateral statements one way or the other, I submit that we should not assume that the text of Rule 804(b)(3), which is silent about collateral statements, in fact incorporates one of the competing positions. The Rule's silence no more incorporates Jefferson's position respecting collateral statements than it does McCormick's or Wigmore's....

II

First, the Advisory Committee Note establishes that some collateral statements are admissible. In fact, it refers in specific terms to the issue we here confront: "[o]rdinarily the third-party confession is thought of in terms of exculpating the accused, but this is by no means always or necessarily the case: it may include statements implicating him, and under the general theory of declarations against interest they would be admissible as related statements." 28 U.S.C. App., p. 790. This language seems a forthright statement that collateral statements are admissible under Rule 804(b)(3)....

Absent contrary indications, we can presume that Congress intended the principles and terms used in the Federal Rules of Evidence to be applied as they were at common law. *See Daubert v. Merrell Dow Pharmaceuticals, Inc.*, 509 U.S. ___, ___, 113 S.Ct. 2786, 2793-2794, 125 L.Ed.2d 469 (1993); *see also Midlantic Nat. Bank v. New Jersey Dept. of Environmental Protection*, 474 U.S. 494, 501, 106 S.Ct. 755, 759-760, 88 L.Ed.2d 859 (1986) ("if Congress intends for legislation to change the interpretation of a judicially created concept, it makes that intent specific"). Application of that principle indicates that collateral statements should be admissible.... Indeed, the Advisory Committee Note itself, in stating that collateral statements would be admissible, referred to the "general theory" that related statements are admissible, an indication of the state of the law at the time the rule was enacted. Rule 804(b)(3) does not address the issue, but Congress legislated against the common law background allowing admission of some collateral statements, and I would not assume that Congress gave the common law rule silent burial in Rule 804(b)(3)....

....

2. HEARSAY EXCEPTIONS PROBLEMS

1. "Missing ... "

Shawn went to a party one chilly January night to take a break from entering data on her computer. The last time anyone saw her was when she left the party, apparently alone. Peter is charged with Shawn's murder. Which of the following testimony is admissible?

a. Susan: I heard Shawn say at the party: "I'm just going to go to the liquor store with Peter; I'll be back."
b. Susan: I told Shawn, "Is that a gun Peter is showing Diane over there? It looks like a Smith and Wesson."
c. Susan: Peter said as he left the party that he was going to go home to sleep because he was feeling very tired.
d. Susan: Shawn knew that I was doing my neurology residency and she asked me what to do about some dizzy spells she had been having.

2. Shepard's Pie

Several hours after eating some Shepard's Pie, Mrs. Connolly shrieked, "My hands are tingling; that snake Mr. Connolly must have poisoned me!" Mrs. Connolly then collapsed and died. Mr. Connolly was charged with her murder. Are Mrs. Connolly's statements admissible at trial? Why?

3. Records

In a prom-night accident, a joy-riding, intoxicated high school senior named Royce drives at high speed into a group of freshmen and sophomores gathered at a street corner near the high school. Miraculously, no one is killed. Several serious injuries, however, occur. In a subsequent trial brought by the parents of the injured bystanders, which records are admissible?

a. The hospital records reflecting the injuries of the bystanders.
b. The repair records of the car that crashed as regularly maintained by Briarcliff Service Station and Auto Repair.
c. The notes taken by one of the parents detailing the torturous recovery of one of the victims.
d. The records of the weather bureau for that day regarding rain, and time of sunset.
e. The police report providing a description of the accident and its cause.

C. HEARSAY EXCEPTIONS 151

4. "I Swear To Tell ..."

A witness, Arton Serma, testified at a Congressional oversight hearing on subcontracting irregularities in the Army and then promptly disappeared. In a subsequent criminal trial brought against one of the subcontractors, can the defendant offer the videotape of Arton's testimony against the prosecution? Why?

5. The Fugitive

A significant issue in a probate proceeding was whether the fugitive, Frank, who was wanted in the death of his wife, was still alive. Two months earlier, Arturo knowingly lay dying at the hands of an intruder. He blurted out, "Jermaine killed Frank last month!" Arturo then died. Are these statements admissible at trial? Why?

6. Dead Overdrive

Joel's best friend Pasquale was charged with improperly charging for "overdrive" on various model cars when the "overdrive" was merely decorative. When Joel was asked why he did not come to his friend's defense, Joel stated, "because they would've found out that I knew more about those charges than Pasquale did." If Joel suffers a stroke and is unable to testify, can Pasquale offer Joel's statement at his trial on fraud charges?

7. Grand Jury

A witness, Davey, testified before the grand jury investigating claims of child abuse at a day-care center. Prior to the trial, Davey suffers an incapacitating stroke. Can Davey's grand jury testimony be offered at trial? By the prosecution? By the defendant? Why?

VIII. THE CONFRONTATION CLAUSE

In all criminal prosecutions, the accused shall enjoy the right ... to be confronted with the witnesses against him.

U.S. Const. amend. VI

A. CONFRONTATION CLAUSE CASES

BRUTON v. UNITED STATES
391 U.S. 123 (1968)

JUSTICE BRENNAN delivered the opinion of the Court:

This case presents the question, last considered in *Delli Paoli v. United States*, 352 U.S. 232, 77 S.Ct. 294, 1 L.Ed.2d 278, whether the conviction of a defendant at a joint trial should be set aside although the jury was instructed that a codefendant's confession inculpating the defendant had to be disregarded in determining his guilt or innocence.

A joint trial of petitioner and one Evans in the District Court for the Eastern District of Missouri resulted in the conviction of both by a jury on a federal charge of armed postal robbery, 18 U.S.C. § 2114. A postal inspector testified that Evans orally confessed to him that Evans and petitioner committed the armed robbery. The postal inspector obtained the oral confession, and another in which Evans admitted he had an accomplice whom he would not name, in the course of two interrogations of Evans at the city jail in St. Louis, Missouri, where Evans was held in custody on state criminal charges. Both petitioner and Evans appealed their convictions to the Court of Appeals for the Eighth Circuit. That court set aside Evans' conviction on the ground that his oral confessions to the postal inspector should not have been received in evidence against him. 375 F.2d 355, 361. However, the court, relying upon *Delli Paoli*, affirmed petitioner's conviction because the trial judge instructed the jury that although Evans' confession was competent evidence against Evans it was inadmissible hearsay against petitioner and therefore had to be disregarded in determining petitioner's guilt or innocence. 375 F.2d, at 361-363. We granted certiorari to reconsider *Delli Paoli*. 389 U.S. 818. The Solicitor General has since submitted a memorandum stating that "in the light of the record in this particular case and in the interests of justice, the judgment below should be reversed and the cause remanded for a new trial." The Solicitor General states that this disposition is urged in part because "(h)ere it has been determined that the confession was wrongly admitted against [Evans] and his conviction has been reversed, leading to a new trial at which he was acquitted. To argue, in this situation, that [petitioner's] conviction should nevertheless stand may be to place too great a strain upon the [*Delli Paoli*] rule — at least, where, as here the other evidence against [petitioner] is not strong." We have concluded, however, that *Delli Paoli* should be overruled. We hold that, because of the substantial risk that the jury, despite instructions to the contrary, looked to the incriminating extrajudicial statements in determining petitioner's guilt, admission of Evans' confession in this joint trial violated petitioner's right of cross-examination secured by the Confrontation Clause of the Sixth Amendment. We therefore overrule *Delli Paoli* and reverse.

The basic premise of *Delli Paoli* was that it is "reasonably possible for the jury to follow" sufficiently clear instructions to disregard the confessor's extrajudicial statement that his codefendant participated with him in committing the crime. 352 U.S., at 239, 77 S.Ct., at 299. If it were true that the jury disregarded the reference to the codefendant, no question would arise under the Confrontation Clause, because by hypothesis the case is treated as if the confessor made no statement inculpating the nonconfessor. But since *Delli Paoli* was decided this Court has effectively repudiated its basic premise....

... True, the repudiation was not in the context of the admission of a confession inculpating a codefendant but in the context of a New York rule which submitted to the jury the question of the voluntariness of the confession itself. *Jackson v. Denno*, 378 U.S. 368, 84 S.Ct. 1774, 12 L.Ed.2d 908. Nonetheless the message of *Jackson* for *Delli Paoli* was clear. We there held that a defendant is constitutionally entitled at least to have the trial judge first determine whether a confession was made voluntarily before submitting it to the jury for an assessment of its credibility. More specifically, we expressly rejected the proposition that a jury, when determining the confessor's guilt, could be relied on to ignore his confession of guilt should it find the confession involuntary. *Id.*, at 388-389. Significantly, we supported that conclusion in part by reliance upon the dissenting opinion of Mr. Justice Frankfurter for the four Justices who dissented in *Delli Paoli*. *Id.*, at 388, n. 15.

That dissent challenged the basic premise of *Delli Paoli* that a properly instructed jury would ignore the confessor's inculpation of the nonconfessor in determining the latter's guilt. "The fact of the matter is that too often such admonition against misuse is intrinsically ineffective in that the effect of such a nonadmissible declaration cannot be wiped from the brains of the jurors. The admonition therefore becomes a futile collocation of words and fails of its purpose as a legal protection to defendants against whom such a declaration should not tell." 352 U. S., at 247. The dissent went on to say, as quoted in the cited note in *Jackson*, "The Government should not have the windfall of having the jury be influenced by evidence against a defendant which, as a matter of law, they should not consider but which they cannot put out of their minds." *Id.*, at 248....

The significance of *Jackson* for *Delli Paoli* was suggested by Chief Justice Traynor in *People v. Aranda*, 63 Cal.2d 518, 528-529, 47 Cal.Rptr. 353, 358-359, 407 P.2d 265, 271-272:

A. CONFRONTATION CLAUSE CASES

"Although Jackson was directly concerned with obviating any risk that a jury might rely on an unconstitutionally obtained confession in determining the defendant's guilt, its logic extends to obviating the risks that the jury may rely on any inadmissible statements. If it is a denial of due process to rely on a jury's presumed ability to disregard an involuntary confession, it may also be a denial of due process to rely on a jury's presumed ability to disregard a codefendant's confession implicating another defendant when it is determining that defendant's guilt or innocence.

"Indeed, the latter task may be an even more difficult one for the jury to perform than the former. Under the New York procedure, which Jackson held violated due process, the jury was only required to disregard a confession it found to be involuntary. If it made such a finding, then the confession was presumably out of the case. In joint trials, however, when the admissible confession of one defendant inculpates another defendant, the confession is never deleted from the case and the jury is expected to perform the overwhelming task of considering it in determining the guilt or innocence of the declarant and then of ignoring it in determining the guilt or innocence of any codefendants of the declarant. A jury cannot 'segregate evidence into separate intellectual boxes.' ... It cannot determine that a confession is true insofar as it admits that A has committed criminal acts with B and at the same time effectively ignore the inevitable conclusion that B has committed those same criminal acts with A."

....

Those who have defended reliance on the limiting instruction in this area have cited several reasons in support. Judge Learned Hand, a particularly severe critic of the proposition that juries could be counted on to disregard inadmissible hearsay, wrote the opinion for the Second Circuit which affirmed *Delli Paoli*'s conviction. 229 F. 2d 319. In Judge Hand's view the limiting instruction, although not really capable of preventing the jury from considering the prejudicial evidence, does as a matter of form provide a way around the exclusionary rules of evidence that is defensible because it "probably furthers, rather than impedes, the search for truth ...." *Nash v. United States*, 54 F. 2d 1006, 1007. Insofar as this implies the prosecution ought not to be denied the benefit of the confession to prove the confessor's guilt, however, it overlooks alternative ways of achieving that benefit without at the same time infringing the nonconfessor's right of confrontation. Where viable alternatives do exist, it is deceptive to rely on the pursuit of truth to defend a clearly harmful practice.

Another reason cited in defense of *Delli Paoli* is the justification for joint trials in general, the argument being that the benefits of joint proceedings should not have to be sacrificed by requiring separate trials in order to use the confession against the declarant. Joint trials do conserve state funds, diminish inconvenience to witnesses and public authorities, and avoid delays in bringing those accused of crime to trial. But the answer to this argument was cogently stated by Judge

Lehman of the New York Court of Appeals, dissenting in *People v. Fisher*, 249 N.Y. 419, 432, 164 N.E. 336, 341:

> "We still adhere to the rule that an accused is entitled to confrontation of the witnesses against him and the right to cross-examine them .... We destroy the age-old rule which in the past has been regarded as a fundamental principle of our jurisprudence by a legalistic formula, required of the judge, that the jury may not consider any admissions against any party who did not join in them. We secure greater speed, economy and convenience in the administration of the law at the price of fundamental principles of constitutional liberty. That price is too high."

Finally, the reason advanced by the majority in *Delli Paoli* was to tie the result to maintenance of the jury system. "Unless we proceed on the basis that the jury will follow the court's instructions where those instructions are clear and the circumstances are such that the jury can reasonably be expected to follow them, the jury system makes little sense." 352 U.S., at 242, 77 S.Ct., at 300. We agree that there are many circumstances in which this reliance is justified. Not every admission of inadmissible hearsay or other evidence can be considered to be reversible error unavoidable through limiting instructions; instances occur in almost every trial where inadmissible evidence creeps in, usually inadvertently. "A defendant is entitled to a fair trial but not a perfect one." ... It is not unreasonable to conclude that in many such cases the jury can and will follow the trial judge's instructions to disregard such information. Nevertheless, as was recognized in *Jackson v. Denno, supra*, there are some contexts in which the risk that the jury will not, or cannot, follow instructions is so great, and the consequences of failure so vital to the defendant, that the practical and human limitations of the jury system cannot be ignored.... Such a context is presented here, where the powerfully incriminating extrajudicial statements of a codefendant, who stands accused side-by-side with the defendant, are deliberately spread before the jury in a joint trial. Not only are the incriminations devastating to the defendant but their credibility is inevitably suspect, a fact recognized when accomplices do take the stand and the jury is instructed to weigh their testimony carefully given the recognized motivation to shift blame onto others. The unreliability of such evidence is intolerably compounded when the alleged accomplice, as here, does not testify and cannot be tested by cross-examination. It was against such threats to a fair trial that the Confrontation Clause was directed. *Pointer v. State of Texas, supra*.

... Here the introduction of Evans' confession posed a substantial threat to petitioner's right to confront the witnesses against him, and this is a hazard we cannot ignore. Despite the concededly clear instructions to the jury to disregard Evans' inadmissible hearsay evidence inculpating petitioner, in the context of a joint trial we cannot accept limiting instructions as an adequate substitute for

A. CONFRONTATION CLAUSE CASES 157

petitioner's constitutional right of cross-examination. The effect is the same as if there had been no instruction at all....

Reversed.

....

OHIO v. ROBERTS

448 U.S. 56 (1980)

Mr. Justice Blackmun delivered the opinion of the Court:

This case presents issues concerning the constitutional propriety of the introduction in evidence of the preliminary hearing testimony of a witness not produced at the defendant's subsequent state criminal trial....

... Roberts was charged with forgery of a check in the name of Bernard Isaacs, and with possession of stolen credit cards belonging to Isaacs and his wife Amy.

A preliminary hearing was held in Municipal court.... Respondent's appointed counsel had seen the Isaacs' daughter, Anita, in the courthouse hallway, and called her as the defense's only witness. Anita Isaac testified that she knew respondent, and that she permitted him to use her apartment for several days while she was away. Defense counsel questioned Anita at some length and attempted to elicit from her an admission that she had given respondent checks and the credit cards without informing him that she did not have permission to use them. Anita, however, denied this. Respondent's attorney did not ask to have the witness declared hostile and did not request permission to place her on cross-examination. The prosecutor did not question Anita.

A county grand jury subsequently indicted respondent for forgery, for receiving stolen property ... and for possession of heroin....

Between November 1975 and March 1976, five subpoenas for four different trial dates were issued to Anita.... She did not telephone and she did not appear at trial.

In March 1976, the case went to trial before a jury in the Court of Common Pleas. Respondent took the stand and testified that Anita Isaacs had given him her parents' checkbook and credit cards with the understanding that he could use them. Relying on Ohio Rev.Code Ann. § 2945.49 (1975), which permits the use of preliminary examination testimony of a witness who "cannot for any reason be produced at the trial," the State, on rebuttal, offered the transcript of Anita's testimony.

Asserting a violation of the Confrontation Clause and indeed, the unconstitutionality thereunder of § 2945.49, the defense objected to the use of the transcript.... The trial court admitted the transcript into evidence. Respondent was convicted on all counts.

The Court of Appeals of Ohio reversed ... conclud[ing] that the prosecution had failed to make a showing of a "good-faith effort" to secure the absent witness' attendance....

The Supreme Court of Ohio ... affirmed....

The historical evidence leaves little doubt ... that the Confrontation Clause was intended to exclude some hearsay.... Moreover, underlying policies support the same conclusion. The Court has emphasized that the Confrontation Clause reflects a preference for face-to-face confrontation at trial, and that "a primary interest secured by [the provision] is the right of cross-examination." *Douglas v. Alabama*, 380 U.S. 415, 418 (1965). In short, the Clause envisions

> "a personal examination and cross-examination of the witness in which the accused has an opportunity, not only of testing the recollection and sifting the conscience of the witness, but of compelling him to stand face to face with the jury in order that they may look at him, and judge by his demeanor upon the stand and the manner in which he gives his testimony whether he is worthy of belief." *Mattox v. United States*, 156 U.S., at 242-243....

The Court, however, has recognized that competing interests, if "closely examined," *Chambers v. Mississippi*, 410 U.S., at 284, 295, 93 S.Ct. 1045, may warrant dispensing with confrontation at trial....
....

The Confrontation Clause operates in two separate ways to restrict the range of admissible hearsay. First, in conformance with the Framers' preference for face-to-face accusation the Sixth Amendment establishes a rule of necessity. In the usual case (including cases where prior cross-examination has occurred), the prosecution must either produce, or demonstrate the unavailability of, the declarant whose statement it wishes to use against the defendant....

The second aspect operates once a witness is shown to be unavailable. Reflecting its underlying purpose to augment accuracy in the factfinding process by ensuring the defendant an effective means to test adverse evidence, the Clause countenances only hearsay marked with such trustworthiness that "there is no material departure from the reason of the general rule." *Snyder v. Massachusetts*, 291 U.S. at 107.... The principle recently was formulated in *Mancusi v. Stubbs*:

> "The focus of the Court's concern has been to insure that there 'are indicia of reliability which have been widely viewed as determinative of whether a statement may be placed before the jury though there is no confrontation of the declarant,' ... and to 'afford the trier of fact a satisfactory basis for evaluating the truth of the prior statement.' ... It is clear from these statements and from numerous prior decisions of this Court, that even though the witness be unavailable his prior testimony must bear some of these 'indicia of reliability.'" 408 U.S., at 213, 92 S. Ct., at 2313.

The Court has applied this "indicia of reliability" requirement principally by concluding that certain hearsay exceptions rest upon such solid foundations that admission of virtually any evidence within them comports with the "substance of the constitutional protection."...

A. CONFRONTATION CLAUSE CASES

In sum, when a hearsay declarant is not present for cross-examination at trial, the Confrontation Clause normally requires a showing that he is unavailable. Even then, his statement is admissible only if it bears adequate "indicia of reliability." Reliability can be inferred without more in a case where the evidence falls within a firmly rooted hearsay exception. In other cases, the evidence must be excluded, at least absent a showing of particularized guarantees of trustworthiness.

III

We turn first to that aspect of confrontation analysis deemed dispositive by the Supreme Court of Ohio, and answered by it in the negative — whether Anita Isaacs' prior testimony at the preliminary hearing bore sufficient "indicia of reliability."...

....

... [W]e reject respondent's attempt to fall back on general principles of confrontation, and his argument that this case falls among those in which the Court must undertake a particularized search for "indicia of reliability." Under this theory, the factors previously cited — absence of face-to-face contact at trial ... and the lack of classic cross-examination — combine with consideration uniquely tied to Anita to mandate exclusion of her statements.... Given these facts, her prior testimony falls on the unreliable side, and should have been excluded.

In making this argument, respondent in effect asks us to disassociate preliminary hearing testimony previously subjected to cross-examination from previously cross-examined prior-trial testimony, which the Court has deemed generally immune from subsequent confrontation attack. Precedent requires us to decline this invitation....

In sum, ... "[s]ince there was an adequate opportunity to cross-examine [the witness], and counsel ... availed himself of that opportunity, the transcript ... bore sufficient 'indicia of reliability' and afforded the '"trier of fact a satisfactory basis for evaluating the truth of the prior statement."'" (Citations omitted.)

....

UNITED STATES v. INADI

475 U.S. 387 (1985)

JUSTICE POWELL delivered the opinion of the Court:

This case presents the question whether the Confrontation Clause requires the Government to show that a nontestifying co-conspirator is unavailable to testify, as a condition for admission of that co-conspirator's out-of-court statements.

I

Following a jury trial in the Eastern District of Pennsylvania, respondent Joseph Inadi was convicted of conspiring to manufacture and distribute methamphetamine, and related offenses.... The evidence at trial showed that in September 1979, respondent was approached by unindicted co-conspirator Michael McKeon, who was seeking a distribution outlet for methamphetamine....

In the course of manufacturing and selling methamphetamine, McKeon, Levan, and respondent met with another unindicted co-conspirator, John Lazaro, at an empty house in Cape May, New Jersey.... In the early morning hours of May 23, 1980, two Cape May police officers, pursuant to a warrant, secretly entered the house and removed a tray covered with drying methamphetamine....

From May 23 to May 27, 1980, the Cape May County Prosecutor's Office lawfully intercepted and recorded five telephone conversations between various participants in the conspiracy. These taped conversations were played for the jury at trial. The conversations dealt with various aspects of the conspiracy, including planned meetings and speculation about who had taken the missing tray from the house and who had set Lazaro up for the May 25 stop and search. Respondent sought to exclude the recorded statements of Lazaro and the other unindicted co-conspirators on the ground that the statements did not satisfy the requirements of Federal Rule of Evidence 801(d)(2)(E), governing admission of co-conspirator declarations. After listening to the tapes the trial court admitted the statements, finding that they were made by conspirators during the course of and in furtherance of the conspiracy, and thereby satisfied Rule 801(d)(2)(E).

Respondent also objected to admission of the statements on Confrontation Clause grounds, contending that the statements were inadmissible absent a showing that the declarants were unavailable. The court suggested that the prosecutor bring Lazaro to court in order to demonstrate unavailability. The court also asked defense counsel whether she wanted the prosecution to call Lazaro as a witness, and defense counsel stated that she would discuss the matter with her client. The co-conspirators' statements were admitted, conditioned on the prosecution's commitment to produce Lazaro. The Government subpoenaed Lazaro, but he failed to appear, claiming car trouble. The record does not indicate that the defense made any effort on its own part to secure Lazaro's presence in court.

Respondent renewed his Confrontation Clause objections, arguing that the Government had not met its burden of showing that Lazaro was unavailable to testify. The trial court overruled the objection, ruling that Lazaro's statements were admissible because they satisfied the co-conspirator rule.

The Court of Appeals for the Third Circuit reversed. 748 F. 2d 812 (1984). The court agreed that the Government had satisfied Rule 801(d)(2)(E), but decided that the Confrontation Clause established an independent requirement that the Government, as a condition to admission of any out-of-court statements, must show the unavailability of the declarant. 748 F. 2d, at 818. The court derived this "unavailability rule" from *Ohio v. Roberts*, 448 U.S. 56 (1980). The Court of Appeals rejected the Government's contention that *Roberts* did not require a showing of unavailability as to a nontestifying co-conspirator, finding that *Roberts* created a "clear constitutional rule" applicable to out-of-court statements

A. CONFRONTATION CLAUSE CASES

generally. 748 F.2d, at 818. The court found no reason to create a special exception for co-conspirator statements, and therefore ruled Lazaro's statements inadmissible. *Id.*, at 818-819.

We granted certiorari, 471 U.S. 1124 (1985), to resolve the question whether the Confrontation Clause requires a showing of unavailability as a condition to admission of the out-of-court statements of a nontestifying co-conspirator, when those statements otherwise satisfy the requirements of Federal Rule of Evidence 801(d)(2)(E). We now reverse.

II

A

The Court of Appeals ... quoted *Roberts* as holding that "in conformance with the Framers' preference for face-to-face accusation, the Sixth Amendment establishes a rule of necessity. In the usual case ... the prosecution must either produce, or demonstrate the unavailability of, the declarant whose statement it wishes to use against the defendant." 448 U.S., at 65. The Court of Appeals viewed this language as setting forth a "clear constitutional rule" applicable before any hearsay can be admitted. 748 F.2d, at 818. Under this interpretation of *Roberts*, no out-of-court statement would be admissible without a showing of unavailability.

Roberts, however, does not stand for such a wholesale revision of the law of evidence, nor does it support such a broad interpretation of the Confrontation Clause. *Roberts* itself disclaimed any intention of proposing a general answer to the many difficult questions arising out of the relationship between the Confrontation Clause and hearsay.... In addition, the Court specifically noted that a "demonstration of unavailability ... is not always required." 448 U.S., at 65, n. 7.

The Confrontation Clause analysis in *Roberts* focuses on those factors that come into play when the prosecution seeks to admit testimony from a prior judicial proceeding in place of live testimony at trial. See Fed. Rule Evid. 804(b)(1). In particular, the *Roberts* Court examined the requirement, found in a long line of Confrontation Clause cases involving prior testimony, that before such statements can be admitted the government must demonstrate that the declarant is unavailable....

Roberts must be read consistently with the question it answered, the authority it cited, and its own facts. All of these indicate that *Roberts* simply reaffirmed a longstanding rule, ... that applies unavailability analysis to prior testimony. *Roberts* cannot fairly be read to stand for the radical proposition that no out-of-court statement can be introduced by the government without a showing that the declarant is unavailable.

B

There are good reasons why the unavailability rule, developed in cases involving former testimony, is not applicable to co-conspirators' out-of-court statements....

... Because ... [statements] are made while the conspiracy is in progress, such statements provide evidence of the conspiracy's context that cannot be replicated, even if the declarant testifies to the same matters in court. When the Government — as here — offers the statement of one drug dealer to another in furtherance of an illegal conspiracy, the statement often will derive its significance from the circumstances in which it was made. Conspirators are likely to speak differently when talking to each other in furtherance of their illegal aims than when testifying on the witness stand. Even when the declarant takes the stand, his in-court testimony seldom will reproduce a significant portion of the evidentiary value of his statements during the course of the conspiracy.

In addition, the relative positions of the parties will have changed substantially between the time of the statements and the trial. The declarant and the defendant will have changed from partners in an illegal conspiracy to suspects or defendants in a criminal trial, each with information potentially damaging to the other. The declarant himself may be facing indictment or trial, in which case he has little incentive to aid the prosecution, and yet will be equally wary of coming to the aid of his former partners in crime. In that situation, it is extremely unlikely that in-court testimony will recapture the evidentiary significance of statements made when the conspiracy was operating in full force.

These points distinguish co-conspirators' statements from the statements involved in *Roberts* and our other prior testimony cases.... No such strong similarities exist between co-conspirator statements and live testimony at trial. To the contrary, co-conspirator statements derive much of their value from the fact that they are made in a context very different from trial, and therefore are usually irreplaceable as substantive evidence.... The admission of co-conspirators' declarations into evidence thus actually furthers the "Confrontation Clause's very mission" which is to "advance 'the accuracy of the truth-determining process in criminal trials.'" (Citation omitted.)

C

There appears to be little, if any, benefit to be accomplished by the Court of Appeals' unavailability rule. First, if the declarant either is unavailable, or is available and produced by the prosecution, the statements can be introduced anyway. Thus, the unavailability rule cannot be defended as a constitutional "better evidence" rule, because it does not actually serve to exclude anything, unless the prosecution makes the mistake of not producing an otherwise available witness.... In this case, for example, out-of-court statements by Michael McKeon and Marianne Lazaro, who testified under immunity, could be introduced based on their testimony in court. The statements of William Levan were admissible

A. CONFRONTATION CLAUSE CASES

because he properly asserted his Fifth Amendment privilege and thereby was unavailable.

Second, an unavailability rule is not likely to produce much testimony that adds anything to the "truth-determining process" over and above what would be produced without such a rule. *Dutton, supra*, at 89. Some of the available declarants already will have been subpoenaed by the prosecution or the defense, regardless of any Confrontation Clause requirements. Presumably only those declarants that neither side believes will be particularly helpful will not have been subpoenaed as witnesses. There is much to indicate that Lazaro was in that position in this case. Neither the Government nor the defense originally subpoenaed Lazaro as a witness....

While the benefits seem slight, the burden imposed by the Court of Appeals' unavailability rule is significant. A constitutional rule requiring a determination of availability every time the prosecution seeks to introduce a co-conspirator's declaration automatically adds another avenue of appellate review in these complex cases. The co-conspirator rule apparently is the most frequently used exception to the hearsay rule.... A rule that required each invocation of Rule 801(d)(2)(E) to be accompanied by a decision on the declarant's availability would impose a substantial burden on the entire criminal justice system.

Moreover, an unavailability rule places a significant practical burden on the prosecution. In every case involving co-conspirator statements, the prosecution would be required to identify with specificity each declarant, locate those declarants, and then endeavor to ensure their continuing availability for trial....

An unavailability rule would impose all of these burdens even if neither the prosecution nor the defense wished to examine the declarant at trial. Any marginal protection to the defendant by forcing the government to call as witnesses those co-conspirator declarants who are available, willing to testify, hostile to the defense, and yet not already subpoenaed by the prosecution, when the defendant himself can call and cross-examine such declarants, cannot support an unavailability rule. We hold today that the Confrontation Clause does not embody such a rule....

MARYLAND v. CRAIG

497 U.S. 839 (1990)

JUSTICE O'CONNOR delivered the opinion of the Court:

This case requires us to decide whether the Confrontation Clause of the Sixth Amendment categorically prohibits a child witness in a child abuse case from testifying against a defendant at trial, outside the defendant's physical presence, by one-way closed circuit television....

....

The Confrontation Clause of the Sixth Amendment, made applicable to the States through the Fourteenth Amendment, provides: "In all criminal prosecutions, the accused shall enjoy the right ... to be confronted with the witnesses against him.''

We observed in *Coy v. Iowa* that "the Confrontation Clause guarantees the defendant a face-to-face meeting with witnesses appearing before the trier of fact." ...

....

We have never held, however, that the Confrontation Clause guarantees criminal defendants the *absolute* right to a face-to-face meeting with witnesses against them at trial. Indeed, in *Coy v. Iowa*, we expressly "le[ft] for another day ... the question whether any exceptions exist" to the "irreducible literal meaning of the Clause: 'a right to *meet face to face* all those who appear and give evidence *at trial.*'" ... The procedure challenged in *Coy* involved the placement of a screen that prevented two child witnesses in a child abuse case from seeing the defendant as they testified at trial.... In holding that the use of this procedure violated the defendant's right to confront witnesses against him, we suggested that any exception to the right "would surely be allowed only when necessary to further an important public policy" — i.e., only upon a showing of something more than the generalized, "legislatively imposed presumption of trauma" underlying the statute at issue in that case.... We concluded that "[s]ince there ha[d] been no individualized findings that these particular witnesses needed special protection, the judgment [in the case before us] could not be sustained by any conceivable exception." ... Because the trial court in this case made individualized findings that each of the child witnesses needed special protection, this case requires us to decide the question reserved in *Coy*.

The central concern of the Confrontation Clause is to ensure the reliability of the evidence against a criminal defendant by subjecting it to rigorous testing in the context of an adversary proceeding before the trier of fact. The word "confront," after all, also means a clashing of forces or ideas, thus carrying with it the notion of adversariness....

The combined effect of these elements of confrontation — physical presence, oath, cross-examination, and observation of demeanor by the trier of fact — serves the purposes of the Confrontation Clause by ensuring that evidence admitted against an accused is reliable and subject to the rigorous adversarial testing that is the norm of Anglo-American criminal proceedings....

....

Although face-to-face confrontation forms "the core of the values furthered by the Confrontation Clause," ... we have nevertheless recognized that it is not the *sine qua non* of the confrontation right....

For this reason, we have never insisted on an actual face-to-face encounter at trial in *every* instance in which testimony is admitted against a defendant. Instead, we have repeatedly held that the Clause permits, where necessary, the admission of certain hearsay statements against a defendant despite the defendant's inability to confront the declarant at trial....

....

A. CONFRONTATION CLAUSE CASES

In sum, our precedents establish that "the Confrontation Clause reflects a *preference* for face-to-face confrontation at trial," ... a preference that "must occasionally give way to considerations of public policy and the necessities of the case,".... Thus, though we reaffirm the importance of face-to-face confrontation with witnesses appearing at trial, we cannot say that such confrontation is an indispensable element of the Sixth Amendment's guarantee of the right to confront one's accusers....

Maryland's statutory procedure, when invoked, prevents a child witness from seeing the defendant as he or she testifies against the defendant at trial. We find it significant, however, that Maryland's procedure preserves all of the other elements of the confrontation right: The child witness must be competent to testify and must testify under oath; the defendant retains full opportunity for contemporaneous cross-examination; and the judge, jury, and defendant are able to view (albeit by video monitor) the demeanor (and body) of the witness as he or she testifies. Although we are mindful of the many subtle effects face-to-face confrontation may have on an adversary criminal proceeding, the presence of these other elements of confrontation — oath, cross-examination, and observation of the witness' demeanor — adequately ensures that the testimony is both reliable and subject to rigorous adversarial testing in a manner functionally equivalent to that accorded life, in-person testimony.... We are therefore confident that use of the one-way closed circuit television procedure, where necessary to further an important state interest, does not impinge upon the truth-seeking or symbolic purposes of the Confrontation Clause....

We have of course recognized that a State's interest in "the protection of minor victims of sex crimes from further trauma and embarrassment" is a "compelling" one.... "[W]e have sustained legislation aimed at protecting the physical and emotional well-being of youth even when the laws have operated in the sensitive area of constitutionally protected rights." *Ferber, supra,* at 757 ....

We likewise conclude today that a State's interest in the physical and psychological well-being of child abuse victims may be sufficiently important to outweigh, at least in some cases, a defendant's right to face his or her accusers in court. That a significant majority of States has enacted statutes to protect child witnesses from the trauma of giving testimony in child abuse cases attests to the widespread belief in the importance of such a public policy.... Thirty-seven States, for example, permit the use of videotaped testimony of sexually abused children; 24 States have authorized the use of one-way closed circuit television testimony in child abuse cases; and 8 States authorize the use of a two-way system in which the child-witness is permitted to see the courtroom and the defendant on a video monitor and in which the jury and judge is permitted to view the child during the testimony....

... Accordingly, we hold that, if the State makes an adequate showing of necessity, the state interest in protecting child witnesses from the trauma of testifying in a child abuse case is sufficiently important to justify the use of a special procedure that permits a child witness in such cases to testify at trial against a defendant in the absence of face-to-face confrontation with the defendant.

....

IDAHO v. WRIGHT
497 U.S. 805 (1990)

JUSTICE O'CONNOR delivered the opinion of the Court:

This case requires us to decide whether the admission at trial of certain hearsay statements made by a child declarant to an examining pediatrician violates a defendant's rights under the Confrontation Clause of the Sixth Amendment.

I

Respondent Laura Lee Wright was jointly charged with Robert L. Giles of two counts of lewd conduct with a minor under 16, in violation of Idaho Code § 18-1508 (1987). The alleged victims were respondent's two daughters, one of whom was 5½ and the other 2½ years old at the time the crimes were charged.

....

At the joint trial of respondent and Giles, the trial court conducted a *voir dire* examination of the younger daughter, who was three years old at the time of trial, to determine whether she was capable of testifying.... The court concluded, and the parties agreed, that the younger daughter was "not capable of communicating to the jury." ...

At issue in this case is the admission at trial of certain statements made by the younger daughter to Dr. Jambura in response to questions he asked regarding the alleged abuse....

From the earliest days of our Confrontation Clause jurisprudence, we have consistently held that the Clause does not necessarily prohibit the admission of hearsay statements against a criminal defendant, even though the admission of such statements might be thought to violate the literal terms of the Clause.... We reaffirmed only recently that "[w]hile a literal interpretation of the Confrontation Clause could bar the use of any out-of-court statements when the declarant is unavailable, this Court has rejected that view as 'unintended and too extreme.'" *Bourjaily v. United States*, 483 U.S. 171, 182 (1987) (quoting *Ohio v. Roberts*, 448 U.S. 56, 63 (1980); ....

....

In *Ohio v. Roberts*, we set forth "a general approach" for determining when incriminating statements admissible under an exception to the hearsay rule also meet the requirements of the Confrontation Clause. 448 U.S., at 65. We noted that the Confrontation Clause "operates in two separate ways to restrict the range of admissible hearsay." *Ibid*. "First, in conformance with the Framers' preference for face-to-face accusation, the Sixth Amendment establishes a rule of necessity. In the usual case ..., the prosecution must either produce or demonstrate the unavailability of the declarant whose statement it wishes to use

A. CONFRONTATION CLAUSE CASES

against the defendant.'' *Ibid.* Second, once a witness is shown to be unavailable, "his statement is admissible only if it bears adequate 'indicia of reliability.' Reliability can be inferred without more in a case where the evidence falls within a firmly rooted hearsay exception. In other cases, the evidence must be excluded, at least absent a showing of particularized guarantees of trustworthiness.'' *Id.,* at 66 (footnote omitted) (citations omitted).

....

Applying the *Roberts* approach to this case, we first note that this case does not raise the question whether, before a child's out-of-court statements are admitted, the Confrontation Clause requires the prosecution to show that a child witness is unavailable at trial — and, if so, what that showing requires.... For purposes of deciding this case, we assume without deciding that, to the extent the unavailability requirement applies in this case, the younger daughter was an unavailable witness within the meaning of the Confrontation Clause.

The crux of the question presented is therefore whether the State, as the proponent of evidence presumptively barred by the hearsay rule and the Confrontation Clause, has carried its burden of proving that the younger daughter's incriminating statements to Dr. Jambura bore sufficient indicia of reliability to withstand scrutiny under the Clause....

In *Roberts*, we suggested that the "indicia of reliability" requirement could be met in either of two circumstances: where the hearsay statement "falls within a firmly rooted hearsay exception," or where it is supported by "a showing of particularized guarantees of trustworthiness."...

....

We note at the outset that Idaho's residual hearsay exception, Idaho Rule Evid. 803(24), under which the challenged statements were admitted ... is not a firmly rooted hearsay exception for Confrontation Clause purposes....

The State in any event does not press the matter strongly and recognizes that, because the younger daughter's hearsay statements do not fall within a firmly rooted hearsay exception, they are "presumptively unreliable and inadmissible for Confrontation Clause purposes," ... and "must be excluded, at least absent a showing of particularized guarantees of trustworthiness ....'' The court below concluded that the State had not made such a showing, in large measure because the statements resulted from an interview lacking certain procedural safeguards. The court below specifically noted that Dr. Jambura failed to record the interview on videotape, asked leading questions, and questioned the child with a preconceived idea of what she should be disclosing....

Although we agree with the court below that the Confrontation Clause bars the admission of the younger daughter's hearsay statements, we reject the apparently dispositive weight placed by that court on the lack of procedural safeguards at the interview.... Although the procedural guidelines propounded by the court below may well enhance the reliability of out-of-court statements of children regarding sexual abuse, we decline to read into the Confrontation Clause a preconceived and artificial litmus test for the procedural propriety of professional interviews in which children make hearsay statements against a defendant.

The State responds that a finding of "particularized guarantees of trustworthiness" should instead be based on a consideration of the totality of the circumstances, including not only the circumstances surrounding the making of the statement, but also other evidence at trial that corroborates the truth of the statement. We agree that "particularized guarantees of trustworthiness" must be shown from the totality of the circumstances, but we think the relevant circumstances include only those that surround the making of the statement and that render the declarant particularly worthy of belief.... In other words, if the declarant's truthfulness is so clear from the surrounding circumstances that the test of cross-examination would be of marginal utility, then the hearsay rule does not bar admission of the statement at trial....

We think the "particularized guarantees of trustworthiness" required for admission under the Confrontation Clause must likewise be drawn from the totality of circumstances that surround the making of the statement and that render the declarant particularly worthy of belief.... Because evidence possessing "particularized guarantees of trustworthiness" must be at least as reliable as evidence admitted under a firmly rooted hearsay exception, ... we think that evidence admitted under the former requirement must similarly be so trustworthy that adversarial testing would add little to its reliability.... Thus, unless an affirmative reason, arising from the circumstances in which the statement was made, provides a basis for rebutting the presumption that a hearsay statement is not worthy of reliance at trial, the Confrontation Clause requires exclusion of the out-of-court statement.

The state and federal courts have identified a number of factors that we think properly relate to whether hearsay statements made by a child witness in child sexual abuse cases are reliable. *See, e.g., State v. Robinson*, 153 Ariz. 191, 201, 735 P.2d 801, 811 (1987) (spontaneity and consistent repetition); *Morgan v. Foretich*, 846 F.2d 941, 948 (CA4 1988) (mental state of the declarant); *State v. Sorenson*, 143 Wis.2d 226, 246, 421 N.W.2d 77, 85 (1988) (use of terminology unexpected of a child of similar age); *State v. Kuone*, 243 Kan. 218, 221-222, 757 P.2d 289, 292-293 (1988) (lack of motive to fabricate). Although these cases (which we cite for the factors they discuss and not necessarily to approve the results that they reach) involve the application of various hearsay exceptions to statements of child declarants, we think the factors identified also apply to whether such statements bear "particularized guarantees of trustworthiness" under the Confrontation Clause. These factors are, of course, not exclusive, and courts have considerable leeway in their consideration of appropriate factors. We therefore decline to endorse a mechanical test for determining "particularized guarantees of trustworthiness" under the Clause. Rather, the unifying principle is that these factors relate to whether the child declarant was particularly likely to be telling the truth when the statement was made.

A. CONFRONTATION CLAUSE CASES

As our discussion above suggests, we are unpersuaded by the State's contention that evidence corroborating the truth of a hearsay statement may properly support a finding that the statement bears "particularized guarantees of trustworthiness." To be admissible under the Confrontation Clause, hearsay evidence used to convict a defendant must possess indicia of reliability by virtue of its inherent trustworthiness, not by reference to other evidence at trial....

In short, the use of corroborating evidence to support a hearsay statement's "particularized guarantees of trustworthiness" would permit admission of a presumptively unreliable statement by bootstrapping on the trustworthiness of other evidence at trial, a result we think at odds with the requirement that hearsay evidence admitted under the Confrontation Clause be so trustworthy that cross-examination of the declarant would be of marginal utility....

....

... Of the factors the trial court found relevant (in considering the reliability of the younger daughter's statements), only two relate to circumstances surrounding the making of the statements: whether the child had a motive to "make up a story of this nature," and whether, given the child's age, the statements are of the type "that one would expect a child to fabricate." *Ibid.* The other factors on which the trial court relied, however, such as the presence of physical evidence of abuse, the opportunity of respondent to commit the offense, and the older daughter's corroborating identification, relate instead to whether other evidence existed to corroborate the truth of the statement. These factors, as we have discussed, are irrelevant to a showing of the "particularized guarantees of trustworthiness" necessary for admission of hearsay statements under the Confrontation Clause.

We think the Supreme Court of Idaho properly focused on the presumptive unreliability of the out-of-court statements and on the suggestive manner in which Dr. Jambura conducted the interview. Viewing the totality of the circumstances surrounding the younger daughter's responses to Dr. Jambura's questions, we find no special reason for supposing that the incriminating statements were particularly trustworthy. The younger daughter's last statement regarding the abuse of the older daughter, however, presents a closer question. According to Dr. Jambura, the younger daughter "volunteered" that statement "after she sort of clammed-up." ... Although the spontaneity of the statement and the change in demeanor suggest that the younger daughter was telling the truth when she made the statement, we note that it is possible that "[i]f there is evidence of prior interrogation, prompting, or manipulation by adults, spontaneity may be an inaccurate indicator of trustworthiness." ... Moreover, the statement was not made under circumstances of reliability comparable to those required, for example, for the admission of excited utterances or statements made for purposes of medical diagnosis or treatment. Given the presumption of inadmissibility accorded accusatory hearsay statements not admitted pursuant to a firmly rooted hearsay exception, ... we agree with the court below that the State has failed to show that the younger daughter's incriminating statements to the pediatrician possessed sufficient "particularized guarantees of trustworthiness" under the Confrontation Clause to overcome that presumption.

... Accordingly, the judgment of the Supreme Court of Idaho is affirmed.

WHITE v. ILLINOIS
502 U.S. 346 (1992)

REHNQUIST, C.J., delivered the opinion of the Court:

In this case we consider whether the Confrontation Clause of the Sixth Amendment requires that, before a trial court admits testimony under the "spontaneous declaration" and "medical examination" exceptions to the hearsay rule, the prosecution must either produce the declarant at trial or the trial court must find that the declarant is unavailable. The Illinois Appellate Court concluded that such procedures are not constitutionally required. We agree with that conclusion.

Petitioner was convicted by a jury of aggravated criminal sexual assault, residential burglary, and unlawful restraint.... The events giving rise to the charges related to the sexual assault of S.G., then four years old. Testimony at the trial established that in the early morning hours of April 16, 1988, S.G.'s babysitter, Tony DeVore, was awakened by S.G.'s scream.... DeVore asked S.G. what had happened. According to DeVore's trial testimony, S.G. stated that petitioner put his hand over her mouth, choked her, and threatened to whip her if she screamed and had "touch[ed] her in the wrong places."...

....

S.G. never testified at petitioner's trial. The State attempted on two occasions to call her as a witness but she apparently experienced emotional difficulty on being brought into the courtroom and in each instance left without testifying.... The defense made no attempt to call S.G. as a witness and the trial court neither made nor was asked to make, a finding that S.G. was unavailable to testify....

Petitioner objected on hearsay grounds to DeVore ... being permitted to testify regarding S.G.'s statements describing the assault.... [T]he trial court concluded that the testimony could be permitted pursuant to an Illinois hearsay exception for spontaneous declarations....

....

... We note first that the evidentiary rationale for permitting hearsay testimony regarding spontaneous declarations and statements made in the course of receiving medical care is that such out-of-court declarations are made in contexts that provide substantial guarantees of their trustworthiness. But those same factors that contribute to the statements' reliability cannot be recaptured even by later in-court testimony. A statement that has been offered in a moment of excitement — without the opportunity to reflect on the consequences of one's exclamation — may justifiably carry more weight with a trier of fact than a similar statement offered in the relative calm of the courtroom. Similarly, a statement made in the course of procuring medical services, where the declarant

A. CONFRONTATION CLAUSE CASES 171

knows that a false statement may cause misdiagnosis or mistreatment, carries special guarantees of credibility that a trier of fact may not think replicated by courtroom testimony. They are thus materially different from the statements at issue in *Roberts*, where the out-of-court statements sought to be introduced were themselves made in the course of a judicial proceeding, and where there was consequently no threat of lost evidentiary value if the out-of-court statements were replaced with live testimony.

The preference for live testimony in the case of statements like those offered in *Roberts* is because of the importance of cross examination, "the greatest legal engine ever invented for the discovery of truth." ... Thus courts have adopted the general rule prohibiting the receipt of hearsay evidence. But where proffered hearsay has sufficient guarantees of reliability to come within a firmly rooted exception to the hearsay rule, the Confrontation Clause is satisfied.

We therefore think it clear that the out-of-court statements admitted in this case had substantial probative value, value that could not be duplicated simply by the declarant later testifying in court. To exclude such probative statements under the strictures of the Confrontation Clause would be the height of wrong-headedness, given that the Confrontation Clause has as a basic purpose the promotion of the "integrity of the facilitating process." ...

As a second line of argument, petitioner presses upon us two recent decisions involving child-testimony in child-sexual assault cases .... Both [*Coy v. Iowa*] and [*Maryland v. Craig*] required us to consider the constitutionality of courtroom procedures designed to prevent a child witness from having to face across an open courtroom a defendant charged with sexually assaulting the child. In *Coy* we vacated a conviction that resulted from a trial in which a child witness testified from behind a screen, and in which there had been no particularized showing that such a procedure was necessary to avert a risk of harm to the child. In *Craig* we upheld a conviction that resulted from a trial in which a child witness testified via closed circuit television after such a showing of necessity. Petitioner draws from these two cases a general rule that hearsay testimony offered by a child should be permitted only upon a showing of necessity — i.e., in cases where necessary to protect the child's physical and psychological well-being.

Petitioner's reliance is misplaced. *Coy* and *Craig* involved only the question of what *in-court* procedures are constitutionally required to guarantee a defendant's confrontation right once a witness is testifying. Such a question is quite separate from that of what requirements the Confrontation Clause imposes as a predicate for the introduction of out-of-court declarations. *Coy* and *Craig* did not speak to the latter question. As we recognized in *Coy*, the admissibility of hearsay statements raise concerns lying at the periphery of those that the Confrontation Clause is designed to address .... There is thus no basis for importing the "necessity requirement" announced in those cases into the much different context of out-of-court declarations admitted under established exceptions to the hearsay rule.

For the foregoing reasons, the judgment of the Illinois Appellate Court is

Affirmed.

B. CONFRONTATION CLAUSE PROBLEMS

1. Ready and Available

Margot is an eyewitness to a stabbing outside of a New Mexico tavern, La Bonita. At the time of the stabbing, Margot exclaimed, "Look, Ricardo just stabbed Pepe after Pepe punched him!" Ricardo is prosecuted for the stabbing. Margot is available to testify, but prefers not to do so. Can someone who heard Margot's statement testify to it without violating Ricardo's Confrontation Clause rights? Explain.

2. "I Confess"

Nick confesses to the ATM robbery and shooting of a doctor coming off of a late shift at the Graddy Hospital. Nick stated, "Barnes and I thought we would just get some easy money; no one was supposed to get hurt, honest."

Nick and Barnes are jointly tried in state court for the robbery and shooting. Nick's confession is offered by the prosecution against Nick alone. The prosecutor informs the judge that she would not oppose the judge giving the jury a limiting instruction on the evidence. The limiting instruction would inform the jury that the confession is being admitted solely against Nick and should not be used at all against Barnes. (Nick chooses not to testify.) Permissible?

3. Jogger

Carrie was brutally beaten during her afternoon jog. Approximately one week after the beating, Carrie left the hospital and identified Barnett as her attacker in a lineup at the police station (where Barnett was one of six persons in the lineup). Barnett is tried for the beating almost two years after it occurred. If Carrie can no longer identify Barnett as her attacker, will the admission of the line-up identification violate Barnett's Confrontation Clause rights? Explain.

4. Baby Jessica

Jessica, age 4, was allegedly sexually abused by her stepfather. In a prosecution for child molestation against the stepfather, can the prosecution offer Jessica's videotaped deposition instead of her live testimony? Explain.

IX. PRIVILEGES

Article V as submitted to Congress contained thirteen Rules. Nine of those Rules defined specific non-constitutional privileges which the federal courts must recognize (i.e. required reports, lawyer-client, psychotherapist-patient, husband-wife, communications to clergymen, political vote, trade secrets, secrets of state, and other official information, and identity of informer)....

The Committee amended Article V to eliminate all of the Court's specific Rules on privileges. Instead, the Committee, through a single Rule, 501, left the law of privileges in its present state and further provided that privileges shall continue to be developed by the courts of the United States under a uniform standard applicable both in civil and criminal cases....

Fed. R. Evid. 501 Report of the House Committee on the Judiciary

A. PRIVILEGE CASES

UPJOHN CO. v. UNITED STATES
449 U.S. 383 (1981)

JUSTICE REHNQUIST delivered the opinion of the Court:

We granted certiorari in this case to address important questions concerning the scope of the attorney-client privilege in the corporate context and the applicability of the work-product doctrine in proceedings to enforce tax summonses. 445 U.S. 925. With respect to the privilege question the parties and various *amici* have described our task as one of choosing between two "tests" which have gained adherents in the courts of appeals. We are acutely aware, however, that we sit to decide concrete cases and not abstract propositions of law. We decline to lay down a broad rule or series of rules to govern all conceivable future questions in this area, even were we able to do so. We can and do, however, conclude that the attorney-client privilege protects the communications involved in this case from compelled disclosure and that the work-product doctrine does apply in tax summons enforcement proceedings.

Petitioner Upjohn Co. manufactures and sells pharmaceuticals here and abroad. In January 1976 independent accountants conducting an audit of one of Upjohn's foreign subsidiaries discovered that the subsidiary made payments to or for the benefit of foreign government officials in order to secure government business. The accountants so informed petitioner Mr. Gerard Thomas, Upjohn's Vice President, Secretary, and General Counsel.... It was decided that the company would conduct an internal investigation of what were termed "questionable payments." As part of this investigation the attorneys prepared a letter containing a questionnaire which was sent to "All Foreign General and Area Managers" over the Chairman's signature.... Managers were instructed to treat the investigation as "highly confidential" and not to discuss it with anyone other than Upjohn employees who might be helpful in providing the requested information. The responses were to be sent directly to Thomas. Thomas and outside counsel also interviewed the recipients of the questionnaire and some 33 other Upjohn officers or employees as part of the investigation....

... On November 23, 1976, the [Internal Revenue] Service issued a summons ... demanding production of:

> "All files relative to the investigation conducted under the supervision of Gerard Thomas to identify payments to employees of foreign governments ....
>
> "The records should include but not be limited to written questionnaires sent to managers of the Upjohn Company's foreign affiliates, and memorandums or notes of the interviews conducted ... with officers and employees of the Upjohn Company and its subsidiaries...."

The company declined to produce the documents specified ... on the grounds that they were protected from disclosure by the attorney-client privilege ....

Federal Rule of Evidence 501 provides that "the privilege of a witness ... shall be governed by the principles of the common law as they may be interpreted by the courts of the United States in light of reason and experience." The attorney-client privilege is the oldest of the privileges for confidential communications known to the common law.... Its purpose is to encourage full and frank communication between attorneys and their clients and thereby promote broader public interests in the observance of law and administration of justice. The privilege recognizes that sound legal advice or advocacy serves public ends and that such advice or advocacy depends upon the lawyer's being fully informed by the client. As we stated last Term in *Trammel v. United States*, 445 U. S. 40, 51 (1980): "The lawyer-client privilege rests on the need for the advocate and counselor to know all that relates to the client's reasons for seeking representation if the professional mission is to be carried out." And in *Fisher v. United States*, 425 U. S. 391, 403 (1976), we recognized the purpose of the privilege to be "to encourage clients to make full disclosure to their attorneys...." Admittedly complications in the application of the privilege arise when the client is a corporation, which in theory is an artificial creature of the law, and not an individual; but this Court has assumed that the privilege applies when the client is a corporation....

The Court of Appeals, however, considered the application of the privilege in the corporate context to present a "different problem," since the client was an inanimate entity and "only the senior management, guiding and integrating the several operations, ... can be said to possess an identity analogous to the corporation as a whole." 600 F. 2d at 1226. The first case to articulate the so-

A. PRIVILEGE CASES

called "control group test" adopted by the court below ... reflected a similar approach:

> ... "[T]he most satisfactory solution ... is that if the employee making the communication, of whatever rank he may be, is in a position to control or even to take a substantial part in a decision about any action which the corporation may take upon the advice of the attorney, ... then, in effect, *he is (or personifies) the corporation* when he makes his disclosure to the lawyer and the privilege would apply."

Such a view, we think, overlooks the fact that the privilege exists to protect not only the giving of professional advice to those who can act on it but also the giving of information to the lawyer to enable him to give sound and informed advice....

... Middle-level — and indeed lower-level — employees can, by actions within the scope of their employment, embroil the corporation in serious legal difficulties, and it is only natural that these employees would have the relevant information needed by corporate counsel if he is adequately to advise the client with respect to such actual or potential difficulties....

The control group test adopted by the court below thus frustrates the very purpose of the privilege by discouraging the communication of relevant information by employees of the client to attorneys seeking to render legal advice to the client corporation. The attorney's advice will also frequently be more significant to noncontrol group members than to those who officially sanction the advice, and the control group test makes it more difficult to convey full and frank legal advice to the employees who will put into effect the client corporation's policy....

The narrow scope given the attorney-client privilege by the court below not only makes it difficult for corporate attorneys to formulate sound advice when their client is faced with a specific legal problem but also threatens to limit the valuable efforts of corporate counsel to ensure their client's compliance with the law. In light of the vast and complicated array of regulatory legislation confronting the modern corporation, corporations, unlike most individuals, "constantly go to lawyers to find out how to obey the law," Burnham, The Attorney-Client Privilege in the Corporate Arena, 24 Bus. Law. 901, 913 (1969), particularly since compliance with the law in this area is hardly an instinctive matter .... The test adopted by the court below is difficult to apply in practice, though no abstractly formulated and unvarying "test" will necessarily enable courts to decide questions such as this with mathematical precision. But if the purpose of the attorney-client privilege is to be served, the attorney and client must be able to predict with some degree of certainty whether particular discussions will be protected. An uncertain privilege, or one which purports to be certain but results in widely varying applications by the courts, is little better than no privilege at all. The very terms of the test adopted by the court below suggest the unpredictability of its application. The test restricts the availability of the privilege to those officers who play a "substantial role" in deciding and directing a corporation's legal response. Disparate decisions in cases applying this test illustrate its unpredictability....

The communications at issue were made by Upjohn employees to counsel for Upjohn acting as such, at the direction of the corporate superiors in order to secure legal advice from counsel.... The communications concerned matters within the scope of the employees' corporate duties, and the employees themselves were sufficiently aware that they were being questioned in order that the corporation could obtain legal advice.... Pursuant to explicit instructions from the Chairman of the Board, the communications were considered "highly confidential" when made ... and have been kept confidential by the company. Consistent with the underlying purposes of the attorney-client privilege, these communications must be protected against compelled disclosure.

....

... [W]e conclude that the narrow "control group test" ... cannot, consistent with "the principles of common law as ... interpreted ... in light of reason and experience," Fed. Rule Evid. 501, govern the development of the law in this area.

....

NIX v. WHITESIDE

47 U.S. 157 (1986)

CHIEF JUSTICE BURGER delivered the opinion of the Court:

We granted certiorari to decide whether the Sixth Amendment right of a criminal defendant to assistance of counsel is violated when an attorney refuses to cooperate with the defendant in presenting perjured testimony at his trial.

I

A

Whiteside was convicted of second-degree murder by a jury verdict which was affirmed by the Iowa courts. The killing took place on February 8, 1977, in Cedar Rapids, Iowa. Whiteside and two others went to one Calvin Love's apartment late that night, seeking marihuana. Love was in bed when Whiteside and his companions arrived; an argument between Whiteside and Love over the marihuana ensued. At one point, Love directed his girlfriend to get his "piece," and at another point got up, then returned to his bed. According to Whiteside's testimony, Love then started to reach under his pillow and moved toward Whiteside. Whiteside stabbed Love in the chest, inflicting a fatal wound.

Whiteside was charged with murder, and when counsel was appointed he objected to the lawyer initially appointed, claiming that he felt uncomfortable with a lawyer who had formerly been a prosecutor. Gary L. Robinson was then appointed and immediately began an investigation. Whiteside gave him a statement that he had stabbed Love as the latter "was pulling a pistol from

A. PRIVILEGE CASES

underneath the pillow on the bed." Upon questioning by Robinson, however, Whiteside indicated that he had not actually seen a gun, but that he was convinced that Love had a gun....

... About a week before trial, during preparation for direct examination, Whiteside for the first time told Robinson and his associate Donna Paulsen that he had seen something "metallic" in Love's hand. When asked about this, Whiteside responded:

> "[I]n Howard Cook's case there was a gun. If I don't say I saw a gun, I'm dead."

Robinson told Whiteside that such testimony would be perjury and repeated that it was not necessary to prove that a gun was available but only that Whiteside reasonably believed that he was in danger. On Whiteside's insisting that he would testify that he saw "something metallic" Robinson told him, according to Robinson's testimony:

> "[W]e could not allow him to [testify falsely] because that would be perjury, and as officers of the court we would be suborning perjury if we allowed him to do it; ... I advised him that if he did do that it would be my duty to advise the Court of what he was doing and that I felt he was committing perjury; also, that I probably would be allowed to attempt to impeach that particular testimony." App. to Pet. for Cert. A-85.

Robinson also indicated he would seek to withdraw from the representation if Whiteside insisted on committing perjury. (Footnote omitted.)

Whiteside testified in his own defense at trial and stated that he "knew" that Love had a gun and that he believed Love was reaching for a gun and he had acted swiftly in self-defense. On cross-examination, he admitted that he had not actually seen a gun in Love's hand....

....

II

A

The right of an accused to testify in his defense is of relatively recent origin. Until the latter part of the preceding century, criminal defendants in this country, as at common law, were considered to be disqualified from giving sworn testimony at their own trial by reason of their interest as a party to the case....

By the end of the 19th century, however, the disqualification was finally abolished by statute in most states and in the federal courts....

B

In *Strickland v. Washington,* we held that to obtain relief by way of federal habeas corpus on a claim of a deprivation of effective assistance of counsel under the Sixth Amendment, the movant must establish both serious attorney error and prejudice. To show such error, it must be established that the assistance rendered by counsel was constitutionally deficient in that "counsel made errors so serious that counsel was not functioning as 'counsel' guaranteed the defendant by the Sixth Amendment."...

....

In *Strickland*, we recognized counsel's duty of loyalty and his "overarching duty to advocate the defendant's cause." *Ibid*. Plainly, that duty is limited to legitimate, lawful conduct compatible with the very nature of a trial as a search for truth. Although counsel must take all reasonable lawful means to attain the objectives of the client, counsel is precluded from taking steps or in any way assisting the client in presenting false evidence or otherwise violating the law. This principle has consistently been recognized in most unequivocal terms by expositors of the norms of professional conduct since the first Canons of Professional Ethics were adopted by the American Bar Association in 1908....

....

These principles have been carried through to contemporary codifications of an attorney's professional responsibility. Disciplinary Rule 7-102 of the Model Code of Professional Responsibility (1980), entitled "Representing a Client Within the Bounds of the Law," provides:

"(A) In his representation of a client, a lawyer shall not:
....
"(4) Knowingly use perjured testimony or false evidence.
....
"(7) Counsel or assist his client in conduct that the lawyer knows to be illegal or fraudulent."

This provision has been adopted by Iowa, and is binding on all lawyers who appear in its courts. *See* Iowa Code of Professional Responsibility for Lawyers (1985). The more recent Model Rules of Professional Conduct (1983) similarly admonish attorneys to obey all laws in the course of representing a client....

....

It is universally agreed that at a minimum the attorney's first duty when confronted with a proposal for perjurious testimony is to attempt to dissuade the client from the unlawful course of conduct....

The commentary thus also suggests that an attorney's revelation of his client's perjury to the court is a professionally responsible and acceptable response to the conduct of a client who has actually given perjured testimony....

....

On this record, the accused enjoyed continued representation within the bounds of reasonable professional conduct, and did in fact exercise his right to testify; at most he was denied the right to have the assistance of counsel in the presentation of false testimony.... A defendant who informed his counsel that he was arranging to bribe or threaten witnesses or members of the jury would have no "right" to insist on counsel's assistance or silence. Counsel would not be

A. PRIVILEGE CASES

limited to advising against that conduct. An attorney's duty of confidentiality, which totally covers the client's admission of guilt, does not extend to a client's announced plans to engage in future criminal conduct.... In short, the responsibility of an ethical lawyer, as an officer of the court and a key component of a system of justice, dedicated to a search for truth, is essentially the same whether the client announces an intention to bribe or threaten witnesses or jurors or to commit or procure perjury. No system of justice worthy of the name can tolerate a lesser standard.

....

E

We hold that, as a matter of law, counsel's conduct complained of here cannot establish the prejudice required for relief under the second strand of the *Strickland* inquiry....

....

Whiteside's attorney treated Whiteside's proposed perjury in accord with professional standards, and since Whiteside's truthful testimony could not have prejudiced the result of his trial, the Court of Appeals was in error to direct the issuance of a writ of habeas corpus and must be reversed.

....

TRAMMEL v. UNITED STATES

445 U.S. 40 (1980)

Mr. Chief Justice Burger delivered the opinion of the Court:

We granted certiorari to consider whether an accused may invoke the privilege against adverse spousal testimony so as to exclude the voluntary testimony of his wife. 440 U.S. 934, 99 S.Ct. 1277, 59 L.Ed.2d 492 (1979). This calls for a re-examination of *Hawkins v. United States*, 358 U.S. 74, 79 S.Ct. 136, 3 L.Ed.2d 125 (1958).

I

On March 10, 1976, petitioner Otis Trammel was indicted with two others, Edwin Lee Roberts and Joseph Freeman, for importing heroin into the United States from Thailand and the Philippine Islands and for conspiracy to import heroin in violation of 21 U.S.C. §§ 952(a), 962(a), and 963. The indictment also named six unindicted co-conspirators, including petitioner's wife Elizabeth Ann Trammel.

....

Prior to trial on this indictment, petitioner moved to sever his case from that of Roberts and Freeman. He advised the court that the Government intended to call his wife as an adverse witness and asserted his claim to a privilege to prevent her from testifying against him.... [Mrs. Trammel] explained that her cooperation with the Government was based on assurances that she would be given lenient treatment. She then described, in considerable detail, her role and that of her husband in the heroin distribution conspiracy.

After hearing this testimony, the District Court ruled that Mrs. Trammel could testify in support of the Government's case to any act she observed during the marriage and to any communication "made in the presence of a third person"; however, confidential communications between petitioner and his wife were held to be privileged and inadmissible. The motion to sever was denied.

At trial, Elizabeth Trammel testified within the limits of the court's pretrial ruling; her testimony, as the Government concedes, constituted virtually its entire case against petitioner. He was found guilty on both the substantive and conspiracy charges and sentenced to an indeterminate term of years pursuant to the Federal Youth Corrections Act, 18 U.S.C. § 5010(b).

In the Court of Appeals petitioner's only claim of error was that the admission of the adverse testimony of his wife, over his objection, contravened this Court's teaching in *Hawkins v. United States, supra*, and therefore constituted reversible error. The Court of Appeals rejected this contention. It concluded that *Hawkins* did not prohibit "the voluntary testimony of a spouse who appears as an unindicted co-conspirator under grant of immunity from the Government in return for her testimony." 583 F.2d 1166, 1168 (CA10 1978).

II

The privilege claimed by petitioner has ancient roots. Writing in 1628, Lord Coke observed that "it hath been resolved by the Justices that a wife cannot be produced either against or for her husband." ... This spousal disqualification sprang from two canons of medieval jurisprudence: first, the rule that an accused was not permitted to testify in his own behalf because of his interest in the proceeding; second, the concept that husband and wife were one, and that since the woman had no recognized separate legal existence, the husband was that one. From those two now long-abandoned doctrines, it followed that what was inadmissible from the lips of the defendant-husband was also inadmissible from his wife.

....

In *Hawkins v. United States*, 358 U.S. 74, 79 S.Ct. 136, 3 L.Ed.2d 125 (1958), this Court considered the continued vitality of the privilege against adverse spousal testimony in the federal courts. There the District Court had permitted petitioner's wife, over his objection, to testify against him. With one questioning concurring opinion, the Court held the wife's testimony inadmissible .... Also rejected was the Government's suggestion that the Court modify the privilege by vesting it in the witness-spouse, with freedom to testify or not independent of the defendant's control. The Court viewed this proposed modification as antithetical to the widespread belief, evidenced in the rules then in effect in a majority of the States and in England, "that the law should not force or encourage testimony which might alienate husband and wife, or further inflame existing domestic differences." *Id.*, at 79, 79 S.Ct., at 139.

A. PRIVILEGE CASES

Hawkins, then, left the federal privilege for adverse spousal testimony where it found it, continuing "a rule which bars the testimony of one spouse against the other unless both consent." *Id.*, at 78, 79 S.Ct., at 138 (citations omitted). However, in so doing, the Court made clear that its decision was not meant to "foreclose whatever changes in the rule may eventually be dictated by 'reason and experience.'" 358 U.S., at 79, 79 S.Ct., at 139.

III

A

The Federal Rules of Evidence acknowledge the authority of the federal courts to continue the evolutionary development of testimonial privileges in federal criminal trials "governed by the principles of the common law as they may be interpreted ... in the light of reason and experience." Fed.Rule Evid. 501 .... The general mandate of Rule 501 was substituted by the Congress for a set of privilege rules drafted by the Judicial Conference Advisory Committee on Rules of Evidence and approved by the Judicial Conference of the United States and by this Court. That proposal defined nine specific privileges, including a husband-wife privilege which would have codified the *Hawkins* rule and eliminated the privilege for confidential marital communications.... In rejecting the proposed Rules and enacting Rule 501, Congress manifested an affirmative intention not to freeze the law of privilege. Its purpose rather was to "provide the courts with the flexibility to develop rules of privilege on a case-by-case basis," 120 Cong.Rec. 40891 (1974) (statement of Rep. Hungate), and to leave the door open to change....

Although Rule 501 confirms the authority of the federal courts to reconsider the continued validity of the *Hawkins* rule, the long history of the privilege suggests that it ought not to be casually cast aside. That the privilege is one affecting marriage, home, and family relationships — already subject to much erosion in our day — also counsels caution. At the same time, we cannot escape the reality that the law on occasion adheres to doctrinal concepts long after the reasons which gave them birth have disappeared and after experience suggest the need for change....

B

Since 1958, when *Hawkins* was decided, support for the privilege against adverse spousal testimony has been eroded further. Thirty-one jurisdictions, including Alaska and Hawaii, then allowed an accused a privilege to prevent adverse spousal testimony.... The number has now declined to 24.... The trend in state law toward divesting the accused of the privilege to bar adverse spousal testimony has special relevance because the laws of marriage and domestic relations are concerns traditionally reserved to the states.... Scholarly criticism of the *Hawkins* rule has also continued unabated.

C

Testimonial exclusionary rules and privileges contravene the fundamental principle that "'the public ... has a right to every man's evidence.'" *United States v. Bryan*, 339 U.S. 323, 331, 70 S.Ct. 724, 730, 94 L.Ed. 884 (1950). As such, they must be strictly construed and accepted "only to the very limited extent that permitting a refusal to testify or excluding relevant evidence has a public good transcending the normally predominant principle of utilizing all rational means for ascertaining truth." *Elkins v. United States*, 364 U.S. 206, 234, 80 S.Ct. 1437, 1454, 4 L.Ed.2d 1669 (1960) (Frankfurter, J., dissenting) (citations omitted). Here we must decide whether the privilege against adverse spousal testimony promotes sufficiently important interests to outweigh the need for probative evidence in the administration of criminal justice.

It is essential to remember that the *Hawkins* privilege is not needed to protect information privately disclosed between husband and wife in the confidence of the marital relationship — once described by this Court as "the best solace of human existence." *Stein v. Bowman*, 13 Pet., at 223. Those confidences are privileged under the independent rule protecting confidential marital communications. *Blau v. United States*, 340 U.S. 332, 71 S.Ct. 301, 95 L.Ed. 306 (1951); *see* n. 5, *supra*. The *Hawkins* privilege is invoked, not to exclude private marital communications, but rather to exclude evidence of criminal acts and of communications made in the presence of third persons.

No other testimonial privilege sweeps so broadly. The privileges between priest and penitent, attorney and client, and physician and patient limit protection to private communications. These privileges are rooted in the imperative need for confidence and trust....

The *Hawkins* rule stands in marked contrast to these three privileges. Its protection is not limited to confidential communications; rather it permits an accused to exclude all adverse spousal testimony. As Jeremy Bentham observed more than a century and a half ago, such a privilege goes far beyond making "every man's house his castle," and permits a person to convert his house into "a den of thieves." 5 Rationale of Judicial Evidence 340 (1827). It "secures, to every man, one safe and unquestionable and every ready accomplice for every imaginable crime." *Id.*, at 338.

The ancient foundations for so sweeping a privilege have long since disappeared. Nowhere in the common-law world — indeed in any modern society — is a woman regarded as chattel or demeaned by denial of a separate legal identity and the dignity associated with recognition as a whole human being. Chip by chip, over the years those archaic notions have been cast aside so that "[n]o longer is the female destined solely for the home and the rearing of the family, and only the male for the marketplace and the world of ideas." *Stanton v. Stanton*, 421 U.S. 7, 14-15, 95 S.Ct. 1373, 1377-1378, 43 L.Ed.2d 688 (1975).

The contemporary justification for affording an accused such a privilege is also unpersuasive. When one spouse is willing to testify against the other in a criminal proceeding — whatever the motivation — their relationship is almost certainly in disrepair; there is probably little in the way of marital harmony for the privilege to preserve. In these circumstances, a rule of evidence that permits an accused to prevent adverse spousal testimony seems far more likely to frustrate justice than to foster family peace. Indeed, there is reason to believe that vesting the privilege in the accused could actually undermine the marital relationship. For example, in a case such as this the Government is unlikely to offer a wife immunity and lenient treatment if it knows that her husband can prevent her from giving adverse testimony. If the Government is dissuaded from making such an offer, the privilege can have the untoward effect of permitting one spouse to escape justice at the expense of the other. It hardly seems conducive to the preservation of the marital relation to place a wife in jeopardy solely by virtue of her husband's control over her testimony.

IV

Our consideration of the foundations for the privilege and its history satisfy us that "reason and experience" no longer justify so sweeping a rule as that found acceptable by the Court in *Hawkins*. Accordingly, we conclude that the existing rule should be modified so that the witness-spouse alone has a privilege to refuse to testify adversely; the witness may be neither compelled to testify nor foreclosed from testifying. This modification — vesting the privilege in the witness-spouse — furthers the important public interest in marital harmony without unduly burdening legitimate law enforcement needs.

Here, petitioner's spouse chose to testify against him. That she did so after a grant of immunity and assurances of lenient treatment does not render her testimony involuntary.... Accordingly, the District Court and the Court of Appeals were correct in rejecting petitioner's claim of privilege, and the judgment of the Court of Appeals is

Affirmed.

B. PRIVILEGE PROBLEMS

1. CEO

Roberta, the Chief Executive Officer of the Blake Corporation, discusses an investigation of the corporation with the company's attorney, Horatio. Roberta admits that the company had acted unlawfully in the way it provided collateral for its loan agreements. Are Roberta's statements admissible in a subsequent fraud action against the company involving the collateral for the loans? Are Roberta's statements privileged? Explain.

2. The Client

Ned, while meeting with his attorney Cassandra in private, informs her that he has extorted money from several public officials. He provides Cassandra with specific information about the acts of extortion.

   a. Does the attorney-client privilege apply to the conversation between Cassandra and Ned? Why? Would the attorney-client privilege apply if the conversation took place in the middle of a crowded "happy hour" party? How are these changed circumstances significant, if at all?
   b. Could Cassandra waive the attorney-client privilege without the approval of Ned? Why?
   c. If Ned asks Cassandra's help in extorting money from the new mayor, is the conversation privileged? Why?

3. "Till Death Do Us Part..."

Elouisa and Louis, who lived together but were not married, decided to commit a series of crimes as they traveled across the Mid-West. They planned on stealing a car and then robbing the local savings and loan in Cisco, Ohio. The car theft and bank robbery were successful, but Elouisa and Louis were captured when they took a hostage as they fled the bank.

   a. If Louis alone is charged with the crimes of car theft, robbery, and kidnapping because of Elouisa's failing health, can Elouisa be called to testify about what Louis told her in planning the car theft and bank robbery? Could she testify to what she saw during the robbery? Why?
   b. If Louis and Elouisa had been married when the crimes were being planned and committed, would the marital communications privilege apply? Why? Who holds that privilege?
   c. If the nuptials between Louis and Elouisa occurred just prior to trial, would the spousal incapacity privilege apply? Why? Would Elouisa be able to testify at all? Who holds that privilege?
   d. If Louis and Elouisa had been married during the planning and commission of the crimes, but had divorced prior to trial, would the marital communications privilege still apply during trial? Would the spousal incapacity privilege apply? Explain.

X. AUTHENTICATION

Authentication and identification represent a special aspect of relevancy....

This requirement of showing authenticity or identity falls in the category of relevancy dependent upon fulfillment of a condition of fact....

Also, significant inroads upon the traditional insistence on authentication and identification have been made by accepting as at least prima facie genuine items of the kind treated in rule 902 [on self-authentication].

Fed. R. Evid. 901 Advisory Committee's Note

A. AUTHENTICATION CASES

UNITED STATES v. PAULINO
13 F.3d 20 (1st Cir. 1994)

SELYA, CIRCUIT JUDGE:

Defendant-appellant Temistocles Paulino asks us to set aside his conviction and direct his acquittal, or, in the alternative, order a new trial. Having reviewed the record, we decline to disturb the judgment below.

I.

This case finds its genesis in an undercover investigation of narcotics trafficking conducted by the Providence, Rhode Island police department. The investigation focused on an apartment building at 70 Peace Street. In due course, the police began paying special attention to apartment 706. On several occasions in late May and early June of 1992, they observed appellant in and around the apartment.

After intensive surveillance, an informant, acting under police auspices, entered apartment 706 during early June and made a controlled purchase of cocaine from the principal suspect, Moreno, inside the apartment. While the transaction was in progress detectives observed Paulino peering from a window. The officers subsequently obtained a search warrant and executed it on June 11, 1992. They discovered appellant in the kitchen and a stranger, Junior Rodriguez, taking a shower. The man known as "Moreno" was elsewhere when the police arrived, and his whereabouts remain a mystery.

Although the tiny apartment contained little more than a kitchen, bathroom, and bedroom, it nevertheless disclosed bountiful evidence of drug trafficking activities. Detectives found an assortment of drugs in the bedroom, namely, three plastic bags containing 64.02 grams of cocaine in the aggregate, and a fourth bag

containing a "speedball" (a mixture of cocaine and heroin) weighing 11.79 grams....
....

III.

Appellant's most touted assignment of error relates to a so-called "customer's receipt" for a Postal Service money order discovered on a kitchen shelf. The receipt bore appellant's name (although his given name "Temistocles," was spelled with two surplus letters, viz, "Temistomecles"), listed his address as "70 Peace #706 Prov. RI 02907," and purported to corroborate payment to "Tower Management" in an amount of $280. In the "used for" space, someone had written "May rent."

At trial, the prosecution offered the receipt to prove the truth of the matter asserted therein: that appellant had paid the apartment rent for May 1992 — a period when the apartment was used as a drug distribution outlet....

In this court, as below, appellant assigns error. He cites ... the lack of an appropriate foundation....

A.

The logical starting point for consideration of appellant's first asseveration is Fed.R.Evid. 901(a). The rule reminds us that documentary exhibits must be authentic and that "[t]he requirement of authentication or identification as a condition precedent to admissibility is satisfied by evidence sufficient to support a finding that the matter in question is what its proponent claims." Fed.R.Evid. 901(a); *see also United States v. Arboleda*, 929 F.2d 858, 869 (1st Cir. 1991). Under the Evidence Rules, authentication can be accomplished without the direct testimony of either a custodian or a percipient witness.[3] *See* Fed.R.Evid. 903. Thus, for example, a document's "[a]ppearance, contents, substance, internal patterns, or other distinctive characteristics, taken in conjunction with circumstances," can, in cumulation, provide sufficient indicia of reliability to authenticate it. Fed.R.Evid. 901(b)(4); *see also United States v. Newton*, 891 F.2d 944, 947 (1st Cir.1989).

In respect to matters of authentication, the trial court serves a gatekeeping function. *See generally* Fed.R.Evid. 104(a) (discussing handling of preliminary questions of admissibility). If the court discerns enough support in the record to warrant a reasonable person in determining that the evidence is what it purports to be, then Rule 901(a) is satisfied and the weight to be given to the evidence is left to the jury....

---

[3] Notwithstanding this possibility, prudent parties will usually take advantage of direct testimony, especially when it is readily available. In this case, for example, the government jeopardized the entire prosecution by not attempting to authenticate the receipt in better fashion. We should not have to remind experienced prosecutors that, as Benjamin Franklin observed more than two centuries ago, for want of a nail the rider will sometimes be lost.

A. AUTHENTICATION CASES

In this instance, the trial court addressed the issue of authenticity and concluded that the receipt's contents and the attendant circumstances warranted a finding of authenticity. We believe that this determination is supportable. The document was of a type likely to be saved only by a rent-payer (or, perhaps, by a landlord). It was found, neatly stored, in a small, seemingly uninhabited apartment.... [A]ppellant had been in the apartment, on and off, for at least two weeks prior to the searchers' discovery of the document, and, importantly, he had been seen there in May, that is, during the rental period covered by the receipt. To clinch matters, appellant had been in the apartment on the day of the earlier sale; he was there at the time of the raid; and he alone possessed a latchkey. The judge plausibly could infer from those facts that appellant had somehow acquired a right of occupancy in, and a degree of dominion over, the apartment.

The physical setting in which the document surfaced is equally telling. The apartment harbored a large-scale narcotics operation. Drugs, drug paraphernalia, and tools of the trade were strewn about in plain view. The circumstances supported an inference that appellant was part and parcel of the ongoing activities, *see infra* part IV; and, further, that payment in a hard-to-trace manner, such as payment by money order, was compatible with the nature of the illicit enterprise.

Lastly, the content of a disputed document may itself furnish indicia of authenticity.... Here, the document's contents buttress a finding that it is an authentic rent receipt, issued to Paulino. The document bears appellant's name.... And, it refers to a time frame within which the drug distribution center was in operation.

Taking the totality of the circumstances into account, and giving due deference to the wide radius of the trial court's discretion in such matters, we cannot say that the court erred in ruling that, at least presumptively, the document is what it purports to be: a receipt evidencing appellant's payment of rent with respect to apartment 706.

....

We think that the correct approach ... is that "possession plus" can evidence adoption. Put another way, so long as the surrounding circumstances tie the possessor and the document together in some meaningful way, the possessor may be found to have adopted the writing and embraced its contents....

....

V.

We need go no further. Finding no error in the admission of the rent receipt and no shortfall in the government's overall proof of guilt, we remit appellant to his just deserts.

Affirmed.

B. AUTHENTICATION PROBLEMS

1. A Piece of Paper

The defendant, Mary Lou's Books, Inc., allegedly failed to fulfill payment on several promissory notes. The plaintiff, Rasheed, of Rasheed's Book Supplies, testifies in an action for nonpayment about the notes. Rasheed's counsel wishes to introduce the notes in evidence. What must counsel do to authenticate the notes? Explain.

2. "My Baby Just Wrote Me A ..."

Roy, the testator's brother, testified on the issue of whether the letter stating "I bequeath you my entire antique car collection worth approximately $1 million" was an authentic letter from the testator. What must Roy show to properly authenticate the letter? Explain.

3. The Mall

Li Sing was injured when a display at the In Town Shopping Mall fell on her. Li sues the Mall for damages. At trial, Li introduces a photograph of the area in which the display was maintained. What must counsel do to lay a foundation for the photograph of the display? Explain.

XI. THE BEST EVIDENCE RULE

> The rule is the familiar one requiring production of the original of a document to prove its contents, expanded to include writings, recordings, and photographs....

Fed. R. Evid. 1002 Advisory Committee's Note

> In an earlier day, when discovery and other related procedures were strictly limited, the misleading name "best evidence rule" afforded substantial guarantees against inaccuracies and fraud by its insistence upon production of original documents.

Fed. R. Evid. 1001 Advisory Committee's Note

A. BEST EVIDENCE RULE CASES

SEILER v. LUCASFILM, LTD.
808 F.2d 1316 (9th Cir. 1987)

FARRIS, CIRCUIT JUDGE:

Lee Seiler, a graphic artist and creator of science fiction creatures, alleged copyright infringement by George Lucas and others who created and produced the science fiction movie "The Empire Strikes Back." Seiler claimed that creatures known as "Imperial Walkers" which appeared in The Empire Strikes Back infringed Seiler's copyright on his own creatures called "Garthian Striders." The Empire Strikes Back appeared in 1980; Seiler did not obtain his copyright until 1981.

Because Seiler wished to show blown-up comparisons of his creatures and Lucas' Imperial Walkers to the jury at opening statement, the district judge held a pre-trial evidentiary hearing. At the hearing, Seiler could produce no originals of his Garthian Striders nor any documentary evidence that they existed before The Empire Strikes Back appeared in 1980. The district judge, applying the best evidence rule, found that Seiler had lost or destroyed the originals in bad faith under Fed.R.Evid. 1004(1) and denied admissibility of any secondary evidence, even the copies that Seiler had deposited with the Copyright Office. With no admissible evidence, Seiler then lost at summary judgment.

Facts

Seiler contends that he created and published in 1976 and 1977 science fiction creatures called Garthian Striders. In 1980, George Lucas released The Empire Strikes Back, a motion picture that contains a battle sequence depicting giant machines called Imperial Walkers. In 1981 Seiler obtained a copyright on his

Striders, depositing with the Copyright Office "reconstructions" of the originals as they had appeared in 1976 and 1977.

Seiler contends that Lucas' Walkers were copied from Seiler's Striders which were allegedly published in 1976 and 1977. Lucas responds that Seiler did not obtain his copyright until one year after the release of The Empire Strikes Back and that Seiler can produce no documents that antedate The Empire Strikes Back.
....

Discussion

1. *Application of the best evidence rule*

The best evidence rule embodied in Rules 1001-1008 represented a codification of longstanding common law doctrine. Dating back to 1700, the rule requires not, as its common name implies, the best evidence in every case but rather the production of an original document instead of a copy. Many commentators refer to the rule not as the best evidence rule but as the original document rule.
....

We hold that Seiler's drawings were "writings" within the meaning of Rule 1001(1); they consist not of "letters, words, or numbers" but of "their equivalent." To hold otherwise would frustrate the policies underlying the rule and introduce undesirable inconsistencies into the application of the rule.
....

The modern justification for the rule has expanded from prevention of fraud to a recognition that writings occupy a central position in the law. When the contents of a writing are at issue, oral testimony as to the terms of the writing is subject to a greater risk of error than oral testimony as to events or other situations. The human memory is not often capable of reciting the precise terms of a writing, and when the terms are in dispute only the writing itself, or a true copy, provides reliable evidence. To summarize then, we observe that the importance of the precise terms of writings in the world of legal relations, the fallibility of the human memory as reliable evidence of the terms, and the hazards of inaccurate or incomplete duplication are the concerns addressed by the best evidence rule....

Viewing the dispute in the context of the concerns underlying the best evidence rule, we conclude that the rule applies. McCormick summarizes the rule as follows:

> [I]n proving the terms of a writing, where the terms are material, the original writing must be produced unless it is shown to be unavailable for some reason other than the serious fault of the proponent.

McCormick on Evidence § 230, at 704.

The contents of Seiler's work are at issue. There can be no proof of "substantial similarity" and thus of copyright infringement unless Seiler's works are juxtaposed with Lucas' and their contents compared. Since the contents are

A. BEST EVIDENCE RULE CASES

material and must be proved, Seiler must either produce the original or show that it is unavailable through no fault of his own. Rule 1004(1). This he could not do.

The facts of this case implicate the very concerns that justify the best evidence rule. Seiler alleges infringement by The Empire Strikes Back, but he can produce no documentary evidence of any originals existing before the release of the movie. His secondary evidence does not consist of true copies or exact duplicates but of "reconstructions" made after The Empire Strikes Back. In short, Seiler claims that the movie infringed his originals, yet he has no proof of those originals.

The dangers of fraud in this situation are clear. The rule would ensure that proof of the infringement claim consists of the works alleged to be infringed. Otherwise, "reconstructions" which might have no resemblance to the purported original would suffice as proof for infringement of the original. Furthermore, application of the rule here defers to the rule's special concern for the contents of writings. Seiler's claim depends on the content of the originals, and the rule would exclude reconstituted proof of the originals' content. Under the circumstances here, no "reconstruction" can substitute for the original.

....

Affirmed.

UNITED STATES v. DUFFY

454 F.2d 809 (5th Cir. 1972)

WISDOM, CIRCUIT JUDGE:

The defendant-appellant James H. Duffy was convicted by a jury of transporting a motor vehicle in interstate commerce from Florida to California knowing it to have been stolen in violation of 18 U.S.C. § 2312. He was sentenced to imprisonment for a term of two years and six months. On this appeal, Duffy complains of error in the admission of certain evidence and of prejudice resulting from members of the jury having been present during a sentencing in an unrelated case. We affirm.

....

Both the local police officers and the F.B.I. agent testified that the trunk of the stolen car contained two suitcases. Found inside one of the suitcases, according to the witnesses, was a white shirt imprinted with a laundry mark reading "D-U-F". The defendant objected to the admission of testimony about the shirt and asked that the Government be required to produce the shirt. The trial judge overruled the objection and admitted the testimony. This ruling is assigned as error.

The appellant argues that the admission of the testimony violated the "Best Evidence Rule". According to his conception of the "Rule", the Government should have been required to produce the shirt itself rather than testimony about the shirt. This contention misses the import of the "Best Evidence Rule". The "Rule", as it exists today, may be stated as follows:

[I]n proving the terms of a *writing*, where such terms are material, the original writing must be produced, unless it is shown to be unavailable for some reason other than the serious fault of the proponent. (Emphasis supplied.)

Although the phrase "Best Evidence Rule" is frequently used in general terms, the "Rule" itself is applicable only to the proof of the contents of a writing....

The "Rule" is not, by its terms or because of the policies underlying it, applicable to the instant case. The shirt with a laundry mark would not, under ordinary understanding, be considered a writing and would not, therefore, be covered by the "Best Evidence Rule." ... Because the writing involved in this case was simple, the inscription "D-U-F", there was little danger that the witness would inaccurately remember the terms of the "writing". Also the terms of the "writing" were by no means central or critical to the case against Duffy. The crime charged was not possession of a certain article, where the failure to produce the article might prejudice the defense. The shirt was collateral evidence of the crime. Furthermore, it was only one piece of evidence in a substantial case against Duffy.

....

B. BEST EVIDENCE RULE PROBLEMS

1. Blow-Up

A commercial pilot for a commuter airline brought suit against a noted columnist for stating in his column that the pilot, "Tex," dropped bowling balls from his private small plane onto junk cars in a new leisure sport, "air bowling." Tex claimed that the statements in the column were untrue and sued for defamation. Tex testified at trial about the article. If he does not bring the article to court, is the best evidence rule violated? Explain.

2. Through Rain, Sleet or Hail ...

Hassan brought suit against a furniture store, alleging that he had canceled his purchase pursuant to the store's "money back guarantee." Hassan testified at trial that he had also requested a refund by mail within the 90-day refund window permitted by the store.

  a. To assist him with his testimony, Hassan created a worksheet reviewing the timing and description of the events in question. Is the worksheet the best evidence of Hassan's testimony? Why?
  b. If Hassan wrote down the time and date of the mailing in his records but did not bring the records to court, is the "best evidence" rule violated? Explain.
  c. To show that the letter was received, Hassan was given a return receipt from the post office. If Hassan testifies about the receipt without bringing it to court, does that violate the "best evidence" rule? Why?

XII. PROOF ISSUES — PRESUMPTIONS AND JUDICIAL NOTICE

Presumptions

Presumptions are not evidence but ways of dealing with evidence.

Federal Rules of Evidence: Hearings on H.R. 5463 Before the Senate Comm. on the Judiciary, 93d Cong., 2d Sess. 9 (1974) (Statement by the Standing Committee on Practice and Procedure of the Judicial Conference and the Advisory Committee on the Rules of Evidence)

Judicial Notice

The usual method of establishing adjudicative facts is through the introduction of evidence, ordinarily consisting of the testimony of witnesses. If particular facts are outside the area of reasonable controversy, this process is dispensed with as unnecessary. A high degree of indisputability is the essential prerequisite.

Fed. R. Evid. 201 Advisory Committee's Note

A. ISSUES OF PROOF CASES

SANDSTROM v. MONTANA
442 U.S. 510 (1979)

MR. JUSTICE BRENNAN delivered the opinion of the Court:

The question presented is whether, in a case in which intent is an element of the crime charged, the jury instruction, "the law presumes that a person intends the ordinary consequences of his voluntary acts," violates the Fourteenth Amendment's requirement that the State prove every element of a criminal offense beyond a reasonable doubt.

On November 22, 1976, 18-year-old David Sandstrom confessed to the slaying of Annie Jessen. Based upon the confession and corroborating evidence, petitioner was charged on December 2 with "deliberate homicide," Mont. Code Ann. § 45-5-102 (1978), in that he "purposely or knowingly caused the death of Annie Jessen." App. 34. At trial, Sandstrom's attorney informed the jury that, although his client admitted killing Jessen, he did not do so "purposely or knowingly," and was therefore not guilty of "deliberate homicide" but of a lesser crime. *Id.*, at 6-8....

The prosecution requested the trial judge to instruct the jury that "[t]he law presumes that a person intends the ordinary consequences of his voluntary acts." counsel objected, arguing that "the instruction has the effect of shifting the burden of proof on the issue of" purpose or knowledge to the defense, and that "that is impermissible under the Federal Constitution, due process of law."...

....

... We granted certiorari, 439 U.S. 1067 (1979), to decide the important question of the instruction's constitutionality. We reverse.

II

The threshold inquiry in ascertaining the constitutional analysis applicable to this kind of jury instruction is to determine the nature of the presumption it describes. See *Ulster County Court v. Allen, ante,* at 157-163. That determination requires careful attention to the words actually spoken to the jury, see *ante*, at 157-159, n. 16, for whether a defendant has been accorded his constitutional rights depends upon the way in which a reasonable juror could have interpreted the instruction.

Respondent argues, first, that the instruction merely described a permissive inference — that is, it allowed but did not require the jury to draw conclusions about defendant's intent from his actions — and that such inferences are constitutional. Brief for Respondent 3, 15. These arguments need not detain us long, for even respondent admits that "It's possible" that the jury believed they were required to apply the presumption. Tr. of Oral Arg. 18. Sandstrom's jurors were told that "[t]he law presumes that a person intends the ordinary consequences of his voluntary acts." They were not told that they had a choice, or that they might infer that conclusion; they were told only that the law presumed it. It is clear that a reasonable juror could easily have viewed such an instruction as mandatory....

....

... Petitioner's jury was told that *"[t]he law presumes* that a person intends the ordinary consequences of his voluntary acts." They were not told that the presumption could be rebutted, as the Montana Supreme Court held, by the defendant's simple presentation of "some" evidence; nor even that it could be rebutted at all. Given the common definition of "presume" as "to suppose without proof," Webster's New Collegiate Dictionary 911 (1974), and given the lack of qualifying instructions as to the legal effect of the presumption, we cannot discount the possibility that the jury may have interpreted the instruction in either of two more stringent ways.

First, a reasonable jury could well have interpreted the presumption as "conclusive," that is, not technically as a presumption at all, but rather as an irrebuttable direction by the court to find intent once convinced of the facts triggering the presumption. Alternatively, the jury may have interpreted the instruction as a direction to find intent upon proof of the defendant's voluntary actions (and their "ordinary" consequences), unless *the defendant* proved the contrary by some quantum of proof which may well have been considerably greater than "some" evidence — thus effectively shifting the burden of persuasion on the element of intent....

We do not reject the possibility that some jurors may have interpreted the challenged instruction as permissive, or, if mandatory, as requiring only that the defendant come forward with "some" evidence in rebuttal. However, the fact that a reasonable juror could have given the presumption conclusive or persuasion-shifting effect means that we cannot discount the possibility that Sandstrom's jurors actually did proceed upon one or the other of these latter interpretations. And that means that unless these kinds of presumptions are constitutional, the instruction cannot be judged valid....

....

... [A] conclusive presumption in this case would "conflict with the overriding presumption of innocence with which the law endows the accused and which extends to every element of the crime," and would "invade [the] factfinding function" which in a criminal case the law assigns solely to the jury. The instruction announced to David Sandstrom's jury may well have had exactly these consequences. Upon finding proof of one element of the crime (causing death), and of facts insufficient to establish the second (the voluntariness and "ordinary consequences" of defendant's action), Sandstrom's jurors could reasonably have concluded that they were directed to find against defendant on the element of intent. The State was thus not forced to prove "beyond a reasonable doubt ... every fact necessary to constitute the crime ... charged," 397 U.S., at 364, and defendant was deprived of his constitutional rights as explicated in *Winship*.

A presumption which, although not conclusive, had the effect of shifting the burden of persuasion to the defendant, would have suffered from similar infirmities. If Sandstrom's jury interpreted the presumption in that manner, it could have concluded that upon proof by the State of the slaying, and of additional facts not themselves establishing the element of intent, the burden was shifted to the defendant to prove that he lacked the requisite mental state....

Because David Sandstrom's jury may have interpreted the judge's instruction as constituting either a burden-shifting presumption like that in *Mullaney*, or a conclusive presumption like those in *Morissette* and *United States Gypsum Co.*, and because either interpretation would have deprived defendant of his right to the due process of law, we hold the instruction given in this case unconstitutional.

....

COUNTY COURT OF ULSTER COUNTY, N.Y. v. ALLEN

442 U.S. 140 (1979)

Mr. Justice Stevens delivered the opinion of the Court:

A New York statute provides that, with certain exceptions, the presence of a firearm in an automobile is presumptive evidence of its illegal possession by all persons then occupying the vehicle. The United States Court of Appeals for the Second Circuit held that respondents may challenge the constitutionality of this statute in a federal habeas corpus proceeding and that the statute is "unconstitutional on its face." 568 F.2d 998, 1009. We granted certiorari to review these holdings and also to consider whether the statute is constitutional in its application to respondents. 439 U.S. 815.

Four persons, three adult males (respondents) and a 16-year-old girl (Jane Doe, who is not a respondent here), were jointly tried on charges that they possessed two loaded handguns, a loaded machinegun, and over a pound of heroin found in a Chevrolet in which they were riding when it was stopped for speeding on the New York Thruway shortly after noon on March 28, 1973. The two large-caliber handguns, which together with their ammunition weighed approximately six pounds, were seen through the window of the car by the investigating police officer. They were positioned crosswise in an open handbag on either the front floor or the front seat of the car on the passenger side where Jane Doe was sitting. Jane Doe admitted that the handbag was hers. The machinegun and the heroin were discovered in the trunk after the police pried it open....

Counsel for all four defendants objected to the introduction into evidence of the two handguns, the machinegun, and the drugs, arguing that the State had not adequately demonstrated a connection between their clients and the contraband. The trial court overruled the objection, relying on the presumption of possession created by the New York statute....

At the close of the trial, the judge instructed the jurors that they were entitled to infer possession from the defendants' presence in the car. He did not make any reference to the "upon the person" exception in his explanation of the statutory presumption, nor did any of the defendants object to this omission or request alternative or additional instructions on the subject.

Defendants filed a post-trial motion in which they challenged the constitutionality of the New York statute as applied in this case. The challenge was made in support of their argument that the evidence, apart from the presumption, was insufficient to sustain the convictions. The motion was denied, *Id.*, at 775-776, and the convictions were affirmed by the Appellate Division without opinion....

The New York Court of Appeals also affirmed....

Respondents filed a petition for a writ of habeas corpus in the United States District Court for the Southern District of New York contending that they were denied due process of law by the application of the statutory presumption of possession. The District Court issued the writ, holding that respondents had not "deliberately bypassed" their federal claim by their actions at trial and that the mere presence of two guns in a woman's handbag in a car could not reasonably give rise to the inference that they were in the possession of three other persons in the case. App. to Pet. for Cert. 33a-36a.

The Court of Appeals for the Second Circuit affirmed, but for different reasons.... [T]he majority of the court, without deciding whether the presumption was constitutional as applied in this case, concluded that the statute is unconstitutional on its face because the "presumption obviously sweeps within its compass (1) many occupants who may not know they are riding with a gun (which may

A. ISSUES OF PROOF CASES 197

be out of their sight), and (2) many who may be aware of the presence of the gun but not permitted access to it." ...

The petition for a writ of certiorari presented three questions: (1) whether the District Court had jurisdiction to entertain respondents' claim that the presumption is unconstitutional; (2) whether it was proper for the Court of Appeals to decide the facial constitutionality issue; and (3) whether the application of the presumption in this case is unconstitutional. We answer the first question in the affirmative, the second two in the negative. We accordingly reverse....

In this case, the Court of Appeals undertook the task of deciding the constitutionality of the New York statute "on its face." Its conclusion that the statutory presumption was arbitrary rested entirely on its view of the fairness of applying the presumption in hypothetical situations — situations, indeed, in which it is improbable that a jury would return a conviction, or that a prosecution would ever be instituted. We must accordingly inquire whether these respondents had standing to advance the arguments that the Court of Appeals considered decisive. An analysis of our prior cases indicates that the answer to this inquiry depends on the type of presumption that is involved in the case.

Inferences and presumptions are a staple of our adversary system of factfinding. It is often necessary for the trier of fact to determine the existence of an element of the crime — that is, an "ultimate" or "elemental" fact — from the existence of one or more "evidentiary" or "basic" facts.... The value of these evidentiary devices, and their validity under the Due Process Clause, vary from case to case, however, depending on the strength of the connection between the particular basic and elemental facts involved and on the degree to which the device curtails the factfinder's freedom to assess the evidence independently. Nonetheless, in criminal cases, the ultimate test of any device's constitutional validity in a given case remains constant: the device must not undermine the factfinder's responsibility at trial, based on evidence adduced by the State to find ultimate facts beyond a reasonable doubt....

The most common evidentiary device is the entirely permissive inference or presumption, which allows — but does not require — the trier of fact to infer the elemental fact from proof by the prosecutor of the basic one and which places no burden of any kind on the defendant.... In that situation the basic fact may constitute prima facie evidence of the elemental fact.... When reviewing this type of device, the Court has required the party challenging it to demonstrate its invalidity as applied to him.... Because this permissive presumption leaves the trier of fact free to credit or reject the inference and does not shift the burden of proof, it affects the application of the "beyond a reasonable doubt" standard only if, under the facts of the case, there is no rational way the trier could make the connection permitted by the inference. For only in that situation is there any risk that an explanation of the permissible inference to a jury, or its use by a jury, has caused the presumptively rational factfinder to make an erroneous factual determination.

A mandatory presumption is a far more troublesome evidentiary device. For it may affect not only the strength of the "no reasonable doubt" burden but also the placement of that burden; it tells the trier that he or they *must* find the elemental fact upon proof of the basic fact, at least unless the defendant has come forward with some evidence to rebut the presumed connection between the two facts.... In this situation, the Court has generally examined the presumption on its face to determine the extent to which the basic and elemental facts coincide ....

To the extent that the trier of fact is forced to abide by the presumption, and may not reject it based on an independent evaluation of the particular facts presented by the State, the analysis of the presumption's constitutional validity is logically divorced from those facts and based on the presumption's accuracy in the run of cases. It is for this reason that the Court has held it irrelevant in analyzing a mandatory presumption, but not in analyzing a purely permissive one, that there is ample evidence in the record other than the presumption to support a conviction ....

Without determining whether the presumption in this case was mandatory, the Court of Appeals analyzed it on its face as if it were. In fact, it was not, as the New York Court of Appeals had earlier pointed out. 40 N.Y.2d, at 510-511, 354 N.E.2d, at 840.

The trial judge's instructions make it clear that the presumption was merely a part of the prosecution's case,[19] that it gave rise to a permissive inference available only in certain circumstances, rather than a mandatory conclusion of possession, and that it could be ignored by the jury even if there was no affirmative proof offered by defendants in rebuttal.[20] The judge explained that

---

[19] "It is your duty to consider all the testimony in this case, to weigh it carefully and to test the credit to be given to a witness by his apparent intention to speak the truth and by the accuracy of his memory to reconcile, if possible, conflicting statements as to material facts and in such ways to try and get at the truth and to reach a verdict upon the evidence." Tr. 739-740.

"To establish the unlawful possession of the weapons, again the People relied upon the presumption and, in addition thereto, the testimony of Anderson and Lemmons who testified in this case in chief." *Id.*, at 744.

"Accordingly, you would be warranted in returning a verdict of guilt against the defendants or defendant if you find the defendants or defendant was in possession of a machine gun and the other weapons and that the fact of possession was proven to you by the People beyond a reasonable doubt, and an element of such proof is the reasonable presumption of illegal possession of a machine gun or the presumption of illegal possession of firearms, as I have just before explained to you.["] *Id.*, at 746.

[20] "Our Penal Law also provides that the presence in an automobile of any machine gun or of any handgun or firearm which is loaded is presumptive evidence of their unlawful possession."

"In other words, these presumptions or this latter presumption upon proof of the presence of the machine gun and the hand weapons, you may infer and draw a conclusion that such prohibited weapon was possessed by each of the defendants who occupied the automobile at the time when

A. ISSUES OF PROOF CASES 199

possession could be actual or constructive, but that constructive possession could not exist without the intent and ability to exercise control or dominion over the weapons. He also carefully instructed the jury that there is a mandatory presumption of innocence in favor of the defendants that controls unless it, as the exclusive trier of fact, is satisfied beyond a reasonable doubt that the defendants possessed the handguns in the manner described by the judge. In short, the instructions plainly directed the jury to consider all the circumstances tending to support or contradict the inference that all four of the occupants of the car had possession of the two loaded handguns and to decide the matter for itself without regard to how much evidence the defendants introduced.

Our cases considering the validity of permissive statutory presumptions such as the one involved here have rested on an evaluation of the presumption as applied to the record before the Court. None suggests that a court should pass on the constitutionality of this kind of statute "on its face." It was error for the Court of Appeals to make such a determination in this case.

III

As applied to the facts of this case, the presumption of possession is entirely rational. Notwithstanding the Court of Appeals' analysis, respondents were not "hitchhikers or other casual passengers," and the guns were neither "a few inches in length" nor "out of [respondents'] sight." The argument against possession by any of the respondents was predicated solely on the fact that the guns were in Jane Doe's pocketbook. But several circumstances — which, not surprisingly, her counsel repeatedly emphasized in his questions and his argument ... made it highly improbably that she was the sole custodian of those weapons.

Even if it was reasonable to conclude that she had placed the guns in her purse before the car was stopped by police, the facts strongly suggest that Jane Doe was not the only person able to exercise dominion over them. The two guns were too large to be concealed in her handbag. The bag was consequently open, and part of one of the guns was in plain view, within easy access of the driver of the car and even, perhaps, of the other two respondents who were riding in the rear seat.

Moreover, it is highly improbable that the loaded guns belonged to Jane Doe or that she was solely responsible for their being in her purse. As a 16-year-old girl in the company of three adult men she was the least likely of the four to be carrying one, let alone two, heavy handguns. It is far more probable that she

---

such instruments were found. The presumption or presumptions is effective only so long as there is no substantial evidence contradicting the conclusion flowing from the presumption, and the presumption is said to disappear when such contradictory evidence is adduced." *Id.*, at 743

"The presumption or presumptions which I discussed with the jury relative to the drugs or weapons in this case need not be rebutted by affirmative proof or affirmative evidence but may be rebutted by any evidence or lack of evidence in the case." *Id.*, at 760.

relied on the pocketknife found in her brassiere for any necessary self-protection. Under these circumstances, it was not unreasonable for her counsel to argue and for the jury to infer that when the car was halted for speeding, the other passengers in the car anticipated the risk of a search and attempted to conceal their weapons in a pocketbook in the front seat. The inference is surely more likely than the notion that these weapons were the sole property of the 16-year-old girl.

Under these circumstances, the jury would have been entirely reasonable in rejecting the suggestion — which, incidentally, defense counsel did not even advance in their closing arguments to the jury — that the handguns were in the sole possession of Jane Doe. Assuming that the jury did reject it, the case is tantamount to one in which the guns were lying on the floor or the seat of the car in the plain view of the three other occupants of the automobile. In such a case, it is surely rational to infer that each of the respondents was fully aware of the presence of the guns and had both the ability and the intent to exercise dominion and control over the weapons. The application of the statutory presumption in this case therefore comports with the standard laid down in *Tot v. United States*, 319 U.S., at 467, and restated in *Leary v. United States*, 395 U.S., at 36. For there is a "rational connection" between the basic facts that the prosecution proved and the ultimate fact presumed, and the latter is "more likely than not to flow from" the former.

Respondents argue, however, that the validity of the New York presumption must be judged by a "reasonable doubt" test rather than the "more likely than not" standard employed in *Leary*. Under the more stringent test, it is argued that a statutory presumption must be rejected unless the evidence necessary to invoke the inference is sufficient for a rational jury to find the inferred fact beyond a reasonable doubt. See *Barnes v. United States*, 412 U.S., at 842-843. Respondents' argument again overlooks the distinction between a permissive presumption on which the prosecution is entitled to rely as one not necessarily sufficient part of its proof and a mandatory presumption which the jury must accept even if it is the sole evidence of an element of the offense.

In the latter situation, since the prosecution bears the burden of establishing guilt, it may not rest its case entirely on a presumption unless the fact proved is sufficient to support the inference of guilt beyond a reasonable doubt. But in the former situation, the prosecution may rely on all of the evidence in the record to meet the reasonable-doubt standard. There is no more reason to require a permissive statutory presumption to meet a reasonable-doubt standard before it may be permitted to play any part in a trial than there is to require that degree of probative force for other relevant evidence before it may be admitted. As long as it is clear that the presumption is not the sole and sufficient basis for a finding of guilt, it need only satisfy the test described in *Leary*.

A. ISSUES OF PROOF CASES

The permissive presumption, as used in this case, satisfied the *Leary* test. And, as already noted, the New York Court of Appeals has concluded that the record as a whole was sufficient to establish guilt beyond a reasonable doubt.

The judgment is reversed.

....

MEREDITH v. BEECH AIRCRAFT CORP.

18 F.3d 890 (10th Cir. 1994)

BRORBY, CIRCUIT JUDGE:

This case comes to us after the district court granted a motion for summary judgment in favor of Beech Aircraft Corporation ("Beech" or "Company") in a Title VII, 42 U.S.C. § 2000(e) et seq., sex discrimination in employment action. Ms. Meredith appeals the order, and we exercise jurisdiction pursuant to 28 U.S.C. § 1291. We reverse in part and affirm in part.

Janis Meredith, a former employee at Beech Aircraft Corporation, alleges sex discrimination in employment. She claims Beech discriminated against her when it failed to promote her to the position of group leader of the department, when it gave her a less than adequate evaluation, and when it finally terminated her employment. The district court granted summary judgment in favor of Beech on each of these claims.

....

Background

The record, when viewed in the light most favorable to Ms. Meredith, reveals Ms. Meredith was denied a promotion to become group leader. Beech considered four employees, three women and one man, for the position of group leader. These four employees were Ms. Meredith, Ms. Charlene Montgomery, Ms. Dixie Adair, and Mr. Chuck Berry. Although Mr. Berry was the least qualified for the position, he was promoted to the position of group leader. When the position was given to Mr. Berry, Ms. Meredith contacted the Equal Employment Opportunity Manager at Beech. Ms. Meredith, as well as Ms. Adair, then filed a complaint with the Kansas Commission on Civil Rights ("KCCR").

....

Discussion

....

... Ms. Meredith invited the district court to consider *Adair v. Beech Aircraft Corp.*, 782 F. Supp. 558 (D. Kan. 1992). *Adair* was decided after a full bench trial in Ms. Adair's sex discrimination suit arising out of the same promotion of Mr. Berry. In *Adair*, the court determined Mr. Berry's promotion was gender based and any other reasons set forth by Beech were mere pretext for sexual discrimination. 782 F. Supp. at 563. The district court in Ms. Meredith's action relied on the *Adair* case to preclude Beech from claiming Mr. Berry's promotion was motivated by nondiscriminatory reasons and also to preclude Ms. Meredith from receiving a remedy. Both Beech and Ms. Meredith challenge the offensive use of issue preclusion by the district court against them....

Courts generally have broad discretion in using offensive estoppel, and offensive estoppel against Beech was proper in this case.

....

We disagree with the district court's use of offensive collateral estoppel against Ms. Meredith who was not a party to the *Adair* suit....

We reject Beech's arguments that the court did not use collateral estoppel against Ms. Meredith but instead applied the basic requirements of stare decisis and judicial notice....

... [T]he district court's use of *Adair* against Ms. Meredith was not an instance of judicial notice. Judicial notice is when a judge recognizes the truth of certain facts, which from their nature are not properly the subject of testimony, or which are universally regarded as established by common knowledge.[3] The recognition of certain facts by the judge is proper without proof because such facts are not subject to reasonable dispute. The fact that Ms. Adair was the most qualified for the position of groups leader is not this kind of universal truth. It is a fact that must be established through the presentation of evidence. This fact is disputed by Ms. Meredith, and therefore judicial notice would be improper.

....

B. ISSUES OF PROOF PROBLEMS

1. Credit Card Balance

Ginny mailed a payment to her credit card company paying off a huge balance. The credit card company claimed it never received the payment and promptly sued for damages, including a substantial late fee. Ginny offered evidence at trial that she had properly addressed the envelope, placed a stamp on it, and mailed it. A presumption exists that "a letter properly addressed, stamped and mailed is presumed to have been received."

a. Does the presumption apply in this case? How should the judge instruct the jury if the company offers no evidence on the issue?
b. What if the company testifies that it did not receive the letter? How should the judge now instruct the jury on this issue?

---

[3] Judicial Notice of Adjudicative Facts

....

(b) Kinds of facts. A judicially noticed fact must be one not subject to reasonable dispute in that it is either (1) generally known within the territorial jurisdiction of the trial court or (2) capable of accurate and ready determination by resort to sources whose accuracy cannot reasonably be questioned. Fed. R. Evid. 201.

B. ISSUES OF PROOF PROBLEMS

c. What if the company had stated that it had no knowledge of whether it had received payment because its records were missing, but that Ginny had failed to properly mail the letter because she did not place a stamp on the envelope? How should the judge now instruct the jury on this question?

2. A Question of Criminal Law

Suzanne is charged with the possession of a firearm after being arrested in a hotel room with four other people. Suzanne was a guest of one of the other occupants, Jimi. The room was not registered in her name. The firearm was found in an unlocked drawer of the nightstand. At trial, the prosecutor asked the judge to instruct the jury on the presumption in the jurisdiction that "a person found in a hotel room containing a firearm is presumed to constructively possess that firearm." Should the judge instruct the jury on this presumption? If so, how?

3. On a Roll

A car parked on a steep hill crashed into a car at the bottom of the hill after its parking brake gave out. The owner of the demolished car, Taylor, sued Emma, who was found holding the keys to the runaway car. In the jurisdiction a presumption existed that "ownership of an automobile is presumed from the possession of the automobile's ignition key."

a. If Fed. R. Evid. 301 applies, how would defendant Emma "burst the bubble" of the presumption at trial?
b. If this presumption had shifted the burden of persuasion, what would be required for Emma to overcome the presumption?

4. Judicially Noticed

a. In a breach of contract action brought by Rose Hosiery Mills, Inc. against Burlington Hosiery Mills, Inc., can the court take judicial notice that socks and sweaters are usually prepared through a process involving knitting?
b. In an action involving the redistricting of certain voting districts in Kentucky, the judge wishes to take judicial notice of the location of the state capitol. One of the parties, an out-of-state attorney, says "We do not object to the court taking judicial notice of the state capitol. Is it pronounced 'Louie'ville or "Low-e"ville, your honor?" The judge replied, "It is pronounced 'Frankfort' counsel, and I will take judicial notice." Is judicial notice proper? Explain.
c. If the redistricting case was appealed, could the appellate court take judicial notice as to the location of certain towns in Kentucky? Why?
d. In a robbery trial, the court took judicial notice of the effect of a certain anesthetic in ruling that the defendant's confession was involuntary. The

judge relied solely on his own experience with this anesthetic. Was the judge's decision proper?

XIII. MISCELLANEOUS PROBLEMS

A. *The Answering Machine*

Alan received a phone call at the auto body shop from his wife, Sarah, right before he was about to close up. Just after she called, and before he had a chance to turn off the answering machine, Alan exclaimed, "Hold on just a second, Sarah, it looks like Tommy is at the door." Sarah heard the "rat-a-tat-tat" of a gun and nothing further. Tommy is subsequently charged with the murder of Alan.

Can Detective Tony O'Villa testify as to the conversation on the answering machine tape? What evidentiary objections will most likely be made? How should the judge rule on those objections? Explain your answer.

B. *"Not Again!"*

Ramesh Sinhah owned a small corner pharmacy. One night at 8 p.m. he came across Jennifer surreptitiously placing cosmetics in her pocketbook. Ramesh exclaimed, "I can't believe you just put some cosmetics in your pocketbook, Miss; that is the third time this past month you have done something like that!" If Jennifer is subsequently charged with shoplifting, are Ramesh's statements admissible when offered by the prosecution? Why?

C. *A Marital Partnership*

Melody is charged with conspiracy to bribe an immigration official concerning an allegedly illegal alien employed by Melody. At trial, the government offers the testimony of Yanni, Melody's husband, to testify "I told Melody 'the maid is definitely illegal, Mel, so we'd better do what we can to cover up any trace of her status around here and to minimize any indication that we knew about it. You know, deniability.'" Is Yanni's testimony admissible? Explain.

D. *Tenth Avenue Punch-Out*

On Tenth Avenue, several groups of teenagers met and fought with each other over turf. Joseph was caught and prosecuted. Pursuant to a valid search warrant of Joseph's apartment, the police uncovered a variety of boxing gloves totaling twenty in number. If the prosecution offers these boxing gloves in evidence, are they admissible?

E. *Von Goodenough*

Arthur S. Murray is charged with assault and battery on one of his neighbors, Samantha. In his defense, Murray offers the testimony of Dr. Boris Von Goodenough, a geneticist. Von Goodenough testifies at trial on Murray's behalf:

Defense Attorney: "Doctor, are you a qualified geneticist?"

Dr. Von Goodenough: "Yes, of course."

Defense Attorney: "What is your opinion, then, Doctor, of Murray's mental state at the time of the alleged crime?"

Dr. Von Goodenough: "Violence is hereditary and based on my observations of Murray, he has an aggressive genetic code that caused him to commit the crime."

Is Dr. Von Goodenough's testimony objectionable? Discuss.